URBAN ECOLOGY

URBAN ECOLOGY

THE SECOND EUROPEAN ECOLOGICAL SYMPOSIUM

BERLIN, 8–12 SEPTEMBER 1980

EDITED BY

R. BORNKAMM

Institut für Ökologie, Technische Universität Berlin
Rothenburgstrasse 12, 1000 Berlin 41

J. A. LEE

Department of Botany, The University,
Manchester, M13 9PL, U.K.

AND

M. R. D. SEAWARD

School of Studies in Environmental Science,
University of Bradford,
Bradford, West Yorkshire, BD7 1DP, U.K.

SPONSORING SOCIETIES

The British Ecological Society

The Ecological and Ethological Section of
the Royal Zoological Society of Belgium

Gesellschaft für Ökologie

Oecologische Kring

Polish Academy of Sciences

Scandinavian Society Oikos

Societa Italiana di Ecologia

Société d'Écologie

BLACKWELL SCIENTIFIC PUBLICATIONS

OXFORD LONDON EDINBURGH

BOSTON MELBOURNE

© 1982 by Blackwell Scientific Publications
Editorial offices:
Osney Mead, Oxford, OX2 OEL
8 John Street, London, WC1N 2ES
9 Forrest Road, Edinburgh, EH1 2QH
52 Beacon Street, Boston
    Massachusetts 02108, U.S.A.
99 Berry Street, Carlton
    Victoria 3053, Australia

First published 1982

Printed in Great Britain at
the Alden Press, Oxford
and bound by
Butler & Tanner Ltd
Frome, Somerset

Distributed in U.S.A. and Canada by
Halsted Press, a division of
John Wiley & Sons Inc
New York

British Library
Cataloguing in Publication Data

European Ecological Symposium *(2nd: Berlin: 1980)*
    Urban ecology.
    1. Sociology, Urban—Congresses
    2. Urban ecology (Biology)—Congresses
    I. Title   II. Bornkamm, R. III. Lee, J.A.
    IV. Seaward, M.R.D.
    307.76 (expanded)   HT151

ISBN 0-632-00943-8

CONTENTS

I · URBAN ECOSYSTEMS AND THEIR CONSTITUTION

II · ECOLOGICAL EFFECTS OF HUMAN ACTIVITY IN URBAN AREAS

IV · ABSTRACTS OF POSTER PAPERS

V · INDEXES

PLANNING COMMITTEE

H. P. BLUME *Institut für Ökologie, Technische Universität Berlin, Rothenburgstrasse 12, 1000 Berlin 41*

R. BORNKAMM *Institut für Ökologie, Technische Universität Berlin, Rothenburgstrasse 12, 1000 Berlin 41*

P. H. ENCKELL *Department of Animal Ecology, Ecology Building, S-223 62 Lund, Sweden*

J. A. LEE *Department of Botany, The University, Manchester, M13 9PL, U.K.*

S. W. F. VAN DER PLOEG *Milletstraat 12–4, 1077 ZD Amsterdam, The Netherlands*

K.-F. SCHREIBER *Robert-Koch-Strasse, D-4400 Münster, West Germany*

H. SUKOPP *Institut für Ökologie, Technische Universität Berlin, Rothenburgstrasse 12, 1000 Berlin 41*

PREFACE

The Second European Ecological Symposium was held in West Berlin from 8–12 September 1980. The subject was Urban Ecology, and this attracted 400 participants drawn from 18 countries. The First European Ecological Symposium, entitled *Ecological Processes in Coastal Environments*, dealt with habitats which have fascinated ecologists for many years and which have been much researched. Urban ecology has received much less attention, despite the fact that many ecologists live and find employment in large cities. Although changes in the flora and fauna of cities have been recorded since at least the middle of the nineteenth century, few integrated attempts have been made to examine the ecological relationships between plants and animals and the urban environment. This Symposium was an attempt to bring together the limited information available, to encourage further interest and research in urban ecology, and to encourage the use of ecological inputs to the planning process.

To many ecologists it may seem unreal to consider the assemblages of plants and animals interacting with the urban environment as ecosystems; but it is not clear how extensive human interference needs to be before the term ecosystem ceases to be applicable. Urban ecosystems vary widely, from little-altered relics of forest and grassland to highly modified or new ones in concrete wildernesses. Perhaps all these can be regarded as an extension of Tansley's 'anthropogenic ecosystems'. The Berlin school of ecologists in recent years has been particularly associated with the evaluation of human influence in urban ecosystems, and it was for this reason that the venue for the symposium was chosen by the European Ecological Societies.

The Symposium originally had five themes, but some of these have been combined to produce the three main sections of this volume. The first deals with the description and functioning of urban ecosystems and their component animal and plant communities. The second is concerned with the effects of human activity, including atmospheric pollution, on the biota. The third section considers the teaching of ecology in cities, and the application of ecological knowledge in the planning and management of urban areas. A fourth section contains the abstracts of the poster papers.

Extensive revision of the original translations have been undertaken in a number of cases, and it has also been necessary to condense several of the longer papers; in both cases, the editors trust that the authors' intentions have been faithfully presented.

The members of the other European Ecological Societies are indebted to the Gesellschaft für Ökologie for hosting the meeting and for the excellent

arrangements they made for it. The editors are grateful to Dr J.M. Cherrett,
Dr N.P. Ferguson and Dr J.H. Tallis for their help in the preparation of this
volume.

I

URBAN ECOSYSTEMS AND THEIR CONSTITUTION

1. FLUXES AND ACCUMULATION OF ORGANIC CARBON IN URBAN ECOSYSTEMS ON A GLOBAL SCALE

TORLEIF BRAMRYD
Department of Plant Ecology,
University of Lund, Ecology Building,
Helgonavägen 5, S-223 62 Lund, Sweden

SUMMARY

In connection with studies of human impact on the global carbon cycle it is of great importance to study the role of urban ecosystems. This paper gives a budget on a global scale for organic carbon in urban ecosystems including human settlements. Estimates of carbon in urban soil and vegetation are presented as well as calculations of carbon in the human population, pets, etc. Attempts are made to calculate the CO_2-fluxes to the atmosphere from mineralization and incineration.

Most products from forestry and agriculture are transported into human society. Large amounts of carbon are accumulated for a long time in building material, furniture and books.

Solid waste generated each year in the world contains about 160×10^{12} g C. In addition to this, large amounts of sludge and different types of industrial wastes are produced. Incineration means a rapid oxidation of the carbon, while landfills can have similar carbon-accumulating effects to peatlands. Therefore, this paper also includes calculations concerning waste production, incineration and accumulation on landfills.

INTRODUCTION

Accelerated burning of fossil fuels and human disturbance of the CO_2 balance in terrestrial ecosystems have resulted in a rapid increase in the atmospheric CO_2 concentration.

In 1977 the consumption of oil and condensed gas amounted to about 3.10×10^{15} g C (Shell 1978). The annual release of CO_2 from fossil fuels has been estimated at *c.* 5×10^{15} g C per year (Keeling 1973). In addition to combustion of fossil fuels, activities in terrestrial ecosystems result in the release of large amounts of carbon dioxide.

Intensive management of forests and agricultural lands has resulted in a

3

net flux of CO_2 to the atmosphere (Bramryd 1979, 1980a). Drainage of peatlands and exploitation of peat for fuel have rapidly increased the oxidation of the accumulated organic matter at the same time as the carbon-accumulating capacity of the area has been lost (Bramryd 1980b).

Different estimates of the annual carbon release from terrestrial ecosystems range from $1.2–3.2 \times 10^{15}$ g (Baes *et al* 1976) to a maximum value of 18×10^{15} g C per year (Woodwell *et al* 1978). Since the beginning of industrialization about 120×10^{15} g C might have been released to the atmosphere due to combustion or a net shift in the difference between biological fixation and release (Olson *et al* 1978).

The concentration of CO_2 in the atmosphere has increased steadily from about 295 ppm in 1860 to a current value (1980) of about 330 ppm (Baes *et al* 1976). Estimates have shown that about 56% of the CO_2 released from fossil fuel utilization between 1958 and 1979 has remained in the atmosphere (Keeling & Bacastow 1977).

However, the CO_2 concentration in the atmosphere has only increased by about 50% of what could be expected from fossil fuel burning. In terms of the global carbon budget, one must consider probable feedback mechanisms as net accumulation in the oceans and in some terrestrial ecosystems especially in the temperate and boreal zones. Long-term accumulation in soil organic matter and in peatlands seems to be the most probable natural mechanism.

In most studies of the global carbon cycle, urban areas and their man-made biological processes are ignored. Urban agglomerations cover an increasing area of the land surface, and sometimes contain more organic carbon per area unit than many natural ecosystems. Most products from agriculture and forestry are transported into human society. Large amounts of carbon are accumulated for a long time in building material, furniture, books, etc., but most products are quickly turned into garbage. Thus different methods for dealing with solid waste are of interest from a global CO_2 viewpoint (Bramryd 1977, 1979).

This paper gives an overview of carbon accumulation and man-made carbon fluxes in urban areas.

CARBON IN URBAN AREAS

Long-term accumulated organic carbon in cities and other urban agglomerations can be divided into four main categories:

1. Biomass in humans and animals.
2. Biomass in trees and other plants.
3. Carbon in construction material, furniture, books.
4. Soil organic carbon and organic carbon accumulated in landfills.

Humans and higher animals

Organic carbon is stored for longer or shorter times in the tissues of all living organisms. Whittaker and Likens (1975) estimated the total biomass of animals in the world at 906×10^{12} g C. About 457×10^{12} g C is bound in land animals. The annual animal production is about 372×10^{12} g C for the land fauna and about 138×10^{12} g C for marine animals.

In this paper calculations only include pet animals and assume that dogs have a clear dominance.

In Sweden a mean value of 0.05 dogs per capita is found for large cities (e.g. Stockholm and Malmö) while smaller towns and villages have a somewhat higher figure of 0.06–0.07 dogs per capita. Similar values can be calculated from, for example, Duvigneaud (1975) giving the figure 0.05 dogs per inhabitant in Brussels. In many countries in, for example, south Europe and in many developing countries much higher dog populations can be found. Thus 0.06 dogs per capita is a probable average for the world. With $c.\ 4 \times 10^9$ people in the world this would give a total number of 0.24×10^9 dogs. If we estimate the mean weight for a dog as 10 kg this means a total biomass of 2.4×10^6 tons. With 30% dry matter containing $c.\ 50\%$ carbon the total carbon content in dogs can be estimated to 0.36×10^6 tons C. These dogs produce about 3.3×10^6 tons C in faeces per year. It can be assumed that the biomass of other pets is negligeable in comparison with dogs. Cattle are excluded from these calculations.

At the end of the 1970s the world's human population amounted to approximately 4×10^9 persons. With an assumed mean weight of 50 kg, 30% dry matter containing 50% carbon, this gives a figure of 30×10^6 tons C in the human population. With an annual increase of the population of $c.\ 60 \times 10^6$ persons this would mean an increase in fixed carbon in Man with 0.45×10^6 tons C per year. The United Nations have estimated that the world's population of humans in the year 2000 will be about 5.8×10^9 persons, equivalent to 43.5×10^6 tons C.

Trees and other plants

Urban areas have an appreciable plant biomass. Most cities have parks and plantations and large residential districts in the outskirts where gardens often are large and productive. According to Abrams (1965), 18% of the central parts of some North American cities are open areas. Duvigneaud (1975) found that up to 50% of the city area of Brussels was open space with relatively high productivity. Bolin *et al* (1979) calculated that towns have an average living plant biomass of 3.5 kg dry wt m^{-2} in open areas. This figure compares with an estimated plant biomass for grasslands of 2.0 kg dry wt m^{-2} (Bolin *et al* 1979). If villages and smaller urban communities with more green areas than

Municipal waste contains approximately 75–85% organic matter with a dry matter content of about 60% and a carbon concentration around 50% (Besley & Reed 1972; Hovsenius 1979). Thus a figure of 0.15 tons organic C per capita and year can be calculated for heavily industrialized parts of Europe, Australia and Japan and 0.30 tons organic C for the United States.

With these figures as starting points and based on the paper-consumption in different countries (*Yearbook of Environmental Statistics 1979*) the estimates given in Table 1.1 are made concerning organic carbon in solid waste. The data show good agreement with available statistics on solid-waste production from different countries.

Around 30% of the solid municipal waste in Europe was burned in incinerators at the end of the 1970s. In the United States only 15–20% was

TABLE 1.1. *Solid-waste production in different parts of the world.*

	Solid waste per capita and year (tons of carbon)	Solid waste per year (tons of carbon $\times 10^6$)
Heavy industrialized parts of Europe	0.15	20.6
Less industrialized parts of Europe	0.06	19.7
United States	0.30	64.6
Canada	0.30	6.0
South America	0.05	18.0
Africa	0.008	3.5
Asia (except Japan)	0.004	9.3
Japan	0.15	18.0
Australia, New Zealand	0.13	2.0
Others in South Pacific	0.006	0.03
Total		161.73

incinerated. Incinerators are used in many big cities in Africa, Asia and South America but most of the garbage is deposited in landfills. Sydney in Australia has incinerators, but most garbage in Australia and New Zealand is deposited or composted (Auckland). However, landfills with open burning are common in many countries and up to 30% of the dumped garbage is burned in some countries. Including burning of garbage by the individual producer it may be realistic to assume that 30–40% of the solid municipal waste in the world is burned and 50–60% deposited in landfills. Although commonly used in many countries in Europe (Holland, Germany, Sweden, etc.), in China and in many other parts of the world, controlled composting of municipal solid waste together with sewage sludge probably only makes up a few percent of the total solid-waste management. However, this practice will probably increase rapidly in all parts of the world within a few years. According to the estimates above, approximately $50–60 \times 10^6$ tons C are released to the atmosphere by solid-waste burning, while about 100×10^6 tons C are deposited on landfills and only slowly released to the atmosphere. It should be emphasized that these calculations only concern municipal refuse. Considerably higher amounts would be obtained if agricultural, forestry and chemical wastes were included. Many of these types of wastes, however, are mineralized or accumulated in the ecosystems where they are produced.

Most countries in the industrialized world have sewage treatment producing approximately 0.03 tons dry wt of solid residues per year and capita corresponding to 0.009 tons of organic carbon (assuming 30% carbon in sludge) (e.g. Duvigneaud 1975; Hökervall 1977; *Yearbook of Environmental Statistics 1979*). Large amounts of organic material from sewage are distributed into the sea either without any treatment or as sludge from sewage plants. About 1×10^6 tons of organic carbon in sewage sludge are used on land every year. About 40% of this is used in agriculture and about 50% is dumped in landfills, etc.

Organic carbon accumulated in landfills

Landfills can often be regarded as long-term accumulators of carbon and in this respect can be compared with the natural peatland ecosystems. Often wet areas have been used as dumps for garbage, and due to anaerobic conditions mineralization is very slow. In modern landfills the garbage is well compacted which decreases the aeration and thus the decomposition rate.

Investigations (Bramryd, in preparation) have shown that relatively well-aerated 25–30-year-old landfills contain over 10% organic carbon. In the 1940s and 1950s the relative amount of organic matter in garbage was lower than today, probably around 60–65%, compared with the present ratio of 75–85% in industrialized countries. This means an average carbon concentration in the dumped material of about 30%. Thus, one-third of the organic carbon is still unmineralized after 30 years. No significant difference in carbon concentration could be found between 20 and 30-year-old landfill sites and it can be expected that the remaining carbon is bound in long-lived humus substances and will remain unmineralized for a very long time (Bramryd, in preparation). Present garbage contains a significant fraction of plastics and other resistant organic matter. This fact, together with a harder compaction, will probably leave up to 50% or more of the carbon for long-term accumulation in present landfills. Thus, 50×10^6 tons of C of the total annually dumped municipal garbage (100×10^6 tons of C) will be accumulated, long-term, in landfills around the world and withdrawn from the CO_2 cycle. These figures can be compared with the estimated figure 220×10^6 ton C for the annual accumulation in the world's peatlands (Bramryd 1980b). Thus it seems relevant to conclude that landfills could help to moderate the increased atmospheric CO_2 concentrations.

U.S. Department of Health, Education and Welfare (1968) *Quad-city Solid Wastes Project, Interim Report*, Cincinnati, Ohio.

Whittaker R.H. & Likens G.E. (1975) The biosphere and man. *Primary Productivity of the Biosphere* (Ed. by H. Lieth & R.H. Whittaker), pp. 305–328. Ecological Studies 14. Springer-Verlag, Berlin.

Woodwell G.M., Whittaker R.H., Reiners W.A., Likens G.E., Delwiche C.C. & Botkin D.B. (1978) The biota and the world carbon budget. *Science*, 199, 141–146.

Yearbook of Environmental Statistics (1979) National Central Bureau of Statistics, Stockholm. 196 pp.

2. COMPARISON OF THE FLORA OF SOME CITIES OF THE CENTRAL EUROPEAN LOWLANDS

WOLFRAM KUNICK

Eugenstrasse 23, 7302 Ostfildern 4 (Kemnat),
West Germany

SUMMARY

Urban floras of nine cities are compared with regard to the shares of different vegetation types. This demonstrates a generally high percentage of ruderal plants in all cities, an increasing proportion of plants of moist or wet habitats towards the West and, on the contrary, an increase of dry-grassland species towards the East. The transition area between both regions lies between the rivers Elbe and Oder. Species common everywhere as well as species showing increasing frequency in the eastern or in the western part were analysed concerning their geographical origin and their ecological demands using the indicator indices of Ellenberg (1979).

INTRODUCTION

Recent research projects carried out in several cities have shown that the composition of the urban flora differs in many regards from that of the surrounding habitats. In order to complement such individual research, an attempt was made to determine to what extent urban floras of widely separated areas exhibit common or differing features. Eight cities situated in the Central European Lowlands, and in addition the city of Vienna, were compared (Fig. 2.1, Table 2.1). The data available appear to be rather heterogeneous with regard to the extent of the area considered and the completeness of the lists of species. Particularly great differences resulted in the case of casual aliens or ephemerophytes, i.e. species growing wild only temporarily, the relative proportion of which can reach a very high share (see Table 2.2).

CLASSIFICATION OF THE FLORA ACCORDING TO VEGETATION TYPES

The number of species occurring in the cities mentioned totals 2,061, of which

13

TABLE 2.1. *Some data about the cities.*

City:	Amsterdam	Brussels	Duisburg	Hanover	Berlin	Poznán	Łódź	Warsaw	Vienna
Authors of the floras:	Bolman (1976 & in litt.)	Holland (1976–77)	Düll & Kutzelnigg (1980)	Haeupler (1976)	Kunick (1974)	Krawiecowa (1951)	Krawiecowa & Rostański (1976)		Forstner & Hübl (1971)
Average altitude above sea level:	2 m	108 m	20–50 m	57 m	35 m	58 m	97 m	121 m	200 m
Average annual temperature (°C):	10.0	9.7	9–10	9.0	8.4	8.3	7.9	7.6	9.5
Average annual rainfall (mm):	648	835	750–800	644	577	513	567	545	600–700
Surface: (km²):	314	160	1280	225	480	115	214	445	414

TABLE 2.2. *Composition of the wild flora of some Central European cities*

Vegetation type:	City: n =	Am 390	Br 458	Du 1036	Ha 914	Be 994	Po 539	Ło 545	Wa 474	Vi 1348
1. Coast vegetation (%)		3.6	0.4	0.3	0.9	0.7	0.2	0.7	0.4	0.7
2. Extra-alpine rock vegetation (%)		0.5	0.4	0.4	0.8	1.0	1.5	0.9	1.1	0.9
3. Alpine vegetation (%)		0.3	0.2	—	—	0.1	0.2	—	—	—
4. Hygrophilous pioneer vegetation (%)		3.8	1.7	3.3	3.2	1.9	3.5	3.7	4.9	1.7
5. Weeds of arable fields and gardens; pioneer vegetation on ruderal sites (%)		20.3	15.7	13.5	15.4	14.2	28.6	23.9	22.8	15.1
6. Perennial tall herb vegetation on ruderal sites (%)		16.1	14.6	12.7	12.4	11.6	16.7	16.3	16.0	11.9
7. Flood meadows and trampled grounds (%)		5.9	5.7	3.4	3.5	2.9	3.5	4.0	5.5	2.3
8. Rough grassland dominated by *Agropyron repens* (L.) P.B. (%)		2.9	2.4	1.7	1.6	1.8	2.6	3.1	3.8	1.8
9. Semi-dry and dry grassland (%)		5.9	5.3	7.6	8.4	11.2	11.5	10.8	8.9	9.5
10. Eutrophic waters (%)		6.7	6.3	7.5	8.2	4.8	0.7	1.5	2.5	3.7
11. Spring fens (%)		—	0.4	0.6	0.7	0.1	—	—	—	0.1
12. Raised bogs and oligotrophic waters (%)		1.5	0.9	3.2	3.1	2.2	0.2	—	0.2	0.5
13. Herbaceous and low shrub heathland (%)		0.8	1.5	1.9	2.3	1.9	0.6	1.1	0.2	0.9
14. Fresh and fertile meadows and pastures (%)		12.0	10.7	6.5	6.7	6.0	7.8	8.8	9.5	4.6
15. Moist meadows (%)		5.6	5.2	4.9	5.9	4.5	0.7	0.9	3.6	3.3
16. Subalpine vegetation (%)		0.5	0.2	0.7	0.7	0.6	—	—	0.2	0.7
17. Woodland on moist or wet sites (%)		2.6	4.4	4.9	4.8	3.8	1.1	0.9	1.9	2.2
18. Xerothermic bushes (%)		1.8	2.2	4.5	3.8	4.7	1.5	3.1	2.1	5.4
19. Woodland on acid soils (%)		1.0	7.2	5.2	5.6	5.1	0.9	1.3	1.3	2.0
20. Mesophilous woodlands (%)		1.0	8.5	6.8	7.3	5.3	1.8	4.8	2.7	4.9
Species not classified (%)		7.2	5.9	10.4	4.5	15.5	16.3	14.1	12.4	27.7

number the individual urban floras reach a share of between 20% (Amsterdam) and 65% (Vienna). The classification was carried out according to Sukopp *et al.* (1978). Table 2.2 shows that, without consideration of the very different share of species not classified (mainly ephemerophytes), the groups of weeds and ruderal plants are always the most numerous. Hence short-lived or perennial species of habitats strongly influenced by man predominate.

Figure 2.2 shows the percentage of the flora from different vegetation types in the nine cities without consideration of the species not classified. It is particularly striking that plants of moist or wet habitats, partly also those of the woodlands, show higher shares in the cities situated west of the Oder river,

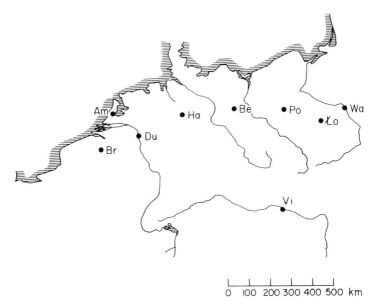

FIG. 2.1. Location of the cities: Am, Amsterdam; Br, Brussels; Du, Duisburg; Ha, Hanover; Be, Berlin; Po, Poznán; Ło, Łodz; Wa, Warsaw; Vi, Vienna.

whilst east of the Elbe river the percentage of dry-grassland species increases slightly.

THE DISTRIBUTION OF SEVERAL SPECIES ACCORDING TO THE GEOGRAPHICAL LOCATION

An attempt was made on the one hand to find those species common everywhere and on the other hand those plants whose distribution clusters in the eastern or western part of the whole area. These are analysed concerning their geographical origin (Fig. 2.4) and their ecological demands (Fig. 2.5).

Three hundred and twelve species in all, that is about 15% of the total number of species, occur in (almost) every city. Predominant among these are plants of ruderal sites and those of fresh and fertile meadows and pastures. Many of them are also very common outside the cities, some others however are typical urban plants which, especially in the oceanic region, scarcely occur beyond the urban fringes as, for example, *Hordeum murinum* L. (see Fig. 2.3), *Diplotaxis tenuifolia* (L.) DC., *Lactuca serriola* L. or *Malva neglecta* Wallr. Trees and shrubs have a low share with only 6.5%. The most important are *Acer pseudoplatanus* L., *A.platanoides* L., *Aesculus hippocastanum* L., *Cle-*

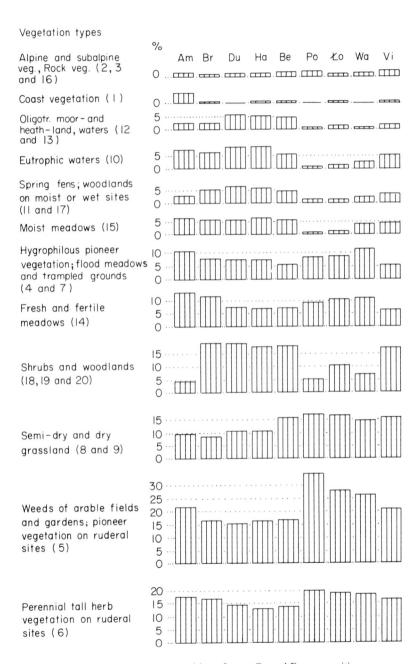

Fig. 2.2.   Floristic composition of some Central European cities.

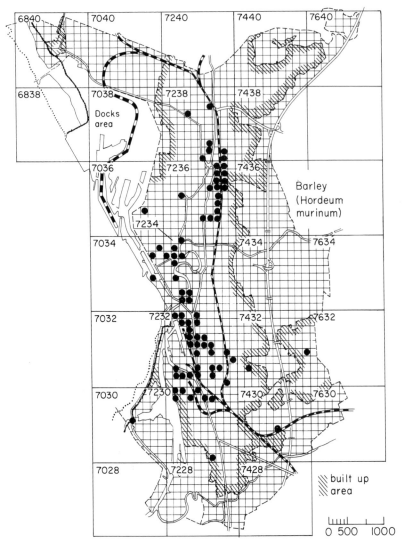

FIG. 2.3. Distribution of *Hordeum murinum* L. in the city of Bremerhaven (from Kunick 1974).

matis vitalba L., *Parthenocissus quinquefolia* agg., *Populus tremula* L., *Rosa canina* L., *Rubus caesius* L., *R.fruticosus* agg., *R.idaeus* L., some *Salix* species (*S.alba* L., *S.caprea* L.) and *Sambucus nigra* L., i.e. mostly components of pioneer stages of mesophilous woodlands. I suppose, however, that the phenomenon of spontaneously growing ligneous plants is not sufficiently taken into account.

Only a few species of foreign continents have been able to become naturalized in all cities. These are mainly from North America (beside the previously mentioned *Parthenocissus*) some *Aster* taxa, *Conyza canadensis* (L.) Cronq., *Erigeron annuus* (L.) Pers., *Galinsoga ciliata* (Rafin.) Blake, *G.parviflora* Cav., some *Oenothera* taxa, *Solidago canadensis* L., *S.gigantea* Ait., and from East Asia, *Impatiens parviflora* DC. and *Reynoutria japonica* Houtt.

Two hundred and twenty-four species (11% of the total species number) are characteristic of eastern cities. Among these, the share of plants of European–West Asian origin is the highest (see Fig. 2.4). Examples that can be mentioned are *Atriplex* taxa (*A.nitens* Schkuhr, *A.tatarica* L., *A.oblongifolia* W. & K.), *Chenopodium* taxa (*C.hybridum* L., *C.strictum* Roth, *C.murale* L.), *Descurainia sophia* (L.) Webb ex Prantl, *Kochia scoparia* (L.) Schrad., *Leonurus cardiaca* L. and some *Sisymbrium* taxa (*S.loeselii* L., *S.orientale* L., *S.irio* L.), as well as some plants of North American origin like *Amaranthus albus* L., *A.retroflexus* L., *Iva xanthiifolia* Nutt., *Lepidium densiflorum* Schrad. and *Xanthium spinosum* L.

In addition to these components of ruderal vegetation, some species of dry grassland are also represented, for example *Artemisia campestris* L., *Helichrysum arenarium* (L.) Moench, *Poa bulbosa* L. or *Potentilla arenaria* Borkh.

Among the woody plants the following seem to become more frequent towards the East: *Lycium barbarum* L., *Populus alba* L., spontaneously growing fruit trees (*Malus domestica* Borkh., *Pyrus communis* L.), as well as the North American species *Acer negundo* L., *Rhus typhina* L. and *Robinia pseudoacacia* L.

Only a few species, namely 45 or 2.2% of the total number, occur

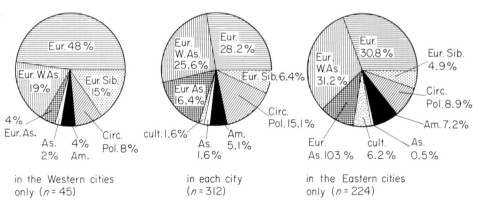

in the Western cities
only (*n* = 45)

in each city
(*n* = 312)

in the Eastern cities
only (*n* = 224)

FIG. 2.4. Classification of the species according to their geographical origins (following Rothmaler 1976): Eur., species of European origin; Eur.–W.As., European–West Asian; Eur.–As., European–Asian; As., Asian; Am., American; Circ.Pol., Circumpolar; Eur.–Sib., European–Siberian; cult., cultivated plants.

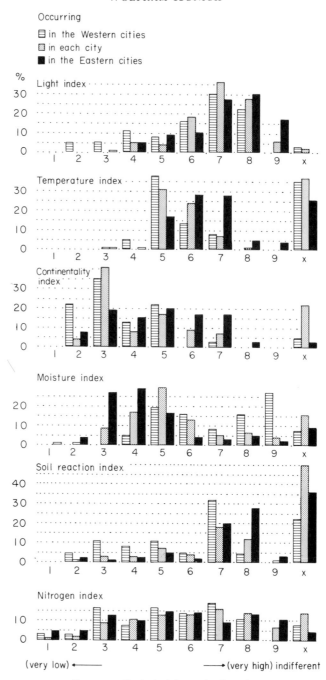

FIG. 2.5. Ecological demands of species.

exclusively in the western cities. Among this group, the percentage of plants of European distribution is particularly high. Plants of acidophilous woodlands, eutrophic waters and moist grassland prevail, for example *Lotus uliginosus* Schkuhr., *Lysimachia nummularia* L., *Petasites hybridus* L., G., M. & Sch., *Rumex hydrolapathum* Huds., *Teucrium scorodonia* L., as well as the following trees and shrubs: *Frangula alnus* Mill., *Ilex aquifolium* L., *Lonicera periclymenum* L., *Prunus serotina* Ehrh., *Sarothamnus scoparius* (L.) Wimm. ex Koch, and *Viburnum opulus* L.

Fig. 2.5 shows the indicator values concerning the factors light, temperature, continentality, moisture, soil reaction and nitrogen, as worked out by Ellenberg (1979) in a nine-part scale, for those species occurring with frequency everywhere or with increasing frequency towards the eastern or western part of the whole area.

The figure indicates, first of all, that with regard to most of the factors mentioned except nitrogen, there are clearly marked maxima characterizing the chosen species as mainly preferring light, as being suboceanic, as enduring moderate dryness and as preferring basic soils. Comparing those species which occur mainly in the eastern cities with those of West European distribution, they have higher demands for light, temperature and soil reaction. Species occurring everywhere show the highest percentage of indifferents concerning each of these factors.

CONCLUSION

The comparison of the floras of several cities proves first of all that the geographical differences existing over larger distances between the oceanic and the continental region are also reflected in the composition of the urban floras. It is true that the generally high share of annual or perennial ruderal plants distinguishes the urban regions from their rural environment but the specific urban conditions are certainly a little blurred, because most of the areas considered contain urban fringe situations too. A comparison of species lists from urbanized areas alone would emphasize more clearly the specifics of the urban flora. It is, therefore, desirable to compile such lists.

REFERENCES

Bolman J. (1976) *Wilde Planten in en bij Amsterdam.* Thieme, Zutphen.
Düll R. & Kutzelnigg H. (1980) *Punktkartenflora von Duisburg und Umgebung.* Westdeutscher Verlag, Opladen.
Ellenberg H. (1979) Zeigerwerte der Gefäßpflanzen Mitteleuropas. *Scripta Geobotanica* **9**, second edition, E. Goltze-Verlag, Göttingen.
Forstner W. & Hübl E. (1971) *Ruderal-, Segetal- und Adventivflora von Wien.* Verlag Notring, Wien.

22 WOLFRAM KUNICK

Haeupler H. (1976) Flora von Südniedersachsen, 1. Atlas zur Flora von Südniedersachsen. *Scripta Geobotanica*, 10, E. Goltze-Verlag, Göttingen.

Holland F. (1976) Contribution à l'Étude de l'Écologie Urbaine. Aperçu de la Flore et de la Végétation Bruxelloise. *Mémoires de la Faculté des Sciences Botaniques*, Bruxelles.

Krawiecowa A. (1951) *Analiza geograficzna flory synantropijnej miasta Poznania*. Poznàn.

Krawiecowa A. & Rostański K. (1976) Zalezność flory synantropijnej wybranych miast polskich od ich warunków przyrodniczych i rozwoju. *Acta Universitatis Wratislavensis*, 303, 1–61.

Kunick W. (1974) *Veränderungen von Flora und Vegetation einer Großstadt, dargestellt am Beispiel von Berlin (West)*. Dissertation, Technical University of Berlin.

Rothmaler W. (1976) *Exkursionsflora für die Gebiete der DDR und der BRD*. Kritischer Band. VEB Volk und Wissen, Berlin.

Sukopp H., Trautmann W. & Korneck D. (1978) Auswertung der Roten Liste gefährdeter Farn- und Blütenpflanzen in der Bundesrepublik Deutschland für den Artenund Biotopschutz. *Schriftenreihe für Vegetationskunde*, 12, 1–131, Bonn-Bad Godesberg.

3. ECOLOGICAL INDICATOR-VALUE SPECTRA OF SPONTANEOUS URBAN FLORAS

RÜDIGER WITTIG AND KARL-JOSEF DURWEN

Botanisches Institut der Universität D 4000 Düsseldorf
and *Institut für Geographie der Universität D 4400 Münster,*
West Germany

SUMMARY

The indicator-value spectra of spontaneous floras in the cities of Bielefeld, Dortmund, Münster and Köln are different from the spectra of the floras of their environs: a greater proportion of higher values are found in respect of light, temperature, continentality, soil reaction and nitrogen, but the reverse is the case for moisture. It is notable that the proportion of species which are ecologically indifferent to soil reaction and continentality is always higher in the cities than in their environs.

INTRODUCTION

Climatic and edaphic factors operating in large towns differ from those of the environs, for example the mean annual temperature rises about 0.5 to 1.5°C (Kratzer 1956), the soils are much altered and often eutrophicated (Sukopp *et al.* 1974; Blume *et al.* 1978) and the ground water-table is lowered. In the present paper, four large towns in North-Rhine-Westfalia are examined to see whether such differences are reflected in the indicator-value spectrum of vascular plants (Ellenberg 1974).

METHODS

Floral lists were obtained from the following cities:

Bielefeld: Observations in the years 1973–1979 were combined with the data of Trinczek (1975).

Dortmund: Observations in 1980.

Köln: The floral list was compiled from Bornkamm (1974b), but those species which were not expected to occur in the plant communities of the city centre of Köln (Bornkamm 1974a) were omitted.

Münster: The list of Wittig (1974) was combined with that of Runge (1972), but species from non-urban sites were excluded.

In all cases the field records of the floral mapping of Central Europe served as a basis for the floral lists of the respective environs. In the case of topographical maps of Bielefeld, Dortmund and Münster (scale of 1:25.000), those species which according to the authors' knowledge of the flora of these towns are only found in urban-industrial regions were omitted. As the conditions in Köln are unfamiliar to the authors, a similar procedure was impractical. Instead, the total flora of the nearest non-urban mapped area (No. 5006: 'Frechen') was used for the 'environs-list'. Cultivated and casual alien species were not included in either the 'city-lists' or the 'environs-lists'.

The processing, calculation and production of the indicator-value spectra were made with the help of the computer program 'FLORA'. 'FLORA' is a new part of the landscape-ecological-information-system 'LÖKIS' (see Durwen 1979).

RESULTS

In all four cities there are relatively more species with high indicator values for light (Fig. 3.1), temperature (Fig. 3.2), continentality (Fig. 3.3), soil reaction (Fig. 3.5) and nitrogen (Fig. 3.6), but less in the case of moisture (Fig. 3.4), than in the respective environs. In the cities there is also a higher percentage of species which are ecologically indifferent to continentality and soil reaction. If the corresponding averages are compared with one another, it is apparent that the averages in all cities are nearly the same. Weighting the species had very little effect on the form of the spectra. As weighting has a certain degree of subjectivity and was not practicable for Köln, Figures 3.1–3.6 show only unweighted results.

ACKNOWLEDGEMENTS

We are indebted to the following for their help: Prof. Dr A. Gerhardt, Mr H. Lienenbecker, Dr H.G. Fink and Dr F. Runge.

REFERENCES

Blume H.-P., Horbert M., Horn R. & Sukopp H. (1978) Zur Ökologie der Grossstadt unter besonderer Berücksichtigung von Berlin (West). *Schriftenreihe des Deutschen Rates für Landespflege*, **30**, 658–677.
Bornkamm R. (1974a) Die Unkrautvegetation im Bereich der Stadt Köln. I. Die Pflanzengesellschaften. *Decheniana*, **126**, 267–306.

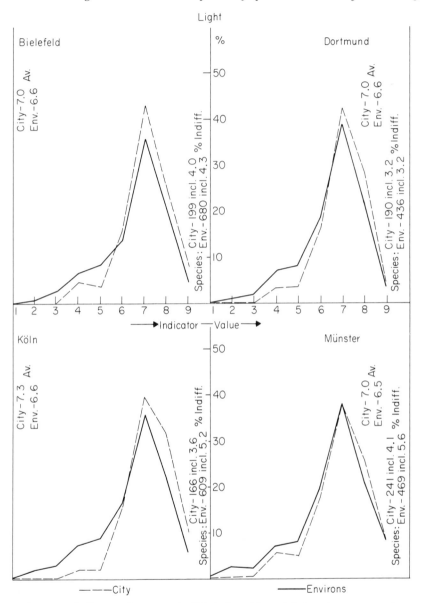

FIG. 3.1.   Indicator-value spectra for light in four cities and their environs, expressed as a percentage. Indifferent species are not considered.

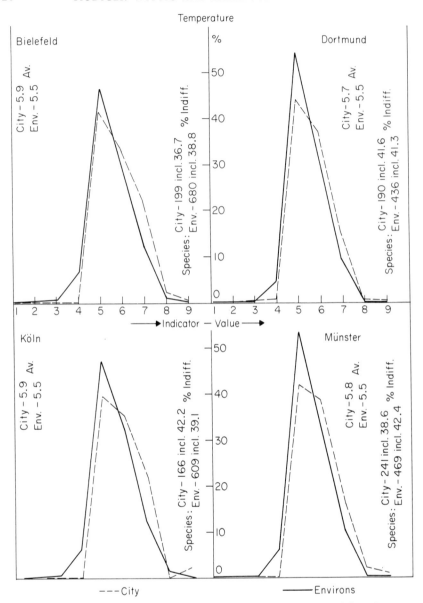

FIG. 3.2.   Indicator-value spectra for temperature in four cities and their environs, expressed as a percentage. Indifferent species are not considered.

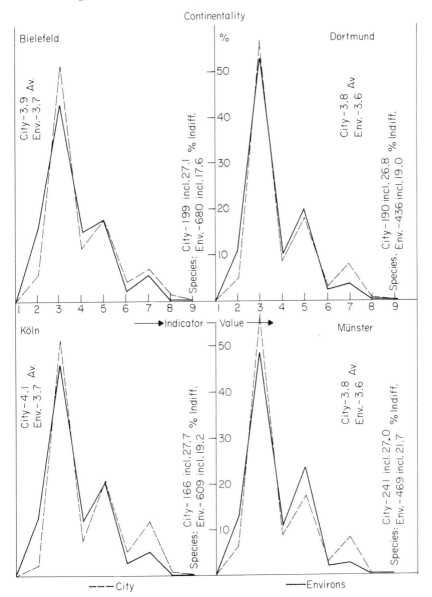

FIG. 3.3.   Indicator-value spectra for continentality in four cities and their environs, expressed as a percentage. Indifferent species are not considered.

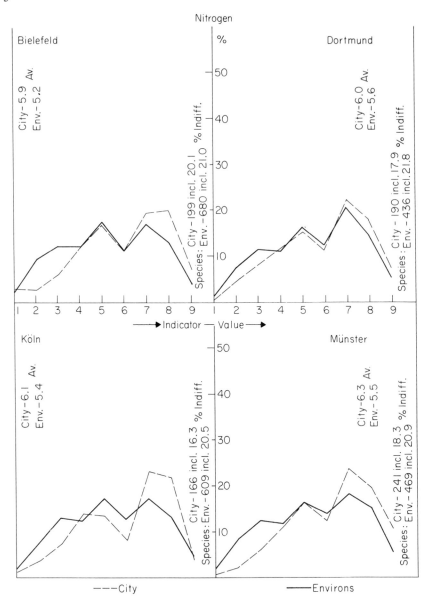

FIG. 3.6.   Indicator-value spectra for nitrogen in four cities and their environs, expressed as a percentage. Indifferent species are not considered.

Bornkamm R. (1974b) Die Unkrautvegetation im Bereich der Stadt Köln. II. Der soziologische Zeigerwert der Arten. *Dechenia*, **126**, 307–332.

Durwen K.-J. (1979) Das Landschaftsökologische Informationssystem LÖKIS-Eine einführende Beschreibung. *Arbeitsberichte des Lehrstuhls Landschaftsökologie Münster*, 1. Selbstverlag, Münster.

Ellenberg H. (1974) Zeigerwerte der Gefässpflanzen Mitteleuropas. *Scripta Geobotanica*, 9, E. Goltze-Verlag, Göttingen.

Kratzer A. (1956) Das Stadtklima. *Die Wissenschaft*, 90, Braunschweig.

Runge F. (1972) Adventivpflanzen der beiden Kanalhälften in Münster während der Jahre 1965–1971. *Natur und Heimat*, **32**, 49–51.

Sukopp H., Blume H.-P., Chinnow D., Kunick W., Runge M. & Zacharias F. (1974) Ökologische Charakteristik von Grossstädten, besonders anthropogene Veränderungen von Klima, Boden und Vegetation. *Zeitschrift der Technischen Universität Berlin*, **6**, 469–488.

Trinczek D. (1975) *Ruderalgesellschaften der Bielefelder Innenstadt.* Staatsexamensarbeit Pädagogische Hochschule, Westfalen-Lippe. Bielefeld.

Wittig R. (1974) Die Ruderalflora der Münsterschen Innenstadt im Jahre 1972. *Göttinger Floristische Rundbriefe*, **8**, 58–62.

industrial habitats around Greater Manchester and I will discuss the conservation of existing habitats and opportunities to create new ones.

CALCAREOUS WASTE HABITATS

Several types of industrial waste form calcareous habitats in Greater Manchester (Table 4.1). The most important orchidiferous site in the county is on alkali waste from the obsolete Leblanc process. Tipped at least 70 years ago, the waste was initially strongly alkaline due to calcium hydroxide. Rainfall has since leached the strong base from the surface to leave a highly

TABLE 4.1. *Types of industrial waste forming calcareous plant habitats in Greater Manchester.*

Material and origin	Initial pH
Leblanc process alkali waste from manufacture of sodium carbonate	Up to 12.7
Blast furnace slag from smelting of iron ores	Up to 10.6
Pulverized fuel ash from coal-burning power stations	Up to 9.5
Calcium carbonate slurry from chemical works	Up to 8.6
Calcareous boiler ash	Up to 8.2
Colliery washery waste	Up to 8.0
Calcareous colliery spoil	Up to 8.0
Demolition rubble	Up to 7.8

calcareous material overlying unweathered alkaline waste (Table 4.2). The soil is also extremely deficient in nitrogen and phosphorus.

The flora of Leblanc waste (Table 4.3) is unusual, its closest natural counterparts being the vegetation of calcareous dune slacks and calcareous soils over chalk and limestone. The flora is very open, species-rich, with a high proportion of dicotyledonous plants. There are several calcicoles, notably *Carlina vulgaris*, *Erigeron acer* and *Linum catharticum*. Garden escapes such as *Aster novi-belgii* and *Solidago* spp. occur, *Sisyrinchium bermudiana* being a presumed garden escape on one site.

Natural calcareous habitats such as chalk and limestone grasslands do not occur in Greater Manchester. This makes the Leblanc waste sites particularly interesting and important. A comparable situation has arisen in the adjacent county of Cheshire where Lee and Greenwood (1976) have described a similar flora on lime-beds from the Solvay process.

Compared with Leblanc waste, pulverized fuel ash from power stations has formed habitats of relatively recent origin. One site, on which ash was

5. MACRO-FUNGAL FLORA OF ŁÓDŹ

MARIA ŁAWRYNOWICZ
Department of Botany,
Institute of Environmental Biology,
University of Łódź, Poland

SUMMARY

The macro-fungal flora of lawns, squares, parks, urban woods and ruderal places of Łódź, a town (214 km², 800,000 inhabitants) situated in central Poland, was studied. Macro-fungi occur throughout the urban area, including the 'lichen desert', and the total number of species recorded exceeds that of wild higher plants. Three zones were recognized: central, urban and suburban. The central zone contained 72 species but lacked epiphytes with woody, perennial fruit bodies and had few mycorrhizal symbionts. Saprophytes of open grassy areas predominated. The urban zone contained 162 species, including epiphytes with woody, perennial fruit bodies and many mycorrhizal symbionts of native forest trees; however, parasites were not abundant. The suburban zone contained 403 species, predominantly forest symbionts and saprophytes.

INTRODUCTION

Fungi are a functional element of all terrestrial ecosystems including urban ones. The vascular and lichen flora of many European towns has been well studied, but little is known of urban macro-fungi. Observations of fungi in towns present numerous interesting problems concerning phenology, adaptation, habitat requirements and response to human activity. However, this paper is concerned principally with their distribution. No complete macro-fungal flora of a town has been found in the literature. In several mycological papers the macro-fungi have been recorded for certain urban areas, mostly botanic gardens, for example Karlvall (1963), Szober (1965), Pegler (1966), Kreisel (1967), Dörfelt and Sommer (1973). Other papers have been concerned with phenological features, for example winter mycoflora (Szulczewski 1930), or the geographical distribution of certain species in urban areas (Skirgiello 1972). This paper examines the fungal flora of Łódź and complements studies of vascular plants (Sowa 1974) and of lichens (Kuziel & Halicz 1979).

AREA OF INVESTIGATION

Łódź is the second largest town in Poland, situated 51°45′ north latitude and
19°28′ east longitude on the watershed of the Wisła and Odra rivers, 190–210
m above sea level. The town covers 214 km², and contains 3,738 inhabitants
per km². Average precipitation is 600 mm annually and the mean annual
temperature is 7.6°C.

The natural environment of Łódź lacks rivers and has few open stretches
of water. The growth of the town during the last 200 years was mainly at the
expense of forest. Łódź is now the centre of the Polish textile industry and has
the highest density of building of any Polish town, but a few vegetated areas
occur in the city centre. Further away from the town centre there are more
green areas, but the greatest number appear in the suburbs, where several
fragments of forest and a nature reserve are maintained between new housing
districts.

The sites colonized by fungi comprise parks, squares and green areas
around buildings and along traffic arteries (there are about 60,000 trees and
400 species of trees and shrubs). Moreover, urban woods amount to 1,300 ha.
Thus there are a large number of microhabitats within the urban area ranging
from semi-natural to artificial.

METHODS

Investigations, begun in 1972 and still in progress, were made at 106 localities
to include a complete variety of habitats. In larger and more natural habitats
(e.g. the nature reserve, the zoo and large parks) regular seasonal examination
of permanent sampling plots was made for 2–3 years. At other sites (e.g.
lawns, squares), fruit bodies were recorded when they appeared. Only the fruit
bodies of macro-fungi were recorded. For analysis the fungi were divided into
three biological groups (symbionts, saprophytes, parasites), and into two
ecological groups (the forest fungi and the fungi of open grassy areas).

MYCOLOGICAL ANALYSIS

Four hundred and seventy-six species of macro-fungi were gathered in Łódź.
(This list forms the basis of Tables 5.1 and 5.2, which summarize the
distribution of the biological and ecological groups.) A few species occur
throughout the urban area, but others are much more local and allow the
identification of three zones: central, urban and suburban.

TABLE 5.1. *The structure of the Łódź macro-fungal flora.*

Zones	Central zone			Urban zone			Suburban zone					Total
Kinds of habitats	Streets	Squares, lawns, ruderal sites	Parks	Streets	Squares, lawns, ruderal sites	Parks	Squares, lawns, ruderal sites, streets	Zoological garden	Parks	Forest reserve	Municipal woodland	
Number of localities	13	3	10	30	12	12	17	1	6	1	1	106
Extent of observed area (ha)	.	.	52	.	.	132	.	17	303	10	1,150	1,664
Biological and ecological groups of species							Number of species					
Forest symbionts	3	2	3	20	8	24	11	62	75	32	112	178
Forest saprophytes	10	10	15	20	22	34	28	44	75	61	107	158
Open area symbionts	6	2	1	12	4	7	6	16	10	2	27	49
Open area saprophytes	18	6	16	40	8	17	6	17	18	17	20	80
Parasites	6	2	3	6	3	4	3	4	7	3	6	11
Total Σ	43	22	38	98	45	86	54	143	185	115	272	476

TABLE 5.2.   *The zonation of the Łódź macro-fungal flora.*

Biological and ecological groups of species	I Central zone	II Urban zone	III Suburban zone	All town area	%
			Total number of species		%
Forest symbionts	8	42	165	178	37.4
Forest saprophytes	22	45	152	158	33.2
Open area symbionts	7	17	37	49	10.3
Open area saprophytes	29	49	41	80	16.8
Parasites	6	9	8	11	2.3
Total $\sum$	72	162	403	476	100
		% of species of the group			
Forest symbionts	4.5	23.6	92.7	—	100
Forest saprophytes	13.9	28.5	96.2	—	100
Open area symbionts	14.3	34.7	75.5	—	100
Open area saprophytes	36.3	61.3	51.3	—	100
Parasites	54.6	81.8	72.7	—	100
All groups together	15.3	34.0	84.7	—	100
		Species occurring in one zone only			
Forest symbionts	2	10	132		
Forest saprophytes	1	5	152		
Open area symbionts	2	8	30		
Open area saprophytes	6	20	16		
Parasites	1	2	1		
Total $\sum$	12	45	331		

Central zone

Buildings and roads occupy between 75 and 90% of the ground area in this zone and vegetation is restricted to roadside verges and small squares and parks. The soil is contaminated with pollutants, the humus layer is often mixed with subsoil and the roadside verges are salted in winter. Herbaceous plants and trees are often present as uniform stands, the lawns are systematically cut and weeded and the trees trimmed or artificially shaped. Natural plant detritus (branches, cones, fruits and leaves) is scrupulously cleared away, thereby limiting normal substrates for fungal growth; however, alternatives in the form of food debris, animal faeces and other urban litter, are often found.

The central zone is wholly situated within the Łódź 'lichen desert' described by Kuziel and Halicz (1979). Altogether 72 species of macro-fungi were collected there (15.3% of the total mycoflora), and these were largely woodland or grassland saprophytes. The most frequently occurring species on lawns were *Panaeolina foenisecii* (Pers. ex Fr.) R.Mre., *Panaeolus fimicola*

(Fr.) Gill., and species of *Conocybe*, *Agrocybe* and *Stropharia*, notably *S. coronilla* (Bull. ex Fr.) Quél. Species of *Agaricus* and *Coprinus* were found on faeces or rotting timber. The most frequently occurring symbiont was *Marasmius oreades* (Bolt. ex. Fr.) Fr., forming fairy rings in grassy areas. A few forest symbionts of the genera *Russula*, *Leccinum* and *Cortinarius* were recorded from parks along with six species which may be parasitic: *Pleurotus ostreatus* (Jacq. ex Fr.) Kummer, *Armillariella mellea* Vahl. in Fl. Dan. ex Fr., *Polyporus squamosus* (Huds.) Fr., *Pholiota squarrosa* (Pers. ex. Fr.) Kummer, *Flammulina velutipes* (Curt. ex Fr.) Sing. and *Agrocybe aegerita* (Brig.) Sing. However, in the surrounding forest these species are more usually saprophytic. All these species have soft and short-lived fruit bodies. There is a lack of species with woody fruit bodies, e.g. *Fomes fomentarius* (L. ex Fr.) Kickx. which is a common species in the surrounding forests. In spite of the presence of many severely mutilated birch trees, typical species such as *Piptoporus betulinus* (Bull. ex Fr.) P. Karst. were not found in this zone. Similarly, many typical birch mycorrhizal symbionts, common in forests, were not observed here.

The limited number of symbionts and the lack of macro-fungi with woody and long-lived fruit bodies are the most striking features of the mycoflora of this zone.

Urban zone

This surrounds the central zone. Macro-fungi occur here in more spacious squares, and in fairly large parks and old established gardens. This is an area of intensive rebuilding, with new housing estates and municipal buildings replacing older houses, resulting in the destruction of former habitats and the creation of new ones. Buildings and roads cover 25–75% of the total area. One hundred and sixty-two species were recorded from this zone (34.0% of the total mycoflora); saprophytes are the most numerous group (45 forest and 49 grassland species). This is nearly double the number of saprophyte species of the central zone, and results from the greater variety of habitats. There is more rotting wood, branches, cones, litter and other plant remains on which fungi can thrive.

Saprophytes and parasites with perennial fruit bodies were recorded (e.g. *Daedalea quercina* L. ex Fr., *Ganoderma applanatum* (Pers. ex Wallr.) Pat.). *Piptoporus betulinus* (Bull. ex Fr.) P. Harst., *Xylosphaera hypoxylon* L. ex Dumort. and species of *Stereum* were frequent. The species recorded in the central zone were also found in the urban zone. An increase in habitat diversity, particularly ruderal ones, accounts for the occurrence of a number of species of the *Pezizales*.

The urban zone has many more forest symbionts than the central zone, (e.g. *Quercus robur*: *Lactarius quietus* Fr., *Amanita citrina* (Schff.) S.F. Gray,

A.rubescens (Pers. ex Fr.) S.F. Gray, *Boletus aestivalis* (Paulet) ex Fr.; *Betula pendula*: *Amanita muscaria* (L. ex Fr.) Hooker, *Lactarius torminosus* (Schff. ex Fr.) S.F. Gray, *Boletus boleticolus* (Vasilk.) Pil. et Derm.; *Pinus sylvestris*: *Lactarius rufus* (Scop.) Fr.; *Carpinus betulus*: *Oudemansiella radicata* (Relhan ex Fr.) Sing). Rare hypogeous fungi (*Hymenogaster tener* Berk. et Br. and *Melanogaster intermedius* Zeller et Dodge) are also present.

Suburban zone

This outer zone consists of big, new housing districts and industrial warehouses mixed with agricultural areas, forests, parks and gardens. Roads and houses account for 10–25% of the surface area. Two big forest complexes occur here: Łagiewniki Forest, preserved as a recreation area, and the People's Park, which has areas set aside as a nature reserve and a zoological garden. Habitats include coniferous and deciduous forests, parks, spacious green areas around housing developments, and also meadows, waste ground and other ruderal localities.

In this zone, 403 macro-fungal species were recorded (84.7% of the total mycoflora), including four hypogeous species. The largest group are forest species (165 symbiotic and 152 saprophytic species). On the other hand, the number of open habitat saprophytes and parasites is lower than in the urban zone. They owe their prevalence in the inner zones to soil cultivation limiting the growth of other fungi. However, fungi of disturbed and modified habitats exist in this zone only with those of natural ones. This results in a rich flora, richer than in some undisturbed forest areas.

CONCLUSIONS

Łódź has a rich and varied fungal flora, in part the result of human activity increasing the variety of potential habitats. Forest symbionts show the greatest reduction in species number in the city centre, and this apparent scarcity of symbionts may adversely affect the growth of trees. In the central zone, saprophytes and parasites with perennial woody fruit bodies are absent, and the distribution of the fruit bodies of some species is restricted. Thus *Armillariella mellea* fruit bodies are found only on tree roots in the city centre, whereas elsewhere they may be found growing on trunks as well. The cause of this is unknown, but may be related to the relative humidity of urban climates. However, although low relative humidity and high levels of pollutants may affect the growth and distribution of some macro-fungi, they are clearly not as sensitive to these factors as lichens since many species of macro-fungi occur in the 'lichen desert'.

REFERENCES

Dörfelt H. & Sommer B. (1973) Pilzfunde im Botanischen Garten Halle. *Mykologisches Mitteilungsblatt*, **17**, 36–43.

Karlvall F. (1963) Larger fungi in the Botanic Gardens in Gothenburg. *Acta Horti Gotoburgensis*, **36**, 19–62.

Kreisel H. (1967) Die Pflanzenbestande des Botanischen Gartens der Ernst-Moritz-Arndt-Universität Greifswald, 3. Die Großpilze des Greifswalder Botanischen Gartens. *Wissenschaftliche Zeitschrift der Ernst-Moritz-Arndt-Universität Greifswald*, **16**, 229–239.

Kuziel S. & Halicz B. (1979) Wystepowanie porostów epifitycznych na obszarze Łodzi. (The occurrence of epiphytic lichens in the area of Łódź.) *Łódzkie Towarzystwo Naukowe— Societas Scientiarum Łodziensis, Sprawozdania z Czynności i Posiedzeń Naukowych*, **33**, 1–7.

Moser M. (1978) Die Röhrlinge und Blätterpilze (Polyporales, Boletales. Agaricales, Russulales). *Kleine Kryptogamenflora*, Band II, Teil b 2. 4. Auflage. Gustav Fischer Verlag, Stuttgart, New York.

Pegler D.N. (1966) Additions to the wild fauna and flora of the Royal Botanic Gardens, Kew. XXVII. A revised list of the Agarics and Boleti. *Kew Bulletin*, **20**, 201–231.

Skirgiello A. (1972) Materiały do poznania rozmieszczenia geograficznego grzybów wyższych w Europie. IV. (Materials to knowledge of the geographical distribution of higher fungi in Europe. IV.) *Acta Mycologica*, **8**, 191–218.

Sowa R. (1974) Wykaz gatunków flory synantropijnej Łodzi oraz zarys ich analizy geograficzno-historycznej. (A list of species of Łodz synanthrophic flora and an outline of their geographic-historical analysis.) *Zeszyty Naukowe Uniwersytetu Lodzkiego, Nauki matematyczno-przyrodnicze*. Seria II, **54**, 11–26.

Szober J. (1965) Grzyby wyższe ogrodu Botanicznego Uniwersytetu Warszawskiego. (Higher fungi of the Botanical Garden of the Warsaw University.) *Hortus Botanicus Universitatis Varsoviensis*. Państwowe Wydawnictwo Naukowe, Warszawa.

Szulczewski J.W. (1930) Prźyczynek do zimowej mykoflory Poznania i okolic (A contribution to the winter mycoflora of Poznan and its vicinity.) *Kosmos*, **55A**, 233–248.

6. HABITAT DIVERSITY AND INVERTEBRATES IN URBAN AREAS

B. N. K. DAVIS

Institute of Terrestrial Ecology,
Monks Wood Experimental Station,
Abbots Ripton, Huntingdon, U.K.

SUMMARY

The diversity of invertebrates in urban areas has been associated with various features including the extent and isolation of suitable habitats, the diversity of planted vegetation, the variety of artificial niches and the degree of pollution and disturbance. A critical appraisal is made of the methodology and rationale used in this synecological approach. Whilst it provides a valuable means of recognizing general trends and of measuring statistical relationships, it is seen as providing only the first step in understanding causal relationships. In particular it is considered important to distinguish three categories of invertebrates: widespread eurytopic species, those that only survive in less disturbed situations because of their specialized requirements, and those that thrive especially in man-made habitats.

Autecological observations form a second stage and two brief studies in the London area are reported:
1 a comparison of litter arthropods in a series of increasingly artificial environments;
2 a survey of phytophagous Hemiptera associated with different families of flowering plants in the Chelsea Physic Garden.
Experimental studies are now required as a third stage in testing hypotheses derived from such observational studies on urban invertebrates.

INTRODUCTION

The development of ecology in Britain has been greatly influenced by Tansley's (1939) perception of natural and semi-natural habitat types. Croplands and other artificial ecosystems managed for economic purposes have attracted the attention of applied ecologists but urbanized environments have been largely ignored. This is demonstrated in past reports of even such an urban-based body as the London Natural History Society. Reading the presidential address to the Society on 'Habitats in the London Area' (Peterken

1953) one would scarcely realize that the area was urban at all: the whole emphasis was on the fragments of semi-natural habitats remaining within the Society's boundary and there was no mention of parks, playing fields, gardens or waste ground that together comprise so much of the open space of our towns and cities. Buildings, parks and gardens *were* recognized as a special category by Elton and Miller (1954) in their classification of animal habitats. They considered them to be 'partly impoverished samples of what would live in a richer mosaic of natural habitats and partly peculiar in so far as man has introduced edible substances and created conditions (especially local high temperatures) that do not occur elsewhere'. Gardens and playing fields alone have been estimated to represent 30% of the total built-up land in the U.K. (Fordham 1975) and the past decade has in fact seen a widespread and increasing interest in the fauna and flora of urban areas both by professional ecologists and by those responsible for shaping and managing the planned open space of urban areas, for example Sukopp *et al* (1974), Euler *et al* (1975), Davis (1976), Frankie and Ehler (1978), Frankie and Koehler (1978), Teagle (1978) and Laurie (1979).

Vertebrates and plants attract most attention but invertebrates present many interesting ecological questions which have been tackled in a variety of ways. Studies of invertebrates in urban areas may be divided into three categories:

1 annotated inventories, for example Groves (1964–7), Pappa (1976);
2 autecological studies, for example Haeseler (1972);
3 synecological studies based on measures of diversity.

I want to examine the rationale and methodology used in this last category before returning to the autecological approach.

SYNECOLOGY AND FAUNAL DIVERSITY

If increasing urbanization leads primarily to a graded impoverishment of the pre-existing fauna, as is often stated, one would expect to detect a trend in species richness along a transect from the edge to the centre of a concentrically developed city like London. I have examined this hypothesis and found it to be substantially correct for ground-living arthropods (Davis 1978, 1979a); the numbers of species declined by nearly 60% between the urban fringe and the City of London. With a total fauna of 111 species spread through seven orders of arthropods, the regression between species-richness at a site and the logarithm of the distance from the city centre was highly significant ($P < 0.001$, correlation coefficient $R^2 = 0.74$). However, this in itself provides no causal explanation and four possible factors can be invoked:

1   increasing disturbance, including the effects of pollution;
2   a reduction in the total area of exploitable habitat with increasing urbanization—a species/area effect;
3   reduction in habitat diversity or variety of niches;
4   some other urban-induced factor such as the heat-island effect.

Disturbance

Disturbance is an important factor limiting vertebrates in urban areas though quite surprising degrees of tolerance can be developed by birds and mammals through behavioural adaptations (Laurie 1979). Such evidence as exists for invertebrates indicates that activities such as trampling, mowing, cultivation and use of pesticides are almost wholly deleterious to species-diversity (Chappell *et al* 1971; Schaefer 1973; Duffey 1975) but there are no quantitative data specifically from towns and cities. The sheer density and activity of people in public recreation areas often causes considerable disturbance, but this cannot be readily dissociated from the deliberate simplification of ecosystems, usually expressed in extensive areas of mown grass, the planting of standard trees, the removal of scrub in woodlands, etc.

Pollution from smoke has been blamed for the scarcity of many common species of spiders in central London (Bristowe 1939) and the lack of insect prey for house martins (*Delichon urbica* (L.)) and swifts (*Apus apus* (L.)) until the 1960s (Cramp & Gooders 1967; Gooders 1968). These suggestions are plausible but there is no experimental evidence to support them. On the other hand, studies on metal pollution from vehicle exhausts have not shown any detectable effects on the invertebrate faunas of road verges in Durham and London (Williamson & Evans 1973; Muskett 1980).

Area

There is good evidence that the extent of suitable habitat is an important factor in determining faunal diversity. This has been shown in the case of highly mobile groups of insects such as Diptera and Coleoptera on herbage in Cincinnati city parks (Faeth & Kane 1978), for gall-forming and leaf-mining insects in Kiel (Segebade & Schaefer 1979) and for ground-living arthropods in London gardens (Davis 1979a). The first two of these studies utilized the concept of habitat islands derived from MacArthur and Wilson's (1967) theories. Faeth and Kane did not in fact show any relationship between species diversity and distance from the presumed source(s) of colonization outside the city. This could be partly because of the somewhat arbitrary assumptions that had to be made: they ignored the presence of gardens and other areas of vegetation that lay around the parks within the city though Owen and Owen (1975) and Owen (1978) have shown how attractive a single herbaceous border can be to hoverflies (Syrphidae) and coccinellid beetles (amongst other insects) and thus how effective gardens could be as 'stepping-stones' for colonization by such groups. Davis and Glick (1978) have made a critical review of the 'habitat island' concept in the urban context and consider that it is probably not relevant to apply the equilibrium model. Urbanization is seen as a negative process causing fragmentation and decrease of available habitats for wildlife together with increasing disturbance which are not matched in the colonization/extinction processes of true islands.

The extent to which habitat islands are isolated from each other and from the surrounding rural reservoir will depend a great deal upon the mobility of the group that is considered as well as upon the actual distances involved. A busy road may provide a considerable barrier for small, crawling invertebrates such as woodlice (Oniscoidea) whilst even a block of terrace buildings or a river may not hinder a bee from passing to and fro, repeatedly. The migration and colonizing ability of terrestrial arthropods is also linked with the permanence of their habitats (Southwood 1962). Thus, to take just two examples from Southwood's review, many studies have shown that calypterate flies which breed in decaying animal and plant material, or fruit flies with a large range of host plants, can travel many miles in a day or two whilst trypetid flies with a limited range of host plants have much smaller mean dispersal distances. Thus the combining of groups with very different powers of dispersal may well obscure any relationships with environmental variables that are measured.

Diversity of habitat

Davis (1979a) listed 15 habitat features of London gardens that could influence ground-living arthropods directly or indirectly but it was not considered feasible to use these in any quantitative analysis because of the inability to assign weighting values to them. There were clearly differences not only in the extent of features such as cultivated ground at any given site but in the relative importance of cultivated ground versus shrubberies etc., for different groups of invertebrates.

Faeth and Kane (1978) did quantify environmental heterogeneity in city parks using a diversity index based on eight habitat types. They found that this index did not add a significant contribution to the multiple regression after considering the effect of area, and concluded that area alone was therefore the determining factor for species richness. However, if habitat diversity and area were themselves closely correlated, it is highly likely that the addition of this term would contribute little to a multiple regression analysis. (In the multiple regression on species-diversity in London gardens, the combination of two terms each with a simple correlation coefficient of 0.73–0.74 gave an improvement of only 0.08.) Figures 3 and 4 in Faeth and Kane's paper suggest that the total number of species of Diptera and Coleoptera collected was of the order of 200 and one may have cause to doubt whether a simple index of habitat diversity could ever be found to 'explain' such species diversity.

On the other hand, Schaefer and Koch (1979) found a correlation between the number of carabid beetle species and the structural diversity of Kiel city parks and nearby woodlands. The fact that a smaller and more homogeneous taxonomic group was studied may have helped to identify relevant habitat features.

Different groups of invertebrates respond quite differently to the same set of habitat features and habitat diversity must, therefore, be seen in relation to the biology of the group. Thus there are distinctive communities of spiders associated with different *physical* characteristics of ground and vegetation layers (Duffey 1962; 1968) whilst phytophagous insects such as Curculionoidea or gall insects are often dependent on particular species of host plants and thus on the *botanical* composition of a plant community. Furthermore, there is a limit to the diversification of habitat which can be reflected in the fauna. Fine-grained, patchy environments will suit euryoecious, highly mobile or polyphagous animals, but not those that need substantial areas of permanent habitat wherein to maintain populations.

Urban climates

Chandler (1976) has described the climate of towns and in the case of London has shown a very clear picture of the heat-island effect based on annual accumulated temperatures (Chandler 1965). For plants, there was estimated to be an 'active growing season' (when temperatures were above 5.5°C) of 279 days near the centre of Regent's Park compared with 261 days only four km further north. Data for the period 1969–78 for two London weather stations and two stations just outside London are given in Figure 6.1. This is equivalent to a considerable difference in latitude and could be expected to affect the life-cycles and survival of some invertebrates. It is not obvious, however, why increasing temperatures towards a city centre should affect faunal diversity and there are many very local factors (greenhouses being an extreme example) which would obscure a linear climatic gradient.

AUTECOLOGY

Whereas the synecological approach provides a valuable means of examining complex ecosystems by yielding statistical relationships, autecology can give a deeper insight into causal relationships. In the urban context, this can be most readily seen in relation to the 'peculiar' conditions referred to by Elton and Miller (1954) quoted earlier; that is, by considering species which are

Ranunculaceae contained only two predatory bugs and this was the only family without *Empoasca* spp.; in contrast, the Labiatae sample contained 245 individuals of 10 species and the Urticaceae + Cannabiaceae produced 93 individuals of 13 species. Of the seven Hemiptera considered to be host-specific, five were indeed confined to the appropriate family beds i.e. *Asciodema obsoletum* and *Orthotylus adenocarpi* on *Ulex* and *Sarothamnus* (Leguminosae), *Orthops campestris* on *Pastinaca* and other Umbelliferae, *Liocoris tripustulatus* and *Eupteryx urticae* on *Urtica*. *Eupteryx melissae* lives on various Labiatae and the large population had evidently spilt over onto other nearby beds but the single *Megalocoleus molliculus* failed to show an association with the cultivated *Achillea* spp. grown in the Compositae bed.

This list could clearly be extended by sampling other family beds and at other times of year or by including phytophagous beetles (numerous in suction samples from Cruciferae) or leaf-mining Diptera (very conspicuous in the Ranunculaceae bed). The degree of host-specificity could also be examined more closely by sampling of individual plants within particular family beds such as the Labiatae or Compositae. In the case of the Urticaceae it was noted that the South European *Urtica pilulifera* L. was attacked by several Homoptera Sternorhyncha specific to native *Urtica* spp. in Britain, namely *Aphis urticata* Fab., *Microlophium carnosum* (Bukt.), *Trioza urticae* (L.) and the flower-beetle *Brachypterus glaber* (Steph.). Likewise, the urticaceous Japanese plant *Boehmeria biloba* Weddell was being fed upon by the pyralid caterpillar *Pleuroptya ruralis* (Scop.) which is monophagous on *Urtica* in Britain.

DISCUSSION

Perivale Wood and similar semi-natural sites form one end of the range of habitats occurring within urban areas whilst the fully built-up environment forms the other. In between, comes a wide range of more or less artificial habitats: public recreational/amenity areas such as Holland Park with its mixture of native and non-native trees and a good development of field and shrub layers; public or private gardens and squares often with a rich mosaic of floristic and structural features but an increasing separation of field, shrub and tree layers and increasing disturbance/management; areas of waste building ground and the legacies of industry, starkly new or converted by time into secondary wilderness ably described by Teagle (1978).

Although the two brief surveys of litter arthropods and phytophagous insects described above only touch upon the autecology of the species concerned, they illuminate various aspects of habitat diversity in the urban environment and carry forward the initial (synecological) study of London's invertebrate fauna (Davis 1978). They lend support to Elton and Miller's

(1954) assessment of urban biotopes both as regards the limited faunas of semi-natural woodland habitats and the specially adapted faunas of artificial habitats like ornamental flower beds and compost heaps. In particular, the studies emphasize the great variation in habitat-specificity among invertebrates and the strong tendency for aggregation around favourable resources or places of refuge, for example *Cylindroiulus teutonicus, C.parisiorum* and *Choneiulus palmatus* among millipedes, *Haplothalmus danicus* and *Trichoniscus pusillus* in the woodlice and *Anthocoris nemoralis, Orthops campestris* and *Eupteryx melissae* in the Hemiptera.

Artificial resources such as alien plant species are sometimes attacked by polyphagous insects or those associated with related, native plants as seen among the Urticaceae at the Chelsea Physic Garden and reported by Owen and Whiteway (1980) for *Buddleia davidii* Franchet in Britain. In other cases they are attacked by introduced insects, for example *Placotettix taeniatifrons* (Kirsch.) collected at the Chelsea Physic Garden in October 1979 and apparently introduced into this country on *Rhododendron* spp. in the last few decades. Similarly, the breakdown of leaf litter from exotic trees and shrubs in urban areas appears to attract an unusual fauna: it is surely significant that such a large proportion of the millipede fauna found consisted of uncommon species (4 out of 14), and that the heaps of leaf compost at Chelsea Physic Garden and the Tavistock Place garden were so dominated by uncommon species. Tischler (1973) has pointed out the increasing degree of synanthropy among arthropods from the south towards the north of Europe through an association with refuse heaps where temperatures are artificially raised. The urban heat-island effect may itself be a significant factor in northern latitudes for species with a southerly distribution in the same way as chalk and limestone quarries appear to extend the northern distribution of certain plants and invertebrates in Britain through locally enhanced temperatures (Davis 1979b). Further experimental work is needed on the biology of such restricted elements of urban faunas to determine their powers of dispersal and competitive abilities and the relative importance of food supply and local micro-climatic conditions.

ACKNOWLEDGEMENTS

I am very grateful to Mr A.P. Paterson, Mrs P. Small (Selborne Society) and Mr A. Janaway (G.L.C. Parks Department) for allowing me to sample invertebrates at the Chelsea Physic Garden, Perivale Wood and Holland Park, respectively. I should also like to thank Mr P.E. Jones for his help in collecting and identifying the material and the Meteorological Office for supplying air temperature data.

2. *Carabid beetles*, as an example of predatory arthropods of the soil surface which walk more than fly and are in part even incapable of flying.

3. *Hover flies*, as an example of flower-visiting insects with a wide dispersal power.

4. *Bumble bees*, as an example of specialized flower-visitors with a limited range in the vicinity of the nest.

THE STUDY SITES

The areas studied are situated in the built-up centre of Berlin, in varying degrees of isolation. They have all developed in the course of 20–30 years from bare-ground sites to relatively similar ruderal plots with grass or tall herb communities containing some woody plants. The soils are pararendzina on rubble.

Site I

An isolated ruderal plot in the heavily built-up city centre (the corner of Fasanenstrasse and Lietzenburger Strasse) of approximately 0.2 ha, protected from visitors by a high fence. The distance to the next large park (the Zoological Garden) is approximately 1 km. The vegetation is a tall herb plant stand which is subject to great anthropogenic disturbance and which had been mown shortly before this study. A few woody and climbing plants are found on the fringe.

Site II

A ruderal site at Lützowplatz in the city centre, approximately 0.8 ha. This site was levelled rubble in 1959, and has been spontaneously colonized by wild plants. It is separated from the very large park 'Grosser Tiergarten' to the north by only 500 m; in between lie vacant lots and a canal. It is surrounded by buildings in the other directions. Area IIa is a young forest of *Robinia* (Chelidonio-Robinietum). Area IIb is a ruderal grassland site with a few patches of tall herbaceous plants.

Site III

A ruderal area on the Tiergartenstrasse, directly adjacent to the 'Grosser Tiergarten'. The area studied is approximately 1 ha, and borders on other ruderal areas and ruins. The vegetation is a mosaic of grassland, tall herbaceous plants and shrubs.

ORIBATID MITES (ACARI, ORIBATEI)

On each site 10 soil samples of 100 cm^3 volume were taken at a depth of 0–4 cm and the fauna extracted with a Berlese-Tullgren apparatus. In total 20 species of oribatid mites occur in the three sites.

Site I, which is the most isolated, is the poorest in species and individuals (Table 8.1). All species found are either drought-tolerant ubiquists or drought-loving species.

TABLE 8.1. *Oribatid mites (Dominance %) in three ruderal areas in the city of Berlin.*

Site	I	IIa	IIb	III
Eupelops occultus (Koch)				7
Liochthonius lapponicus (Träg.)			22	
Oppia minus (Paoli)			9	
Oppiella nova (Oudms.)			1	
O.obsoleta (Paoli)	6			
Oribatella quadricornuta (Mich.)		+	+	
Oribatula tibialis (Nic.)	26	7		
Peloptulus phaenotus (Koch)			+	2
Pilogalumna allifera (Oudms.)		5		5
P.tenuiclava (Berl.)				13
Quadroppia quadricarinata (Mich.)				2
Rhysotritia ardua (Koch)		1	5	1
Scheloribates laevigatus (Koch)				21
Scutovertex minutus (Koch)				+
Steganacarus striculus (Koch)		+		
Suctobelbella nasalis (Forss.)		2		
S.sarekensis (Forss.)	68	17	3	5
S.subcornigera (Forss.)		51	7	8
Tectocepheus sarekensis Träg.		16	51	36
Trichoribates novus Selln.		2		+
Species:	3	9	10	12
Individuals in one l (0–4 cm)	31	184	283	259

The oribatid fauna of the ruderal Sites II and III is, in comparison to that of cultivated park lawns, abundant, but in comparison to that of city forest soils, however, less well-developed (Weigmann & Stratil 1979). Typical forest species are insignificant, even on Site IIa. The colonization of the sites by moss mites and other small arthropods has not been completed and, because of the purely passive dispersal of mites, a balanced, species-rich ruderal fauna will only be observed after a long period of time. Site I is, because of its isolated position from sources of mites, still in the pioneer-colonizer phase with respect to the oribatid mite fauna. The most frequent species in the dry city soils in Berlin, *Tectocepheus sarekensis*, is missing there.

CARABID BEETLES (COLEOPTERA, CARABIDAE)

The carabid fauna as analysed with the help of three pitfall traps per study site, each of which was emptied weekly during the vegetation-growing season from May until October (the total catch was 1,040 carabids). The results in Table 8.2 do not include those species represented by only one individual per site. Thirty-seven species of carabids were found.

TABLE 8.2.   *Carabid beetles (Dominance %) in three ruderal areas in the city of Berlin.*

Site	I	IIa	IIb	III	wings
Amara aenea (Deg.)		1	1	9	m
A.bifrons (Gyll.)	12	2	1	6	m
A.consularis (Dft.)		+		1	m
A.fulva (Müll.)		2			m
Badister bipustulatus (F.)		+	2	+	m
Bembidion lampros (Hbst.)		1			d
Calathus ambiguus (Pay.)		1		2	m
C.fuscipes (Goeze)		23	46	11	b
C.melanocephalus (L.)	27	5	14	4	d
C.mollis (Marsh.)	12	1	1	+	d
C.piceus (Marsh.)	46				d
Harpalus aeneus (F.)		1	1		m
H.rubripes (Dft.)		+	2	1	m
H.rufipes (Deg.)		19	3	1	m
H.smaragdinus (Dft.)		1		1	m
H.tardus (Panz.)		1	2	2	m
H.vernalis (Dft.)			3	2	b
H.winkleri Schaub.		1			m
Licinus depressus (Pay.)				1	b
Masoreus wetterhalli (Gyll.)				1	d
Metabletus foveolatus (Fourc.)			1	2	b
Nebria brevicollis (F.)		38	24	50	m
Synuchus nivalis (Panz.)				+	d
Species, total:	7	24	15	26	
Individuals/one trap, 30 days	4.7	31.3	11.4	36.6	

Rare species are omitted. Wings: m = macropterous; b = brachypterous; d = dimorphic species.

The carabid fauna is composed for the most part of widespread species of dry grass, fallow land and cultivated fields (Thiele 1977; Haeck 1971; Barndt 1976) and differs essentially from the forest carabid fauna in parks (Schaefer & Kock 1979), only one forest species (*Nebria brevicollis*) is abundant. The carabid fauna of Site IIa is not a forest one. Of the brachypterous species (*Calathus fuscipes*, *Harpalus vernalis* and *Metabletus foveolatus*), only *Calathus fuscipes* is frequent at Sites II and III. Of the species which, according to the literature, are dimorphic (i.e. part macropterous (m) and part brachypterous (b)), the following were found: *Bembidion lampros* (100% m), *Calathus melanocephalus* (6% m), *C.mollis* (64% m), *C.piceus* (100% m), *Masoreus wetterhalli* (75% m) and *Synuchus nivalis* (100% m).

The isolated Site I is poor in species (7) and in individuals (Table 8.2); the ruderal meadow of Site III is, with 26 species, as well colonized as dry grassland areas outside the Berlin city region (Barndt 1976). Site IIb (ruderal meadow) is poorer in species than IIa, but has the same dominants with the exception of *Harpalus rufipes*.

HOVER FLIES (DIPTERA, SYRPHIDAE)

The syrphid fauna has not been studied quantitatively. The total species inventory (25 spp) was established by net catches made on 10 catch dates in two summer periods.

The fauna (Table 8.3) consists of generally widespread species. In much

TABLE 8.3. *Hover flies in three ruderal areas in the city of Berlin.*

Site	I	II	III
Chilosia sp.		x	
Chrysotoxum festivum (L.)			r
Epistrophe balteata (Deg.)	x	xx	xx
Eristalis arbustorum (L.)		xx	xx
E.intricarius (L.)		xx	x
E.pertinax (Scop.)			r
Eristalomyia tenax (L.)		xx	xx
Helophilus hybridus Loew.			r
H.pendulus (L.)	x	x	xx
H.trivittatus (Fabr.)	x	x	
Lasiopticus pyrastri (L.)			r
Melanostoma mellinum (L.)		x	x
Myiatropa florea (L.)	x		x
Pipiza festiva Meig.	x		
Sphaerophoria menthastri (L.)			x
Syritta pipiens (L.)			xx
Syrphus albostriatus (Fall.)			r
S.corollae Fabr.	x	x	
S.luniger Meig.		r	
S.ribesii (L.)	x	x	xx
S.tricinctus (Fall.)			r
S.vitripennis Meig.	x	xx	xx
Volucella pellucens (L.)		r	
V.zonaria (Poda)			r
Zelima segnis (L.)	r		
Species:	9	13	18

xx = dominant; x = abundant; r = rare.

more extensive studies in an English suburban garden, Owen (1978) found a
total of 81 species, 47 of these in the first year of study.

Since we must assume that some species do not brood directly in the area,
because their larvae have special needs, for example they live in water, the
species number in the Sites II and III is relatively high for ruderal areas
isolated in the middle of a city. This is probably due to the abundance of
flowers. Site I is presumably thinly populated because of its greater isolation
and the occurrence of fewer flowers. Eleven of the species found feed as larvae
on leaf lice and other homoptera, and eight species require small muddy
bodies of water. Several suitable bodies of water can be found in the vicinity of
Site III, which probably explains why this group of the Syrphids is more
abundant (39% of the total) than at other sites.

BUMBLE BEES (HYMENOPTERA, BOMBUS SPP.)

The species which exist in the three areas were determined on 10 catch dates
each. Exact dominance numbers were not established. Only five species, which
are frequent in the Berlin area, were found in the ruderal sites (Table 8.4).
Cuckoo bees (*Psithyrus* spp.) were not observed.

TABLE 8.4. *Bumble bees in three ruderal areas in the city of Berlin.*

Site	I	II	III
Bombus agrorum (F.)		x	xx
B.hypnorum (L.)		xx	xx
B.lapidarius (L.)	r	xx	xx
B.pratorum (L.)			x
B.terrestris (L.)		x	xx
Species:	1	4	5

xx = dominant; x = abundant; r = rare.

Bumble bees do not fly very far from their nest, seldom more than 2 km. It
can, therefore, be supposed that all species live in the study areas II and III or
in the adjacent ruderal areas and in the 'Grosser Tiergarten'. The rubble soil,
which is rich in openings, offers many nesting possibilities. Bumble bees are
generally short of food sources and nesting sites in the built-up city area, but
these ruderal sites are, for a large city, extremely rich in flowers and therefore
have a high ecological value. Owen (1978) found eight Bombus spp. and two
Psithyrus spp. in an English suburban garden.

DISCUSSION

All animal groups studied show the least number of species (total 18) at Site I, which is the most isolated site from other green areas and lies in a heavily built-up section. All animal groups show the highest numbers of species (total 60) at Site III, which has direct contact to a large city park and to other ruderal sites. The ruderal meadow IIb has, with a total of 41 species, an average value; it is separated only by a canal from Site III, but is surrounded on the other sides by buildings.

It seems probable that, given a relatively similar vegetation development, the faunistic richness is decided by the position of potentially colonizable areas in relation to already colonized regions. In comparison to the easily colonized Site III (next to a park and in a former villa district), Site I harbours only 25% oribatid species, 20% carabid species, no *Bombus* spp. and 50% Syrphid species. The relatively high Syrphid figure relates to dispersal activity. In addition to the isolation from animal populations, Site I is also from a floristic standpoint the poorest, presumably also as a result of isolation. If one supposes, following the ideas of MacArthur and Wilson (1967), that 'biotope islands' in the city also strive for an equilibrium of species numbers, which depends on the size of the island as well as on the ecological variety, then Site I, as the smallest island, will presumably always remain relatively species-poor.

The non-flying brachypterous carabids and the dimorphic species (in part brachypterous) are particularly interesting for our discussion. *Calathus fuscipes* (b), which was dominant in Sites II and III, was very rare on Site I (only one animal was observed) and had possibly only arrived recently (?).

Haeck (1971) found 'almost exclusively winged individuals of dimorphic species' on newly formed polders in Holland. A similar observation does not appear to hold true for all dimorphic species of the 'biotope island' of Site I. All seven *C.melanocephalus* and two of three *C.mollis* individuals were brachypterous, but all 12 *C.piceus* were macropterous.

An empirical rule with regard to island carabids (see Barndt 1976, p. 51) seems, on the other hand, to be substantiated. This rule states that on islands, fewer brachypterous species but more dimorphic species with macropterous individuals occur than on the mainland.

At the isolated Site I, 13 of 22 individuals (59%) of the three dimorphic species were macropterous; at Site III, seven of 24 individuals (29%) of the five dimorphic species were macropterous.

ACKNOWLEDGEMENTS

The author is indebted to Dr R. Böcker and Professor Korge for their help with species identification.

REFERENCES

Barndt D. (1976) *Das Naturschutzgebiet Pfaueninsel in Berlin. Faunistik und Ökologie der Carabiden.* Diss. Freie Universität Berlin.

Blume H.-P., Horbert M., Horn R. & Sukopp H. (1978) Zur Ökologie der Grossstadt unter besonderer Berücksichtigung von Berlin (West). *Schriftenreihe des deutschen Rates für Landespflege*, **30**, 658–677.

Haeck J. (1971) The Immigration and Settlement of Carabids in the new Ijsselmeer-Polders. *Landsbouwhogeschool, Wageningen, Miscellaneous papers*, **8**, 33–52.

MacArthur R.H. & Wilson E.O. (1967) *The theory of island biogeography.* Princeton, N.J., University Press.

Owen D.F. (1978) Insect diversity in an English suburban garden. In, *Perspectives in urban entomology* (Ed. by G.W. Frankie & C.S. Koehler) pp. 13–19. Academic Press, New York, San Francisco, London.

Schaefer M. & Kock K. (1979) Zur Ökologie der Arthropdenfauna einer Stadtlandschaft und ihrer Umgebung. I. Laufkäfer (Carabidae) und Spinnen (Araneida). *Anzeiger für Schädlingskunde, Pflanzenschutz und Umweltschutz*, **52**, 85–90.

Thiele H.U. (1977) *Carabid beetles in their environments.* Zoophysiology and Ecology **10**. Springer; Berlin, Heidelberg, New York.

Weigmann G. & Stratil H. (1979) Bodenfauna im Tiergarten. In, *Ökologisches Gutachten über die Auswirkungen von Bau und Betrieb auf den Grossen Tiergarten* (Ed. by H. Sukopp), pp. 54–71. Senator für Bau- und Wohnungswesen, Berlin.

9. FREE-LIVING INVERTEBRATES WITHIN THE MAJOR ECOSYSTEMS OF VIENNA

WILHELM KÜHNELT

Institut für Zoologie, Universität, Wien I

SUMMARY

Knowledge of the biogeographical and ecological situation (in the widest sense) is necessary to investigate human impact on the living world of a city. Animal species react differently to changes in conditions, and a distinction can be made between susceptible and non-susceptible species. The former can be used as indicators, and the latter are accumulators of contaminants. The most important ecosystem in Vienna (the river-woods) is described.

INTRODUCTION

In order to assess the degree of urban stress by using free-living animals as indicators, the historical background must first be investigated. The first urban settlement in the area of Vienna today was Vindobona, a Roman military camp on the western bank of the River Danube, which bordered the north-eastern corner of the settlement. At this time, the river banks were probably richly wooded. A map dated 1777 A.D. shows the fortified city close to the river-shore and largely surrounded by meadows with isolated trees, arable land and vineyards. Shortly afterwards, the Danube changed its bed during a very high flood, so that the former bed became an oxbow, now the Donaukanal. On the fringes of the inaccessible river-wood area many small villages developed, surrounded by arable fields and kitchen-gardens. The woodland of the western hills (Wienerwald) was intensively used for firewood by the city. Many of these villages were destroyed by a Turkish siege in 1520, after which the fortifications were reinforced and a ring of treeless landscape (*c.* 500 m wide), the Glacis, was established. This was a waste place which was partly used for tipping. Outside of the Glacis, the suburbs developed and were surrounded by arable land and vineyards.

During the expansion of the suburbs fairly large areas of land were incorporated into important wildlife sanctuaries. In 1860 the fortifications were demolished and luxury buildings were erected on the Glacis. The areas between them were planted and no longer contain remnants of the original river-wood vegetation. With the growth of the population, the suburbs have expanded towards the slopes of the Wienerwald, replacing the oak–hornbeam forests. In the south, the agricultural landscape has been replaced by factories, especially brickworks, and abandoned pits filled with groundwater form a characteristic element of this region. In the nineteenth century the streams coming from the Wienerwald and the lower part of the river Wien were culverted and the bed of the Danube was regulated. During the twentieth century the suburban settlements have expanded considerably into the Marchfeld, on the eastern bank of the Danube. A similar process is going on at the southern margin towards the Laaerberg. Even the villages on the eastern rim of the southern Wienerwald (e.g. Mödling) show a tendency to fuse with the main city (see Stahrmühlner & Ehrendorfer 1974).

From this historical review it transpires that the natural vegetation of Vienna stems from the river-woods, the abandoned land of the Glacis, the agricultural land in the east and south and the woodland in the hills of the Wienerwald. Among these the river-woods are the most important because their remnants enter deep into the modern city (e.g. The Augarten). The other communities do approach the centre of the city, for example the deciduous forest of the foothills of the Wienerwald can be traced to within certain parks of the western part of the city which also contain characteristic faunal elements (e.g. *Carabus intricatus* L.). In contrast, the central parts of the city are dominated by descendants of the river-wood ecosystem. The occurrence of *C.hungaricus* Fb, a native of the pannonic region, is limited to the southern part of the city whereas *C.violaceus pseudoviolaceus* Kr. only occurs at the eastern bank of the Danube. Even today these species may be observed in places little disturbed by human activities (Mandl 1968–69).

In the following report rare and conspicuous species, especially when only occasionally observed, will be omitted because they are not useful indicators of actual conditions. (Schweiger 1960 deals extensively with them.)

THE INVERTEBRATE FAUNA

Within the regularly occurring species, a distinction must be made between relict species in the true sense and such species which according to the mobility of certain instars are able to migrate whenever suitable conditions arise. The role of the immigrants should not be overestimated since 2 years of suction-trapping on a roof in the city centre 30 m above ground compared with the catch 1 m above ground were the same. Error could have been caused by animals found near the ground having come by air (e.g. many spiders). Only the presence of all stages of the life-cycle is a sure proof.

Among the species which fulfil the above requirements two groups should be distinguished: animals which persist even under the most severe conditions, and animals which disappear at certain levels of urbanization. The former usually accumulate poisonous substances (e.g. lead) within their bodies (e.g. earthworms, *Porcellio scaber* Latr., *Forficula auricularia* L., and the ants *Lasius niger* L. and *L.alienus* Foerster.). Comparing populations from places with different degrees of pollution the amount of poisonous substances within their bodies varies. Also the animals themselves are not identical since there are genetic differences between the populations. Often a transfer of a population into more severe conditions may cause extinction, as in the case of the carabid beetle *Calathus fuscipes* Goeze).

In general, the number of species diminishes from the outskirts to the centre of the city. Under severe conditions, usually only one species of a taxonomic group (e.g. a genus) remains. Even these species disappear from their innermost sites of occurrence with the progress of urbanization. Two examples may be given here. During the 1950's the grasshopper *Stenobothrus bicolor* Charp. was regularly found within the city centre; now it has practically disappeared and may be found only in the suburbs. A similar shift was observed with the bug *Pyrrhocoris apterus* L. which had several large colonies in the parks of the outer parts of the city and is now only found in certain suburbs. Furthermore, a certain degree of air pollution (especially by SO_2) causes the exclusion of shell-bearing snails, which are otherwise species-rich in the outskirts of the city. Although the distribution of fauna and flora within a city is very patchy, certain zones of urbanization with increasing human influence may be distinguished. Roughly speaking the following ones have been found within Vienna.

Starting from almost undisturbed river-wood, which persists in certain places downstream of the city, the main human influences are as follows. Usually the first step is the construction of dams which prevent inundation during floods. This measure converts 'soft river-wood', originally composed of willows and poplars, into 'hard river-woods' composed of oak, ash and elm. This is the normal successional sequence but damming accelerates it. The number of animal species is greater in the hard river-wood. The next step consists in removing the dead tree stumps and fallen branches and this excludes most of the insects which develop within such substrata (e.g. longicorn beetles, *Prionus coriarius* L. and *Lamia textor* L.) and deprives all those animals which seek shelter behind loose bark of their retreats (e.g. Chilopoda of the genera *Lithobius* Leach and *Geophilus* L., as well as Diplopoda of the genus *Polydesmus* Latz.). In addition, grape vines (*Clematis vitalba* L. and *Vitis sylvestris* Gmel.) as well as epiphytes (*Viscum album* L. and *Loranthus europaeus* Jacq.) are hard-pruned, and their cover is thus removed. Intensive management also removes the annual leaf litter, a measure which is not tolerated by certain very common animals which live there in (e.g. the isopod *Porcellio rathkei* Brandt., *Lepidocyrtus paradoxus* Uel, species of *Entomobrya* Ron. and the earwig *Chelidura acanthopygia* Géné. Among the beetles, *Carabus scheidleri* Panz. and *C.coriaceus* L. also seem to depend on this habitat. Another very common beetle, *Lagria hirta* L., whose larvae live within the litter, is also affected. Among the flies (Diptera), the hard-armoured larvae of the Stratiomyidae (e.g. *Pachygaster* Meig.) depend upon a layer of leaf litter.

The original river-wood has been converted into a park, the grass of which is regularly cut in order to obtain a turf. This measure excludes all animals which depend upon flowers and seeds. A characteristic group which disappears is the flies of the family Trypetidae, the larvae of which live preferably within flower heads. Many of the flower visitors also disappear (Hymenoptera, Lepidoptera). In intensively managed parks, brushwood is also removed to a large extent, especially around tree trunks. This measure causes a marked desiccation of the air, which adversely affects many animals. All these measures result in a close turf which is very poor in animals. Only a few Collembola (*Onychiurus* Gerv.), and some small oribatid mites, Gamasidae and Enchytraeidae remain. Nevertheless, a well-kept turf surrounding tree trunks seems to be better than the most recent trend, which consists in removing the turf itself and planting low bushes (*Myricaria germinica* (L.) Desv. and species of *Berberis* L.). This results in heavy soil erosion, even on gentle slopes, especially when exposed to trampling by children and dogs. Although the bushes produce flowers, these are in most cases only visited by blowflies and rarely by bees.

In certain districts, tree-lined avenues provide very important habitats for the native fauna, especially squirrels and the big green katydids (*Tettiginia viridissima* L.) which find their way along them far into the city.

In places where single trees persist surrounded by a small area of bare soil a partial food-chain may develop. The consumers are sap-sucking insects (aphids and small leaf-hoppers, Typhlocybinae) because the normal leaf-feeders (caterpillars, sawfly larvae and beetles) are excluded by the heavy pollution of the leaf surface; in experiments caterpillars refuse to feed upon such leaves. Ants (mostly *Lasius niger* and *L.alienus*) utilize the aphid honey while ladybirds and their larvae, as well as lacewings (*Chyrsopa* Leach) and Hemerobiid and Syrphid larvae prey upon the aphids. Earwigs (*Forficula auricularia*) feed indiscriminately upon live and dead aphids, and adult Syrphids take aphid honey. In the next trophic level, spiders (especially Thomisidae) are prominent; orb-web spiders are missing in the inner parts of the city.

Another food-chain starts with those herbs which have escaped the lawnmower. Some of them may develop flowers which are visited by flies and bees. Here leaf-eating insects can be found, especially caterpillars of noctuid moths (e.g. *Agrotis* O.) and also larvae and adults of chrysomelid beetles (e.g. *Gastroidea polygoni* L.). This species lives on *Rumex* spp. and occurs in large numbers even in the most polluted central parts of the city wherever a single *Rumex* plant has managed to grow. The explanation of the occurrence of leaf feeders under such conditions may be that the leaf surface of these plants is remarkably clean, as the leaves grow quickly and are eaten before being covered by a film of soot and other contaminants.

Yet another food-chain may exist in the places mentioned above. Although no normal litter fauna can develop here, piles of leaf litter may accumulate around tree bases, in cracks in the soil surface and even within cracks at the base of walls. Here all animals which can resist the severe conditions may find shelter. The largest of them is the isopod *Porcellio scaber* together with some resistant beetles (e.g. *Calathus fuscipes*). There is also a selection of litter and soil surface inhabitants which comprises mainly certain mites (Gamasids and Oribatids) and small beetles (*Tachyporus* spp., *Sericoderus lateralis* Gyll., *Atomaria* spp., *Corticarina* spp. and *Enicmus* spp.).

With the disappearance of trees within the most urbanized areas the fauna shrinks to only a few species. *Porcellio scaber* may still persist, but as a pest on plant material stored by man. Ants (mostly *Lasius* spp.) enter houses and feed upon any available foodstuff, and additionally may visit aphid colonies on house-plants. Within the cracks of pavements, mosses (mostly *Bryum argenteum* L.) form a green lattice which may be inhabited by small collembola (e.g. *Hypogastrura* Bourl.) and certain groups of microscopic animals. In this habitat a series from nearly clean to heavily polluted sites can be traced. In the outermost parts of the city Tardigrada may be present within the moss cushions. In reasonably clean places bdelloid rotifers may exist; these are missing in the more polluted sites, but nematodes still exist. In the most polluted sites only some resistant Protozoa (Ciliata) remain.

With the recent trend to fill cracks in the pavement with asphalt or to use of continuous concrete or asphalt pavements, most animals are excluded. In these areas only the commensals and parasites of man and his pets persist.

The present report is only a summary of an investigation carried out during half a century by the author (e.g. Kühnelt 1955, 1977; Kühnelt *et al.* 1954) and numerous occasional collaborators, supplemented by published and unpublished data from many scientists to whom the author is deeply indebted.

REFERENCES

Kühnelt W. (1955) Gesichtspunkte zur Beurteilung der Grosstadtfauna. *Osterreichische zoologische Zeitschrift*, **6**, 30–54.

Kühnelt W. (1977) Die Grünflachen der Stadte und ihre Tierwelt. In *Stadtökologie 3*. Fachtagung des Institutes für Umweltwissenschaften und Naturschutz, Graz pp. 69–77.

Kühnelt W., Piffl E. & Schremmer F. (1954) Schwärme von Schildwanzen über dem Stadtgebiet von Wien. *Wetter und Leben*, **6**, 34.

Mandl K. (1968–69) Die Carabiden Österreichs VI. *Koleopterologische Rundschau* 46/47, 17–53.

Schweiger H. (1960) Die Insektenfauna des Wiener Stadtgebietes. *XI. internationaler Kongress für Entomologie*, **3**, 184–193.

Stahrmühlner F. & Ehrendorfer F. (Eds.) (1974) *Naturgeschichte Wiens.* 4 vols. Verlag für Jugend und Volk, Wien-München.

10. SUCCESSION AND TROPHIC STRUCTURE OF SOIL ANIMAL COMMUNITIES IN DIFFERENT SUBURBAN FALLOW AREAS

R. STRUEVE-KUSENBERG
II. Zoologisches Institut der Universität
Abteilung Ökologie,
Göttingen, West Germany

SUMMARY

The succession and trophic structure of the soil animal communities in different suburban fallow areas of Göttingen (Germany) were studied from July 1977 to April 1980 using the extraction method of Kempson and pitfall traps. Two of the fallow areas were in a later, stabilized successional stage with high population densities of saprophagous, phytophagous and zoophagous animal groups. The diversity of their carabid fauna was high. On the juvenile soils of the third fallow area a pioneer community of predators (Carabidae, Staphylinidae, Araneida), Collembola and Diptera-larvae (Chironomidae, Sciaridae) was developed. Due to the rapid development of the vegetation, and the island-like location within more mature habitats, the young fallow area was rapidly colonized by Lumbricidae, Diplopoda, Isopoda and Gastropoda. Phytophagous animals were associated with the dominant plants; predators were represented to a large extent by small opportunistic carabid beetles with the ability to fly.

INTRODUCTION

Ecological studies on animal communities in urban environments often deal with habitats newly formed or those modified by urbanization and which are normally subjected to constant human influence (Frankie & Ehler 1978). Vacant lots and fallow areas within cities or nearby urban settlements often originate from previously used sites or agricultural land which is abandoned for an indefinite period, often as future building sites. Normally, human influence is restricted to the formation of these fallow areas.

In the present study different stages of secondary succession (Horn 1974) of animal communities were analysed in three suburban fallow areas differing in age, origin and the successional stage of their vegetation. The two oldest areas were originally arable land and were in an advanced successional stage. The third fallow area was in an early successional stage characterized by extreme environmental conditions. The recolonization of its immature soils by invertebrates was studied for a period of nearly 3 years.

STUDY AREAS AND METHODS

The three fallow areas are located at the outskirts of Göttingen (a city of about 120,000 inhabitants). Two of the areas resulted from former agricultural land which had not been cultivated for 10 and 11 years, respectively. The vegetation was characterized by an undisturbed dense sward with occasional shrubs (*Salix* sp., *Cornus sanguinea* L., *Rosa canina* L.). Most of the 0.5 ha areas were densely covered with *Agropyron repens* L. and *Solidago canadensis* L. In contrast to both old fields the third 2 ha fallow area had been formed in 1975 by bulldozing the earth from construction excavations. In 1977, when the investigations started, most areas of the juvenile soils were stony bare ground with sparse vegetation. The dominant plant was *Melilotus albus* Med. In the course of plant succession the ground cover increased continuously from 1977 to 1980, due to the rapid establishment of grassland plants such as *Poa trivialis* L., *Dactylis glomerata* L., *Trifolium repens* L. and *Medicago lupulina* L. This ameliorated the extreme environmental conditions at the soil surface.

   Animals were sampled by extracting soil samples (314 cm^2 area, depth 5 cm) according to the extraction method developed by Kempson *et al.* (1963) and by using pitfall traps (for details see Strueve-Kusenberg 1980, 1981).

RESULTS

Animal communities extracted from soil samples

Among the large numbers of saprophagous animals in abandoned agricultural areas (average of 664 individuals m^{-2}) the dominant groups were Diplopoda with *Cylindroiulus nitidus* Verhoeff and Isopoda, belonging to the family Trichoniscidae (Fig. 10.1). In comparison, the young fallow area had a very low proportion of saprophagous animals (24 ind. m^{-2}) of which 75% were slugs. In the place of saprovores such as Lumbricidae, Diplopoda or Isopoda the juvenile soils were colonized in 1977 and 1978 by numerous Diptera-larvae of the family Chironomidae and Sciaridae (1902 larvae m^{-2}). On both old fallow areas Diptera-larvae of the family Cecidomyiidae were dominant. From July 1977 to September 1978 dominant predators in the young area were spiders (184.1 ind. m^{-2}), staphylinid beetles (172.1 ind. m^{-2}) and carabid beetles (75.7 ind. m^{-2}). In the old areas the population density of

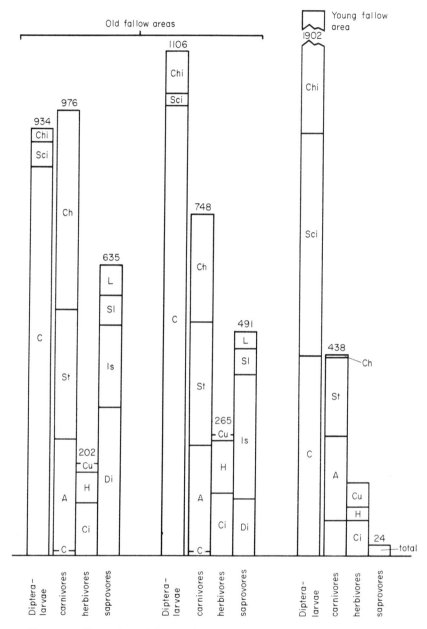

FIG. 10.1 Comparison of the population densities of saprovores, herbivores and of Diptera-larvae between the old fallow areas and the young fallow area from July 1977 to October 1978. Abundance (individuals m⁻²) is calculated as the mean value of abundance based upon the total soil samples in the months of July 1977 to October 1978. *Abbreviations*—saprovores: Di = Diplopoda, Is = Isopoda, Sl = slugs, L = Lumbricidae. Diptera-larvae: C = Cecidomyiidae, Sci = Sciaridae, Chi = Chironomidae. Herbivores: Ci = Cicadina, H = Heteroptera, Cu = Curculionidae. Carnivores: C = Carabidae, A = Araneida, St = Staphylinidae, Ch = Chilopoda.

carabids was very low (8.7 ind. m^{-2}), chilopods, however, with the small species *Lithobius duboscqui* Brolemann were extracted in high numbers.

The difference in the numbers of herbivores between sites was small (Fig. 10.1). This is due to the rapid development of plants and their corresponding fauna in the young fallow area. Among the curculionid beetles species of the genus *Sitona* which feed on clover predominated.

The recolonization of the young fallow area

The continuous colonization of the juvenile soils was studied by means of comparing the abundance of animals in the month of October from 1977 to 1979 and also in April 1980 (Table 10.1). In October 1977 soil samples contained mainly zoophagous animals, curculionid beetles and Diptera larvae. In the decaying vegetation layer of October 1978 larvae of Sciaridae were found in a high density (5,980 ind. m^{-2}). Slugs had doubled their population density in autumn 1979 compared to the preceding year. The snails *Vitrina pellucida* Müller and *Helicella itala* L. reached high densities in 1979 and 1980. Simultaneously—due to the accumulation of litter—the abundance of herbivores, Diplopoda, Isopoda and Lumbricidae increased significantly. Dominant species among Lumbricidae were *Lumbricus rubellus* Hoffmeister, *Allolobophora caliginosa* Savigny and *A.chlorotica* Savigny. The zoophagous Chilopoda (mainly Lithobiidae) colonized the area in high numbers in October 1979 and April 1980. Lower population densities of several animal groups in April 1980 may be due to the season.

TABLE 10.1. *Abundance (individuals m^{-2}) of different saprophagous, phytophagous and zoophagous animal groups in the course of the recolonization of the young fallow area (October 1977–April 1980).*

	October 1977	October 1978	October 1979	April 1980
Lumbricidae		+	49.5	138.1
Gastropoda				
Deroceras spec.	5.8	101.3	219.4	173.1
Vitrina pellucida Müller		+	98.2	503.2
Helicella itala L.		+	87.9	56.1
Diplopoda/Isopoda	+	14.5	61.4	41.6
Diptera-larvae	1798.0	5980.0	1221.3	839.4
Heteroptera	2.3	9.0	71.7	43.8
Cicadina	17.4	99.0	256.6	179.7
Curculionidae				
Sitona sp.	63.7	72.0	151.3	98.6
Carabidae	84.1	127.4	132.3	149.0
Chilopoda	17.4	20.3	116.8	216.8
Araneida	179.5	353.2	642.3	374.8
Staphylinidae	188.2	240.9	430.0	324.4

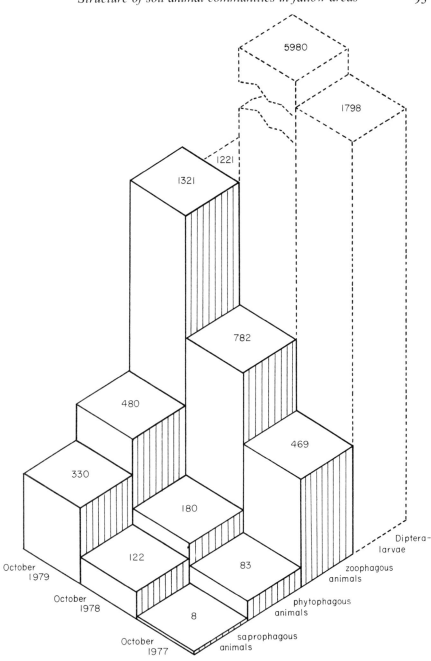

Fɪɢ. 10.2.   Development of the three trophic groups of saprophagous, phytophagous and zoophagous animals and of Diptera-larvae in the young fallow area in October 1977, 1978 and 1979. Total abundances are given as individuals m^{-2}.

Neumann U. (1971) Die Sukzession der Bodenfauna (Carabidae, Coleoptera; Diplopoda und Isopoda) in den forstlich rekultivierten Gebieten des Rheinischen Braunkohlenreviers. *Pedobiologia*, 11, 193–226.

Odum E.P. (1969) The strategy of ecosystem development. *Science*, 164, 262–270.

Schaefer M. & Kock K. (1979) Zur Ökologie der Arthropodenfauna einer Stadtlandschaft und ihrer Umgebung I. Laufkäfer (Carabidae) und Spinnen (Araneida). *Anzeiger Schädlingskunde, Pflanzenschutz, Umweltschutz*, 52, 85–90.

Strueve-Kusenberg R. (1980) Untersuchungen über die Laufkäfer (Coleoptera: Carabidae) verschieden alter Brachlandflächen: Besiedlung und Sukzession. *Drosera*, 80, 25–40.

Strueve-Kusenberg R. (1981) Sukzession und trophische Struktur der Bodenfauna von Brachlandflächen. *Pedobiologia*, 21, 132–141.

Topp W. (1971) Zur Ökologie der Müllhalden. *Annales Zoologici Fennici*, 8, 194–222.

11. SPECIES SIZE DISTRIBUTIONS OF BIRDS AND SNAILS IN AN URBAN AREA

S. H. COUSINS

Energy Research Group,
The Open University, Walton Hall,
Milton Keynes MK7 6AA, Buckinghamshire, U.K.

SUMMARY

Urban ecosystems are hypothesized to present a gradient of declining 'green' patch size towards the urban centre. Small bird species are predicted to survive in urban centres for that reason. Analysis of a London bird atlas shows that average species size per 100 km^2 does decline towards central London. No such relationship is found for land snails and it is suggested that water relations may determine the snails' survival. Trophic structure based on the size of feeder and food 'packet' size is affected by any factor influencing organism size. Human food wastage creates a subsidy of large food 'packets' favouring some larger bird species.

INTRODUCTION

We can suppose that for most species the environment in cities becomes more dissected by human activities and artifacts as one passes from the outskirts to the centre. So although we may not know the dimensions of the patches or 'habitat islands' perceived by different species, we can conclude that for most species (but not all) the 'habitat islands' will become smaller and more isolated towards the city centre. A simple inequality of this type can be a powerful tool with which to analyse the complex problem of ecosystem patchiness.

Schoener (1968) has shown for birds that the territory or area inhabited by a species is positively correlated with its body size. So if we predict that on average green patch size decreases with urbanization, then for birds we should expect the size of species to decline on average also.

Whereas for bird species recolonization of suitable habitats is a relatively simple process, for snails it appears a major problem. Once extinction occurs locally, recolonization may take a long time. Thus for this group of relatively immobile species fecundity might be expected to play an important role in lessening the chances of extinction. Small species have shorter generation times and high rates of reproduction (Fenchel 1974), so small species might be favoured at the city centre. However, large species move more quickly than small ones and would recolonize more rapidly although the rate of colonization must also be a function of species abundance. I shall examine the hypothesis that it is not the speed of recolonization but the reproductive effort that ensures survival in habitat patches perceived by snails. These patches might be expected to become smaller and more isolated near the city centre. So again I predict that smaller species will be favoured in central urban areas.

BIRD SPECIES SIZE IN LONDON

Data are taken from Montier (1977). Species breeding records were collected for each 2 × 2 km grid square and then aggregated to presence or absence of breeding species in each of 24 10 × 10 km contiguous grid squares covering the whole of London. A 25th grid square is included at the centre of the city, also of area 100 km². It overlaps the four central contiguous squares. The accuracy of these data relies on the evenness of observation over London. Montier confirms that there may have been some under-collection of data in North-east London although it should also be noted that the failure of ornithologists to visit an area may mean that it is genuinely species-poor. Figure 11.1 shows both the location of the study area and gives an index of observer effort. Units of the index are absence of breeding records per 2 km square for the ubiquitous species Starling, *Sturnus vulgaris* (Linne), Blackbird, *Turdus merula* (Linne) and Songthrush, *T.philomelos* (Brehm). Data from square 4 (Fig. 11.1) were omitted from further analysis due to the low level of observer effort identified by this method.

Of all the bird species found breeding in London, only land birds are considered here. Different groups of land birds, such as resident species or migrants, are also compared. The single species distributions from Montier (1977) were used to produce composite maps showing the number of species present per 10 km square or some attribute of that collection such as average species weight. Note that average species weight applies to the mean of the weights of a collection of species, and does not reflect the abundance of those species other than their presence or absence. Weight data are from Cousins (1976). Figures 11.2–11.6 were obtained using the SYMAP programme (Dudnik 1972). SYMAP is an interpolative contour mapping programme and the values of the contours are given on each map. Habitat data used here are derived from the records of the London Natural History Society (Sandford 1972, 1975, 1977, 1979) for rainfall, built environment, soils and sulphur dioxide pollution, respectively. All correlations given are Spearman's rank coefficients.

London conforms to the general model of an urban environment, set up by Erz (1966), of concentric rings of habitat; the outermost ring is semi-natural

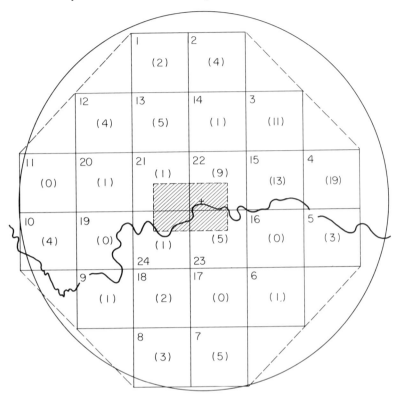

Fɪɢ. 11.1. The study zone of 24 10 × 10 km grid squares and central rectangle is shown within a radius of 32.5 km (20 miles) of St Paul's Cathedral marked by cross. In Figures 11.2–11.6 data are interpolated to the hatched lines. The river Thames is shown. Figures in brackets are an index of observer effort and indicate the number of absent records of three common breeding bird species in 25 4 km² plots of each 100 km².

with a predominance of vegetation leading through dwelling areas to the city centre itself with high-rise close standing buildings and little plant life. Figure 11.2 shows the roughly concentric distribution of an index of London's built environment. For this index Sandford's (1975) land-use classification of each 2 km square was adopted and scored 1.5 for 'settlements without gardens', 1.0 for 'settlements with gardens', and 0.0 if settlements were not the predominant land use. These values were summed for each 10 km square.

The concentric distribution of land bird species density, Figure 11.3, can be seen clearly. The maximum species density of 77 breeding species per 10 km square in outer London was compared to 43 species in the central 10 km square. Species density was negatively correlated with the built environment index at −0.90 significant at $P = 0.001$.

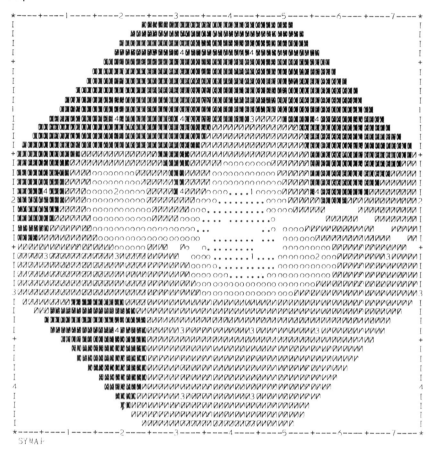

Fig. 11.4. Land bird average species weight/100 km². Contours 1–4 (light to dark),
90.5–98.5 g, 98.6–106.5 g, 106.6–114.5 g, 114.6–122.5 g.

−0.74, P = 0.001. Average species weight of residents was correlated with the built environment index at −0.60, P = 0.001 compared to migrants at −0.47, P = 0.011. Median species weight was significantly correlated with the built environment index at −0.66, P = 0.001 for resident species but was not significant for migrant species.

SNAIL SPECIES SIZE IN LONDON

The size of snail species was estimated from the scale drawings in Cameron and Redfern (1976) by taking the external shell dimensions and approximating the shells to cones or cylinders. Species density and size distribution maps were constructed in the same way as for land birds.

The presence or absence of land snail species in each of the 24 contiguous 10 km grid squares of London was taken from Kerney (1976). An analysis of the number of species in each square showed the species size (volume) distributions were skewed to the left (Kurtosis values −0.68 to −1.9) except for square 3 (Fig. 11.1) which skewed to the right (Kurtosis value 2.6). Data from that square was omitted from Figures 11.5 and 11.6 and the correlations, assuming there to have been under collection that area.

The species density of London's land snails decreases rapidly towards the city centre (see Fig. 11.5). Data extremes are 42 species at the city edge in the North-West and South, and nine species in the North-east square of central

FIG. 11.5. Land snail species density/100 km². Contours 1–4 (light to dark) 9–17 species, 18–25 species, 26–33 species, 34–42 species.

12. THE BREEDING ECOLOGY OF URBAN NESTING GULLS

P. MONAGHAN

Department of Zoology,
University of Glasgow,
Glasgow, G12 8QQ, U.K.

INTRODUCTION

The urban environment provides nesting habitats for numerous bird species, predominantly passerines, which nest in and around inhabited buildings. It is surprising to find, however, that at least 15 species of seabird have been recorded nesting on occupied buildings in a wide variety of localities (Fisk 1978). Seven of these are *Larus* gull species, and the Herring Gull *Larus argentatus* Pontopp. is the most frequently reported. Herring Gulls were first documented as nesting on buildings in a Black Sea port in 1894, and the habit has now been recorded in several European countries and in North America (Witherby *et al.* 1941; Goethe 1960; Mountfort & Ferguson Lees 1961; Paynter 1963; O'Meara 1975; Kosonen & Mäkinen 1978; Hoyer & Hoyer 1978). Like most seabirds, the Herring Gull is a colonial breeder. The adaptive significance of colonial nesting in seabirds is not yet fully understood, though various possible functions have been suggested (Coulson & Dixon 1979). The relationship between breeding success and nesting density is particularly relevant to this issue and Parsons (1976) has shown that breeding success in the Herring Gull is poor at comparatively high and low nesting densities; he suggests that this may be due to high territorial aggression in the former and high predation rates by conspecifics in the latter situation. In order to assess the negative effects of conspecifics, it is necessary to compare colonial breeding gulls with individuals breeding in the absence of intraspecific interference. However, isolated pairs of breeding Herring Gulls are rare: they may be nesting in unsuitable habitats and also lack the social stimulation presumably obtained from neighbouring pairs, which may influence breeding success. In urban colonies, on the other hand, the structure of the buildings in certain areas enforces severe limitations on the amount of interaction between breeding Herring Gulls. A consideration of the colony structure and breeding success of urban nesting gulls may, therefore, contribute to our understanding of the functional significance of colonial breeding.

URBAN NESTING GULLS IN BRITAIN

Throughout much of its range the Herring Gull has undergone a population increase, but nowhere so marked as in the British Isles where the average annual rate of increase is estimated to have been 12.8% since at least 1930 (Chabrzyk & Coulson 1976). Urban nesting was a comparatively rare occurrence prior to 1940 and, while only a small proportion (1%) of British Herring Gulls nest on buildings, urban colonies are expanding extremely rapidly. The first census of urban nesting Herring Gulls in Britain took place in 1969, at which time between 1,300 and 1,400 pairs were involved (Cramp 1971). This was repeated in 1976, when the urban breeding population had reached over 3,000 pairs (Monaghan & Coulson 1977). The distribution and abundance of urban nesting Herring Gulls recorded in both these censuses are shown in Figure 12.1. The average rate of increase in the number of breeding pairs between 1969 and 1976 was 17% per annum. This high rate of increase appears to be due, in part at least, to the saturation or near saturation of more traditional colonies and the movement of young reared in these colonies into urban colonies (Duncan & Monaghan 1977; Monaghan 1979). The number of urban Herring Gull colonies known to be in existence in Britain since 1920 is shown in Figure 12.2; the rate of formation of these colonies has been 9.3% per annum since about 1940. Recent data suggest that the population in North-east Scotland has been underestimated in both censuses (Bourne 1979), and counts obtained in 1977 and 1978 for colonies in Cornwall which were not counted in 1976 indicate that these have been expanding at the typical rate (H.P.K. Robinson, pers. comm.). Urban nesting Lesser Black-backed Gulls *Larus fuscus* Brehm., though less numerous and less widespread than the Herring Gull in urban colonies in Britain, increased by 28% per annum between 1969 and 1976. There is at present no evidence that the population increase in the Herring Gull, both in urban and more traditional colonies in Britain, has ceased.

HERRING GULL BREEDING BIOLOGY
IN URBAN COLONIES

Urban nesting gulls present considerable environmental problems in many towns in Britain, and attempts are now being made to remove birds from certain areas. Prior to, and in the early stages of, control measures being undertaken in two towns in North-east England, South Shields and Sunderland (Tyne & Wear), detailed studies were made of urban gulls between 1974 and 1978. Observations of the breeding birds were made from vantage points overlooking other buildings. Rooftops with nesting gulls were visited

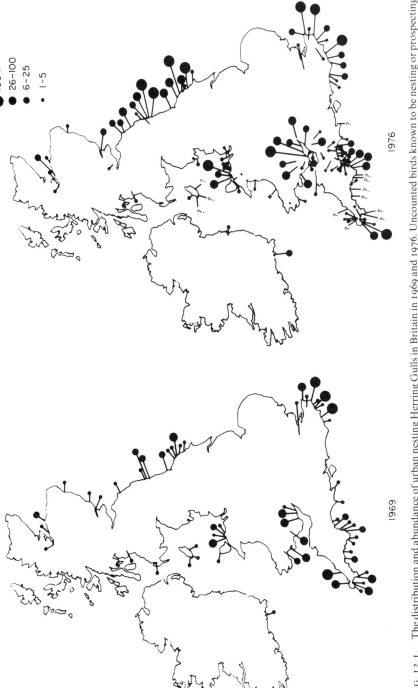

Fig. 12.1. The distribution and abundance of urban nesting Herring Gulls in Britain in 1969 and 1976. Uncounted birds known to be nesting or prospecting are indicated by question marks and crosses respectively.

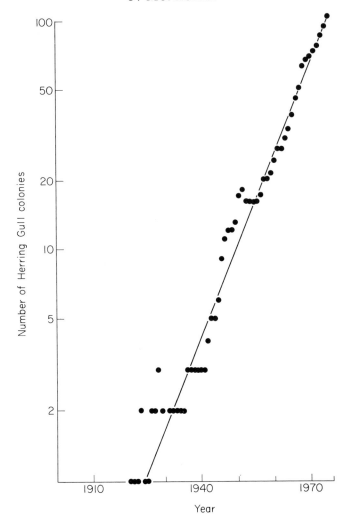

FIG. 12.2. The number of urban Herring Gull colonies (vertical axis) known to exist in Britain since 1920. Numbers on the vertical axis are plotted on a logarithmic scale.

where access was possible; where it was not, and the nests could not easily be viewed, the number of nesting pairs was estimated from the number of birds frequenting the building. It was not possible to ascertain clutch size in inaccessible nests, but chicks, when present, were readily visible. Figure 12.3 shows the rate of increase of nesting Herring Gulls in these towns since the colonies were first established.

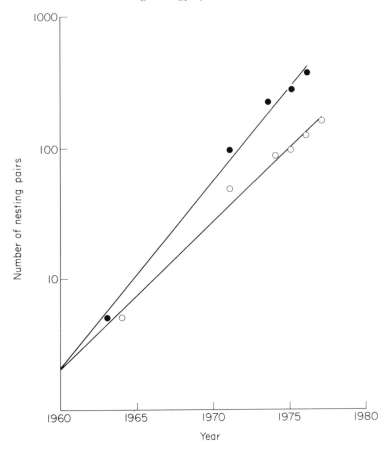

FIG. 12.3. The number of pairs of Herring Gulls nesting in South Shields (solid circles) and in Sunderland (open circles) since these colonies were first recorded. Numbers are plotted on a logarithmic scale (vertical axis), and the lines fitted by least squares regression. The rate of growth has been near constant in both towns, at about 40% per annum in South Shields and 30% per annum in Sunderland.

Nature of the nesting sites

The nesting sites used by Herring Gulls in towns are extremely variable, and range from nests wedged between the pots on top of domestic chimney stacks to nests on the flat roofs characteristic of modern office buildings; the sloping roofs of industrial warehouses are also extensively used. These nesting sites are of two basic types with regards to intraspecific interactions. The first is those sites on which birds are structurally (but not socially) isolated, such as ledges, between chimney pots, etc.; the territories do not border on those of neighbouring pairs. Each pair is effectively nesting on a small stack, and there is no 'land bridge' between adjacent pairs. Chicks are therefore contained within the nest's site and cannot, by virtue of the structure of the buildings, wander between territories. The second type are those on flat or warehouse roofs, at which interaction with other pairs at territory boundaries is possible. Chicks can wander between territories as in a ground nesting situation.

Nesting density

The density of urban nesting gulls is lower than that encountered in more typical colonies on coastal rocky outcrops. Parsons (1976) found the most common nesting density on the Isle of May, Scotland, to be 4–7 nests within a 4.6 m radius around any nest. In South Shields and Sunderland the most common nesting density was 1–2 nests within a 4.6 m radius around a particular nest. Densities higher than this were recorded only on flat roofs supporting multiple nesting sites. On one such roof, on which there were 17 nests in 1974, the density was similar to that recorded on the Isle of May (mean nearest neighbour distances 2.0 m and 2.4 m, respectively). Low nesting density reduces the amount of aggressive interaction between pairs. The number of aggressive encounters per 15-minute period was recorded during the early stages of egg laying for pairs nesting on structurally isolated sites and flat-roof sites in South Shields, and pairs on a nearby coastal stack, Marsden Rock, which supports c. 250 pairs of Herring Gulls nesting at very high densities. (Mean no. of encounters/15 minutes = 0.7, n = 13, 4.1, n = 7 and 3.9, n = 82, respectively.) There was no significant difference between those on the flat roofs and those on Marsden Rock, but the difference between each of these and those on the structurally isolated sites was highly significant. (Mann-Whitney U Test, U = 6 and U = 66, respectively, $P < 0.01$ in both cases.)

Breeding success

The overall breeding success in South Shields in 1974 and 1975 was 1.5 and 1.6 chicks successfully fledged per pair, and similarly in Sunderland 1.2 and 1.3 chicks per pair. This was not due to any difference in clutch size, and details of hatching and fledging success for a number of accessible nests are given in Table 12.1. These figures are high in comparison with the typical breeding success at more traditional colonies (Table 12.1). The breeding success of birds nesting on flat roofs and on structurally isolated sites in the same area and at the same time is given in Table 12.2 for each of the urban colonies. The breeding success at the structurally isolated sites was twice that recorded on the flat roofs. A significantly greater proportion of those on flat roofs (48%)

TABLE 12.1 *The relative breeding success of Herring Gulls in urban colonies and in more traditional colonies.*

	Location	No. nests	Hatching success %	Fledging success %	Chicks/ pair %	Authority
Traditional colonies	Summer Is., Scotland	40	85.7	48.6	0.88	Darling 1938
	Isle of May, Scotland	1,101	64.3	50.8	0.91	Parsons 1971a
	Skomer, Wales	220	63.0	c. 30.0	0.60	Harris 1964
	Skokholm, Wales	366	72.8	30.8	0.60	Davis 1973
	Walney Is., England	139	65.7	52.6	0.87	Brown 1967
Rooftop colonies	(1) Sunderland & South Shields, England	27	43.0	91.0	1.0	Monaghan 1979
	(2) Cardiff	47	64.6	44.0	0.70	Mudge 1978
	(3) Cardiff	14	65.71	69.6	1.14	Mudge 1978

(1) & (3) These refer to commercial premises. (2) This refers to industrial premises.

TABLE 12.2 *The average number of chicks successfully fledged per pair by Herring Gulls nesting on flat roofs and on structurally isolated sites in the same area in 1975.*

		No. chicks fledged/pair	No. nests
South Shields	Flat roof	1.0	14
	Isolated	1.9	27
Sunderland	Flat roof	1.0	13
	Isolated	2.0	18

failed to rear any chicks as compared to the proportion on the structurally isolated sites which failed (11%) ($\chi^2 = 10.4$, d.f. 1, $P < 0.01$).

In general, Herring Gulls are site-tenacious birds, tending to return year after year to the same breeding site (Tinbergen 1953). It was assumed in the urban colonies that, where a site was occupied in consecutive years, the same breeding birds, or at least one member of the previous pair, were present. This was supported by observations on 23 ringed birds. Annual adult mortality is low in the Herring Gull (6% per annum, Chabrzyk & Coulson 1976). Therefore, only a small number of sites will be abandoned due to this factor. Sites which were not occupied in both years were readily identifiable in the urban colonies, and Figure 12.4 shows the proportion of birds changing site in 1975 in relation to their breeding success in 1974. The tendency to change site the following year increases with decreasing breeding success and there was a significant difference between the proportion of birds fledging no chicks and those fledging one or more which changed their breeding site in the following year ($\chi^2 = 21.8$, d.f. 1, $P < 0.001$).

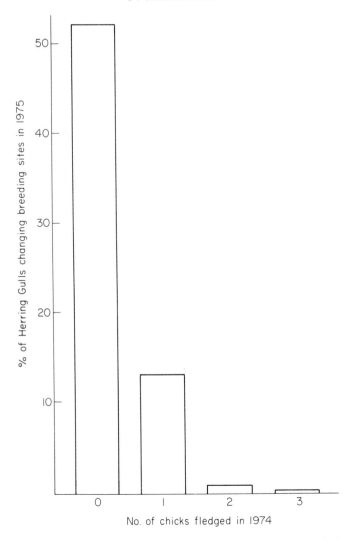

FIG. 12.4. The proportion of Herring Gulls which changed their breeding site in 1975 (vertical axis) in relation to the number of chicks fledged at the site used in 1974 (horizontal axis).

DISCUSSION

The major cause of chick mortality in the Herring Gull is direct interference from conspecifics. Young which wander from their nest into other territories are killed by neighbouring pairs, and a number of birds specialize in preying upon the eggs and young of their own species (Deusing 1939; Paynter 1949; Tinbergen 1953; Brown 1967; Parsons 1971b). Overall breeding success, and particularly fledging success (Table 12.1) is comparatively high in undisturbed urban colonies. Cannibalism was found to be absent in both towns studied, as was also found by Mudge (1978) for an urban gull colony in Cardiff, Wales. Since cannibalistic gulls are relatively infrequent, it is possible that the urban colonies are not sufficiently large for the incidence of cannibals to be appreciable. Alternatively, there may not be enough young chicks in a small colony to enable adults to specialize on them as a food supply. Furthermore, the proximity of urban nesting gulls to their food sources may enable them to feed their chicks more frequently, thereby preventing the heightened activity of hungry chicks which increases the likelihood of their being killed (Hunt & McLoon 1975). At structurally isolated nesting sites in towns both territorial aggression and cannibalism as causes of chick mortality are removed. Therefore, Herring Gulls nesting on such sites are free from the negative effects of conspecifics, while still nesting in close proximity to them. Breeding success is remarkably high at these sites.

The question now arising is why do Herring Gulls nest in colonies, since conspecifics have such a deleterious effect on their breeding success? Possible advantages to be gained from conspecifics in relation to food finding and stimulation of earlier breeding may be important, but there is no evidence to suggest that food is a limiting factor in Herring Gull breeding success (Parsons 1975). It has been suggested that colonial breeding is a response to predation pressure and that the synchronized breeding characteristic of this situation may decrease the chances of an individual's young being taken. Groups of Herring Gulls within a colony are synchronized and, while gulls do mob approaching predators, this tends to deter avian predators only. The response of Herring Gulls to mammalian predation is to increase the spacing of the cryptic eggs and young (Tinbergen 1952). A large colony may serve to attract predators in the first instance, and anti-predator behaviour may there-fore be a consequence rather than a function of colonial nesting. As these urban studies have shown, poor breeding success increases the tendency to change nesting site in the following year. This suggests that finding a suitable site may be an important factor in determining breeding success (though of course a suitable mate must also be found). Young birds prospecting for a nesting site are particularly attracted to the high density areas of existing colonies (Chabrzyk & Coulson 1976), and do not nest in isolation (Coulson & Dixon 1979). The best strategy of a young bird searching for a suitable breeding place may be to join an existing colony, since the existence of this colony is the best indication that the site is safe. The costs of colonial nesting in terms of loss of chicks to conspecifics may not be so great as those incurred by spending potential breeding years in search of a safe, isolated site.

SUMMARY

The numbers of pairs of urban nesting Herring Gulls in Britain in 1976 was over 3,000 pairs, and their rate of increase was 17% per annum between 1969 and 1976. The rate of formation of such urban colonies has been 9.3% since 1940, and there are now over 100 of these. This reflects the general increase in the Herring Gull in much of Europe, and the saturation of more traditional colonies. The breeding success in urban colonies (averaging 1.2–1.6 chicks successfully fledged/pair) is higher than that typical of the traditional colonies. This may be due to the lack of cannibalism in towns, and proximity to food sources. Breeding success is highest at structurally isolated sites in towns (averaging 1.9–2.0 chicks/pair). This is due to the absence of territorial aggression as a cause of chick mortality. It is suggested that Herring Gulls nest in colonies because the existence of the colony is an indication to potential recruits that the site is safe.

REFERENCES

Bourne W.R.P. (1979) Herring Gulls nesting on buildings in Eastern Scotland. *North East Scotland Bird Report*, 1978.

Brown R.G.B. (1967) Breeding success and population growth in a colony of Herring and Lesser Black-backed Gulls *Larus argentatus* and *L.fuscus*. *Ibis*, **109**, 502–515.

Chabrzyk G. & Coulson J.C. (1976) Survival and recruitment in the Herring Gull *Larus argentatus*. *Journal of Animal Ecology*, **45**, 187–203.

Coulson J.C. & Dixon F. (1979) Colonial breeding in seabirds. In *Biology and Systematics of Colonial Organisms*. (Ed. by G. Larwood & B.R. Rosen); pp. 445–458, Academic Press, London.

Cramp S. (1971) Gulls nesting on buildings in Britain and Ireland. *British Birds*, **64**, 476–87.

Darling F.F. (1938) *Bird Flocks and the Breeding Cycle*. Cambridge University Press, Cambridge.

Davis J.W.F. (1973) *Aspects of the Breeding Ecology and Feeding of Certain Gulls*. Unpublished D.Phil. Thesis, University of Oxford.

Deusing M. (1939) The Herring Gulls of Hat Island, Wisconsin. *Wilson Bulletin*, **51**, 170–175.

Duncan W.N.M. & Monaghan P. (1977) Infidelity to the natal colony by breeding Herring Gulls. *Ringing and Migration*, **1**, 166–172.

Fisk E.J. (1978) The growing use of roofs by nesting birds. *Bird-Banding*, **49**, 134–141.

Goethe F. (1960) Felsbrutertum und Weitert Beachfenswerte Tendenzen bei der Silbermöwe. *Proceedings of the International Ornithological Congress*, **12**, 252–258.

Harris M.P. (1964) Aspects of the breeding biology of the gulls *Larus argentatus*, *L.fuscus* and *L.marinus*. *Ibis*, **106**, 432–456.

Hoyer H. & Hoyer G. (1978) Beobachtungen in den Bugutchen salinengieten. *Der Falke*, **25**, 224–228.

Hunt G.L. & McLoon S. (1975) Activity patterns of gull chicks in relation to feeding by parents: their potential significance for density dependent mortality. *Auk*, **92**, 523–527.

Kosonen L. & Mäkinen R. (1978) Harmaalokin posinta rakennukessa. *Ornis Fennica*, **55**, 87.

Monaghan P. (1979) Aspects of the breeding biology of Herring Gulls *Larus argentatus* in urban colonies. *Ibis*, **121**, 475–481.

Monaghan P. & Coulson J.C. (1977) Status of large gulls nesting on buildings. *Bird Study*, **24**, 89–104.

Mountfort G. & Ferguson Lees I.J. (1961) Observations on the birds of Bulgaria. *Ibis*, **103A**, 443–471.

Mudge G.P. (1978) *Ecological Studies of Herring Gulls (Larus argentatus* Pont.*) and other Larini, in an Urban Environment.* Unpublished Ph.D. Thesis, University College, Cardiff.

O'Meara M. (1975) Building-nesting Herring Gulls (*Larus argentatus Pontoppidan*) in Co. Waterford. *Irish Naturalists Journal*, **18**, 152–53.

Parsons J. (1971a) *The Breeding Biology of the Herring Gull Larus argentatus.* Unpublished Ph.D. Thesis, University of Durham.

Parsons J. (1971b) Cannibalism in Herring Gulls. *British Birds*, **64**, 528–537.

Parsons J. (1975) Seasonal variation in the breeding success of the Herring Gull; an experimental approach. *Journal of Animal Ecology*, **44**, 553–573.

Parsons J. (1976) Nesting density and breeding success in the Herring Gull *Larus argentatus*. *Ibis*, **116**, 537–546.

Paynter R.A. (1949) Clutch size and egg and chick mortality of Kent Island Herring Gulls. *Ecology*, **30**, 146–166.

Paynter R.A. (1963) North American Herring Gulls nesting on a building. *Wilson Bulletin*, **75**, 88.

Tinbergen N. (1952) The significance of territory in the Herring Gull. *Ibis*, **94**, 158–159.

Tinbergen N. (1953) *The Herring Gulls' World.* Collins, London.

Witherby H.F., Jourdain F.C.R., Ticehurst N.F. & Tucker B.W. (1941) *The Handbook of British Birds.* Witherby, London.

13. THE DISTRIBUTION AND ECOLOGY OF FOXES, *VULPES VULPES* (L.), IN URBAN AREAS

D. W. MACDONALD AND M. T. NEWDICK

Animal Behaviour Research Group,
Department of Zoology,
South Parks Road, Oxford OX1 3PS

SUMMARY

Foxes, *Vulpes vulpes* (L.), are being studied in Oxford City, where they have been found in all urban habitats within the city boundaries. A questionnaire survey reveals that city-dwelling foxes are widespread throughout England and Wales, although apparently more so in the south and the midlands of England. Preliminary evidence suggests that their pest status in towns is generally minimal. Some results are presented on the movements of radio-tagged foxes of which a sample of 11 had a home-range of 86.2 ha. The home-ranges of city-dwelling foxes in Oxford fell between the sizes of those smaller ranges in the suburbs and larger ones in the adjoining agricultural land.

INTRODUCTION

The red fox, *Vulpes vulpes* (L.), is one of several larger omnivorous mammals that are known to inhabit urban areas. Others include raccoons, *Procyon* spp., skunks, *Mephitis* spp., opossums, *Didelphis* spp., together of course with dogs, *Canis familiaris* (L.), and cats, *Felis catus* (L.), living more or less independently of human owners. The phenomenon of city-dwelling foxes in Britain is popularly thought to be a new one, and is often regarded as somehow unnatural (Vesey-Fitzgerald 1965). To the extent that some towns are probably still being colonized and some urban fox populations still expanding, foxes may indeed be a recent addition to urban faunas. However, foxes have inhabited some towns for at least 40 years, and one garden in our study area in Oxford has regularly supported cubs for 20 years. Since urban habitats clearly provide food and shelter which foxes can utilize, it is more surprising that they were not noted in towns sooner, than it is that they are inhabiting them now.

The recent history of urban-dwelling foxes has been most thoroughly documented for London, where in the 1930s they were found in parkland such as Hampstead Heath and Richmond Common. By 1970 foxes were increasingly familiar in London's inner boroughs and now they occur in the heart of the city—foxes have been seen in Trafalgar Square and around Waterloo Station (Teagle 1967; Beames 1972; Harris 1977a).

Foxes are reported in many towns in Britain and are studied in Bristol, Edinburgh, London and Oxford. Since we have found individual foxes whose ranges encompassed habitats ranging from woodland to terraced housing, it is not easy to define urban foxes. In London, R. Page (pers. comm.) found it helpful to call foxes urban if 80% of their home ranges were comprised of factories, schools, shops, hospitals, roads, railways, high-rise flats and terraced housing, and to distinguish these from suburban foxes whose ranges contained 80% or more of hospitals, schools, shops, cemeteries, parks, market gardens, houses set in their own grounds and semi-detached houses. However, on these criteria almost all of Oxford, a city of over 120,000 inhabitants, would be classed as suburban. This illustrates the great diversity of urban habitats. Our present study is an attempt to investigate these different urban landscapes from the foxes' viewpoint, in terms of the availability of food, the patterns of mortality and the distribution of shelter which each affords.

In this paper we report the preliminary findings of a questionnaire survey of the distribution of urban foxes in England and Wales, together with some representative results of radio-tracking studies of the movement of foxes in Oxford City.

NATIONAL DISTRIBUTION

A questionnaire was distributed throughout England and Wales to each of 328 members of the Inspectorate of the Royal Society for the Prevention of Cruelty to Animals (RSPCA). Each inspector was asked if he had proof of foxes living in towns in his district, whether the foxes were a nuisance and if so, what categories of damage they caused. The RSPCA made completion of the questionnaire compulsory and so 100% response was achieved. RSPCA inspectors are amongst those most likely to know if foxes occur in a town, both through their own work and through frequent contact with other people, such as local environmental health authorities to whom the presence of foxes may be reported.

The 328 records included towns whose human population averaged 71,232 (range 990–1,004,030). Of these, 44% reported evidence of foxes dwelling in urban surroundings (Fig. 13.1). Inspectors from some towns from each of seven regions of England and Wales reported foxes, but there were significant differences ($\chi^2 = 24.2$, d.f. 6, $P < 0.001$) in the proportion of towns within each region which was populated by urban foxes. Most notable were the large number of towns with urban foxes in the South-east, in comparison to their

FIG. 13.1. Towns in which foxes are known to live (▲) and those where there is no evidence of their presence (△), based on a survey of field inspectors from an animal welfare society (RSPCA).

Table 13.1. *Percentage of towns in each of seven regions in which foxes were recorded as present.*

South-east	South	Midlands	Wales	East	South-west	North
74.6	64.0	52.7	47.8	31.4	21.0	15.9

low incidence in the North (Table 13.1). Furthermore, in six out of seven regions, larger conurbations were more inclined to support foxes than were smaller ones, as reflected by the mean human population of towns with and without foxes (see Table 13.2).

Table 13.2. *The mean number of inhabitants (thousands) in towns in each region from which foxes were reported as present or absent.*

	Foxes present	No foxes
South-west	150.5	15.9
South	63.1	28.9
South-east	69.6	53.6
Midlands	136.9	37.3
East	66.6	53.5
North	129.3	78.5
Wales	12.9	61.3

Throughout England and Wales coastal towns were more likely to have evidence of urban foxes than were those inland, ($\chi^2 = 19.6$, d.f. 1, $P < 0.001$) and this trend was apparent for each of the six regions with a coastline. Since coastal towns were not generally bigger than inland ones (e.g. Table 13.3) the effects of a town's population and whether it be coastal or inland were at least partly independent. Furthermore, the midlands has no coastline and towns where foxes were reported had larger populations than those without ($t = 2.7$, $n = 49$, $P < 0.01$). The same tendency was apparent in other regions if only inland towns were considered (e.g., the south, $t = 2.0$, $n = 17$, $P < 0.05$). Presumably there are differences in the habitat structure of larger and smaller towns which may underlie these trends. For example, larger towns may have relatively more suburban habitat.

Table 13.3. *The mean human population ($\pm$s.d.) (in thousands) of coastal and inland towns in the South-East of England which reported foxes as present or absent. n is the number of towns sampled.*

	Foxes present	Foxes absent
Coastal	56.8 ± 44.5	39.0 ± 36.9
	$n = 15$	$n = 4$
Inland	81.1 ± 96.0	59.4 ± 36.0
	$n = 16$	$n = 10$

SPATIAL RELATIONSHIPS AND HABITAT USE

Foxes were captured in and around Oxford City and equipped with radio-transmitters (102.3 MHz), following the design described by Macdonald and Amlaner (1980). Their movements were monitored thereafter using an AVM receiver and Yagi antenna, mounted on a car or on foot using a dipole. To date 47 foxes have been radio-collared in the town and its inner suburbs and over 70 more in rural suburbia. Preliminary analysis shows that foxes utilize every urban habitat in Oxford to at least some extent, including the districts most densely populated by humans. Figure 13.2 shows the approximate locations of some home-ranges. In general, there was evidence that additional adult resident animals (usually females) shared ranges with resident pairs. The spatial organization of neighbouring social groups was of largely exclusive home-ranges and so was compatible with a territorial interpretation, although there were areas of overlap between some adjacent ranges and little indication of defence of boundaries. A sample of 11 home-ranges studied within the city boundary had a mean area of 86.2 ha (s.d. ± 47.2) when the borders of each were drawn by hand along the topographic features believed to embrace each range. In contrast, of seven group-ranges studied on Boars Hill, on the outskirts of Oxford City, the mean area was 45.2 ha (s.d. ± 16.5) (Macdonald 1981).

A categorical division between rural and urban foxes was found to be without foundation. The proportions of urban and rural habitats embraced within the home-ranges of foxes varied from one to the next, and foxes moved readily between them. Some ranges in the suburbs spanned the transition from town to country, and in these cases individuals might sleep by day on farmland and commute to the city by night. Table 13.4 shows the frequency with which radio-location on each of four foxes were in given categories of habitat. Even Fox D No. 4, living in a very built-up district, was nevertheless frequently found in patches of more vegetated habitat, consisting largely of playing fields and allotments.

Dispersing juveniles also crossed back and forth between town and country. Figure 13.3 shows the movements of one sub-adult dog fox which initially occupied a suburban-range and which subsequently travelled cross-country to settle eventually near a village 6 km away. One young vixen, captured in a garden, dispersed successively to four different built-up areas of terraced housing (see Hough 1980).

REPRODUCTION

Twenty-five litters have been observed at their earths in Oxford City. The

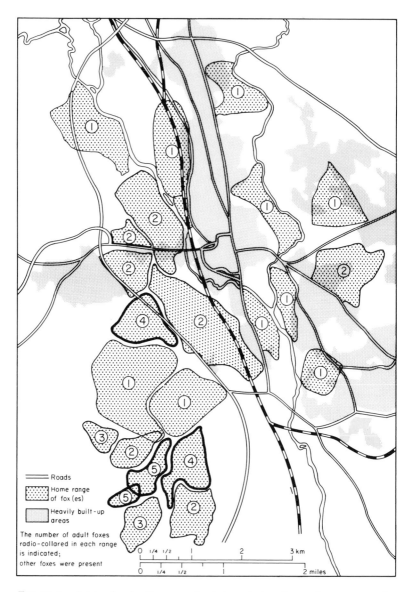

FIG. 13.2. A map showing the approximate boundaries of group home-ranges of a sample of the foxes radio-collared in and around Oxford. Most of the area within the ring road—which approximately encircles the town is built-up, but shading indicates the most developed areas. Numbers indicate the number of radio-collared foxes in each range, but not necessarily the number of foxes present.

TABLE 13.4.   *The percentage of radio fixes taken on each of four foxes which were in different habitat types. All four foxes occupied ranges within Oxford City, but they varied greatly in their utilization of strictly urban environments.*

Habitats	Fox numbers			
	1	2	3	4
Human dependent	0	14.5	19.8	53.3
Agricultural/open	79.6	77.9	52.4	33.8
Woodland	20.4	1.2	23.1	12.8

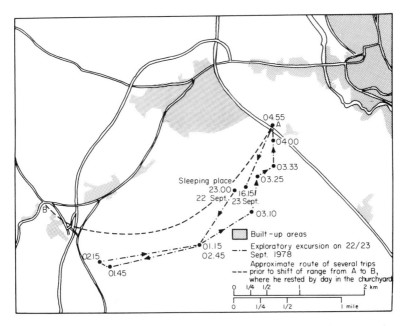

FIG. 13.3.   The dispersal of a 6-month-old dog fox, from a suburban home-range in the city to the environs of a village 6 km away.

mean of the minimum number of cubs at each earth was 4.5. Earths were found in close proximity to houses, beneath outbuildings or warehouses and one in a heap of builder's rubbish. One litter was apparently born above ground in an overgrown garden. However, most (60%) earths were in more 'typical' sites—undisturbed locations in patches of scrubland often on embankments. Fifteen per cent were beneath garden sheds in Oxford, while Harris (1977a) found 37% in similar sites in London and Page (pers. comm.) found 25% of earths under such sheds in Hillingdon, London.

In 1977, Harris reported similar sites of earths in London, but more recently he has found that many earths in Bristol are located beneath houses, with access gained through damaged air-bricks (Harris 1980).

The reproductive productivity of vixens varies from region to region (Englund 1970) and Macdonald (1979) has suggested that this is partly attributable to density-dependent social factors, particularly the inclusion of non-breeding vixens into family groups. In the outskirts of Oxford we have found evidence of non-breeding vixens in every home-range studied and in two out of eight ranges in the City. Up to 52% of yearling vixens were barren in a sample of London's foxes, although their social relationships were unknown, and barren vixens were associated with breeding pairs in Bristol (Harris 1979, 1980).

MORTALITY

Many of the fox populations whose age structures have been studied have been subject to intensive control (e.g. Phillips 1970; Jensen & Nielsen 1968) and this, together with sample bias, is probably reflected in the small number of animals surviving more than 3 years, for example in an intensively controlled area Phillips (1970) reported that 85% of his sample were in their first year. Harris (1977a) found a relatively old fox population in London, with 48% of his sample being over 1 year old.

Although recent escalation in the value of fox furs has resulted in more people attempting to catch foxes in British towns, urban foxes may nevertheless be subject to relatively little deliberate killing although man, at least indirectly, accounts for the deaths of many. Similarly 12 of the 47 foxes radio-tagged in Oxford died while their transmitters were functioning and of these nine were killed by human agencies. Of 62 corpses collected in Oxford between 1977–80, 59% were killed by cars, 13% shot, snared or trapped and 5% succumbed to disease.

In about 2 km² of Boars Hill 11 foxes were killed by cars between 1973–76 and examination of their teeth for cementum annuli (Jensen & Nielsen 1968) revealed that 7 were 5 years old or more. During the same period 33 foxes were examined that had been snared or shot or killed by cars on farmland outside Oxford. Of these only two (6%) were 5 years old or older. These differences, to some extent, reflect the different causes of death.

DIET

Foxes eat a wide variety of prey in towns and countryside, and the popular belief that city foxes are exclusively scavengers while rural foxes are exclusively predators is unfounded. In Oxford City we have observed foxes scavenging from refuse, bird-tables and compost heaps and the greasy wrappers discarded outside fish-and-chip shops. However, we also have evidence of foxes eating fruit and hunting birds, lagomorphs and various invertebrates, especially earthworms, *Lumbricus terrestris* (L.) (Macdonald 1980b). In the rural suburbia of Boars Hill about one half of the diet (% volume) comprised foods that had been scavenged (Macdonald 1981) but the same is also true in a superficially much more rural study area in Switzerland (A. Wandeler pers. comm.). So scavenging from human waste is neither the prerogative of foxes in towns, nor necessarily the most important contribution to their diets.

PEST STATUS

During the past decade opinion has mounted in Oxford City that urban foxes are a pest, and this view has been fuelled by accounts in the press of pets reputedly being preyed upon or savaged by foxes (and also, implausibly, of people and dogs being intimidated). However, a questionnaire survey showed that many people living within the known home-range of a family of foxes were ignorant of their presence. Documented cases of foxes taking pets were very rare, but at least three people rearing chickens or game birds in their gardens on the outskirts of the town have suffered losses repeatedly. The most common damage for which foxes have been blamed has been the appearance of small holes and scrapes in lawns and flowerbeds, the untidying of heaps of lawnmowings and chewing on plastic hoses. Some householders complain of fox faeces, others of the suspected presence of fox urine on their lawns. Fear of disease is used to rationalize these last complaints.

Each RSPCA inspector questioned on the presence of foxes in his town was also required to give details of any evidence of nuisance caused by foxes. Complaints had been made against foxes in 78 (23.8%) of 328 towns, that is in 53.1% of the towns where foxes were reported at all. The number of towns for which each category of nuisance purportedly caused by foxes was recorded is shown in Table 13.5 (which does not indicate the relative frequencies of actual complaints of each type). Some categories of nuisance are rather nebulous, for example in eight towns some people's complaints about foxes stemmed from a fear of disease, but none of these were apparently associated with any discernible disease problem.

TABLE 13.5 *The number of towns in which proven complaints, or hearsay, implicated foxes in each category of nuisance.*

Noise	Loss of cats	Loss of other pets	Raiding dustbins	Loss of fowl	Digging gardens
3	3	13	29	13	34

HEALTH

Studies of disease in wildlife most commonly involve the compilation of lists of conditions and parasites to which a species is susceptible, and rarely provide insight into epizootiology within wild populations, and studies of the maladies of foxes are no exception. Lloyd (1980) has reviewed the known diseases of foxes, but little is known of the relative incidence of each condition in rural versus urban populations. Since at least some urban populations of foxes are at the higher end of the spectrum of known population densities it seems reasonable to assume that they may be more inclined to suffer outbreaks of communicable disease. Certainly, there is a great concern over the possible involvement of urban foxes in any outbreak of rabies (Macdonald 1980a; Bacon & Macdonald 1980). The numbers of foxes in British towns and their frequent encounters with domestic pets could be a recipe for a more destructive rabies epizootic than has occurred in other European countries. These fears have prompted proposals to begin control of fox populations in anticipation of a rabies outbreak but, as Lloyd (1977) has argued, this would be for the most part biologically, economically and morally undesirable.

Amongst the vulpine diseases that might be transmitted to pets, mange (*Sarcoptes* and *Notoedres*) is enzootic in some London boroughs (S. Harris pers. comm.) and is apparently (Stone *et al.* 1972) transmissible to dogs, but not to cats. There is no evidence that mange is necessarily associated more with foxes in urban habitats than in any others. Foxes in Britain are subject to leptospirosis (Weil's disease), but there is no evidence of their involvement in transmission to people or pets. The questionnaire survey revealed that several people complained about foxes because of a fear of distemper, which has never been recorded in foxes in Britain.

There are indications of anatomical traits associated with at least London's urban foxes (Harris 1977b), notably a high incidence of dental impaction.

DISCUSSION

The widespread presence of foxes in British towns raises two questions: first, why should foxes have begun to colonize urban habitats in only the last half century and second, why, as is apparently the case, are urban-dwelling foxes a rarity throughout many other European countries, although probably less so in North America? Neither question can be satisfactorily answered. Numbers of foxes increased on the glut of rabbits, *Oryctolagus cuniculus* (L.), which became available in 1954 when myxomatosis was spreading through their populations, while after the widespread demise of rabbits the diet of foxes probably had to change (Lever 1959). Both the large numbers of foxes and the subsequent widespread disappearance of a principal prey have been mooted as explanation of the movements of foxes into towns. However, foxes were in at least some towns before the 1950s and anyway, if the urban environment could support foxes then it seems likely that there must always have been at least some dispersing individuals who should have capitalized on that food resource. The same argument applies to the suggestion that an increase in urban foxes is a corollary of the decrease in the number of gamekeepers in the surrounding countryside; a smaller pool of foxes from which immigrants could be drawn would reduce the frequency of immigration to new habitats, but would not seem sufficient reason for its total absence. However, Hewson and Kolb (1973) have evidence that certain rural areas of Scotland were only colonized by foxes after their numbers were boosted by the increased availability of rabbits during myxomatosis. There is, nevertheless, an indication that foxes in different regions may treat human settlements differently; foxes radio-tracked around Oxford seemed to move in and out of towns and villages freely. In contrast, foxes radio-tracked in the uplands of the north of England conspicuously avoided human settlements. This may be partly reflected in the rather low incidence of urban foxes in the north as depicted in Figure 13.1. In continental Europe, rabies epizootics move around towns, not through them.

It may be more helpful to look for changes in the urban habitats of Britain rather than change in fox behaviour itself. Food wastage in the British economy is substantial (Roy 1976) and has almost certainly increased during the past 50 years. However, it is not clear if this food has become correspondingly more available to urban scavengers (perhaps through changes in rubbish disposal practice, such as the partial replacement of dustbins with plastic sacks, or the increased provisioning of bird-tables providing foxes with both extra scraps and extra birds). Other aspects of the habitat may have changed also: competitors (or predators) in the form of unrestrained dogs may have decreased and available daytime lairs and breeding sites increased. A. Coleman (pers. comm.) has documented a nationwide increase in the area of wasteland in cities, which in one district in London amounted to 15% of the land area. None of these factors is mutually exclusive of any other, and the colonization of towns by foxes may be a consequence of a combination of them all. The distribution of towns where foxes are reported may hold clues to the origin of colonization. For instance, coastal towns might predominate because the shoreline channelled the movements of the dispersing foxes into them (a similar notion might apply to towns on rivers). Alternatively, coastal towns may attract more tourists and hence available food waste. In some cases towns may have engulfed rural foxes as development eroded the green belt.

One might speculate that dispersing foxes select similar habitats to those in which they were reared. Such habitat preference could contribute to the patterns of distribution and spread of urban foxes.

Although reports are accumulating of urban foxes in Canada (D. Voigt, pers. comm.) and the U.S.A. (A. Carey, pers. comm.) it is still widely believed that in Europe they are largely a British phenomenon. In North America the presence of potential competitors to foxes in towns, such as raccoons and opossums is an additional complication. Nevertheless, Brosset (1975) reported foxes on the outskirts of Paris and there are other reports from Copenhagen and Stockholm. There is no obvious ecological factor which adequately distinguishes all the British towns with foxes from the other European towns without them. The solution to this paradox will have to wait at least until the behaviour and ecology of urban foxes is better known. One thing is clear already: just as rural habitats differ and fox behaviour varies accordingly, so within and between urban areas there is great variation in ecological variables. Doubtless, then, the behaviour of urban-dwelling foxes will be found to vary from one city to the next and from one neighbourhood to the next.

ACKNOWLEDGEMENTS

Our work on foxes in Oxford City has been supported by the Nature Conservancy Council, to whom we are grateful. The Wildlife Department of the RSPCA assisted greatly with the distribution of questionnaires to the Society's inspectors. We are also grateful to N.G. Hough for his collaboration with our work.

REFERENCES

Bacon P.J. & Macdonald D.W. (1980) To control rabies: vaccinate foxes. *New Scientist*, **87**, 640–645.

Beames I. (1972) The spread of the fox in the London area. *Ecologist*, **2**, 25–26.

Brosset A. (1975) Régime alimentaire d'une population suburbaine de renards au cours d'un cycle annual. *Terre et la Vie*, **29**, 20–30.

Englund J. (1970) Some aspects of reproduction and mortality rates in Swedish foxes. *Viltrevy*, **8**, 1–81.

Harris S. (1977a) Distribution, habitat utilization and age structure of a suburban fox (*Vulpes vulpes*) population. *Mammal Review*, **7**, 25–39.

Harris S. (1977b) Spinal arthritis (*Spondylosis deformans*) in the red fox, *Vulpes vulpes*, with some methodology of relevance of zooarchaeology. *Journal of Archaeological Science*, **4**, 183–195.

Harris S. (1979) Age-related fertility and productivity in red foxes, *Vulpes vulpes*, in suburban London. *Journal of Zoology (London)*, **183**, 91–117.

Harris S. (1980) Home ranges and patterns of distribution of foxes (*Vulpes vulpes*) in an urban area, as revealed by radio tracking. In *A Handbook on Biotelemetry and Radio Tracking* (Ed. by C.J. Amlaner and D.W. Macdonald), pp. 685–690. Pergamon Press, Oxford.

Hewson R. & Kolb H.H. (1973) Changes in numbers and distribution of foxes (*Vulpes vulpes*) killed in Scotland from 1948–1970. *Journal of Zoology (London)*, **171**, 285–292.

Hough N.G. (1980) The ranging behaviour of a maturing female red fox, *Vulpes vulpes*, In *A Handbook on Biotelemetry and Radio Tracking* (Ed. by C.J. Amlaner and D.W. Macdonald), pp. 691–696. Pergamon Press, Oxford.

Jensen B. & Nielsen L.B. (1968) Age determination in the red fox (*Vulpes vulpes* L.) from canine tooth sections. *Danish Review of Game Biology*, **5**, 3–15.

Lever J.A.W. (1959) The diet of the fox since myxomatosis. *Journal of Animal Ecology*, **28**, 359–375.

Lloyd H.G. (1977) Wildlife rabies prospects for Britain. In *Rabies: the facts* (Ed. by C. Kaplan), pp. 91–102. Oxford University Press, Oxford.

Lloyd H.G. (1980) *The Red Fox.* Batsford, London.

Macdonald D.W. (1979) 'Helpers' in fox society. *Nature (London)*, **282**, 69–71.

Macdonald D.W. (1980a) *Rabies and Wildlife: a biologist's perspective.* Oxford University Press.

Macdonald D.W. (1980b) The red fox, *Vulpes vulpes* as a predator upon earthworms, *Lumbricus terrestris. Zeitschrift fur Tierpsychologie*, **52**, 171–200.

Macdonald D.W. (1981) Resource dispersion and the social organisation of the red fox, *Vulpes vulpes.* In *Proceedings of the Worldwide Furbearer Conference, Maryland, 1980* (Ed. by J. Chapman and D. Pursely), vol. II, pp. 918–949.

Macdonald D.W. & Amlaner C.J. (1980) A practical guide to radio tracking. In *A Handbook on Biotelemetry and Radio Tracking* (Ed. by C.J. Amlaner and D.W. Macdonald), pp. 143–160. Pergamon Press, Oxford.

Phillips R.L. (1970) Age ratios of Iowa foxes. *Journal of Wildlife Management*, **34**, 52–56.

Roy R. (1976) *Wastage in the UK Food System.* Earth Resources Research publication, London.

Stone W.B., Parkes E., Weber B.L. & Parks F.J. (1972) Experimental transfer of saragstic mange from red foxes, and wild canids to captive wildlife and domestic animals. *New York Fish and Game Journal*, **19**, 1–11.

Teagle W.G. (1967) The fox in the London suburbs. *London Naturalist*, **46**, 44–68.

Vesey-Fitzgerald B. (1965) *Town Fox, Country Fox.* Andre Deutsch, London.

II

ECOLOGICAL EFFECTS OF HUMAN ACTIVITY IN URBAN AREAS

14. CHANGES IN ECOSYSTEM STRUCTURE AND FUNCTION IN TOKYO

MAKOTO NUMATA

Laboratory of Ecology, Faculty of Science,
Chiba University, Yayoi-Cho, Chiba 260, Japan

SUMMARY

An integrated ecological study of the Metropolis of Tokyo has been conducted in relation to the MAB Project 11 and UNESCO/UNEP's working group on ecosystem approaches to human settlements. The characteristics of the urban environment and the dynamics of plant and animal communities under the influence of the urban environment were examined in the first stage of the study. In the second stage an interdisciplinary and integrated study of urban ecosystems was conducted from anthropocentric, zoocentric and phytocentric viewpoints. This is similar to the Clementsian biocentric approach of action and reaction. In the third stage of the study the anthropocentric concept was stressed even more, and ecosystem management and planning are now under consideration in relation to decision-making.

INTRODUCTION

Tokyo has been the capital of Japan for more than 400 years. It developed and expanded very rapidly in the late nineteenth century, and is now the largest city in the world, with a population of 12 million, one tenth of the total population of Japan.

The Tokyo Metropolis was adopted as an urban ecosystem unit for our study. It includes a concrete urban desert as well as suburban and rural areas, and consists of 23 wards (the pre-war City of Tokyo) and many satellite regions. The Tokyo Metropolis is thus a complex of cities and towns.

The 23 wards cover 577 km², with a radius of 15 km, and have a population of 10 million. However, the Capital Region of Tokyo (Tokyo's sphere of influence as defined by the Central Government) encompasses an area within a radius of 100 km from the capital's centre.

The first stage of our studies (1971–73) was concerned with the characteristics of the urban environment, the dynamics of biotic communities under the influence of the urban environment and changes in the human environment. In the second stage of our research (1974–77) an interdisciplinary and integrated study of urban ecosystems was conducted on various aspects of the biotic and abiotic factors from an anthropocentric viewpoint. The third stage of our study (1978–80), an intensive study of coastal cities facing onto the Tokyo Bay, was aimed at the analysis and synthesis of an urban ecosystem, using nine categories: (1) air, (2) soil, (3) water, (4) vegetation, (5) animals, (6) human behaviour, (7) land use and economics, (8) demography and health and (9) city planning.

AIMS OF THE STUDY

Our objectives in studying an urban ecosystem are to clarify the close relationship of the constituents of cities, the process of urbanization, changes in the human environment due to urbanization, changes in the natural environment and their effect on man and changes in environmental perception. The author has proposed the concept of a biocentric environment and its evaluation as a basic ecological concept (Numata 1953).

The term 'urban ecosystem' is used as an analogy to 'natural ecosystem'. Matter, energy, population and information flow into the urban ecosystem, and flow out in different forms. It is basically an entity composed of biotic components and abiotic factors, i.e. an ecologically integrated, holistic entity.

An urban ecosystem can be studied in the following ways:

1. By considering it as a 'quasi-organism'; the transformation of energy, matter, people and information is the chief focus of this approach.
2. By studying the impact of urban environments on terrestrial and aquatic ecosystems; the focus here is the behaviour and responses of the biota to urban as compared to natural environmental conditions.
3. By studying the reaction of human settlement to the abiotic environment.
4. By establishing a simulation model of an urban ecosystem, with networks of actions and reactions of the various components, for use in ecosystem management, planning and decision-making.

In our project, aspects (2) and (3) have been studied most fully and (1) and (4) have been considered in parallel. This paper is largely concerned with aspect (2).

CHANGES IN URBAN ENVIRONMENTS

The urban atmosphere

Changes in the composition of the air, formation of an inversion layer and a climatological dome and the increase in surface temperature, particularly the formation of heat islands, are seen as accompanying the process of urbanization. The annual concentration of SO_2 increased in Tokyo after 1945 and was maximal in 1971. It has gradually declined in recent years because of legal restrictions on emission of smoke from factories and exhaust gases from cars. However, photochemical smog (including NO_x and O_3) has not improved very much. The large cities of Tokyo, Yokohama, Kawasaki, Chiba and Ichihara connected to the coastal industrial zone facing onto Tokyo Bay are all under the influence of these atmospheric pollutants. A characteristic of such coastal cities is a relatively enclosed wind system due to the interaction of land and sea breezes. The concentration of atmospheric pollutants is thus maintained at high levels within such an area (Mitsudera 1979).

The rise in the surface temperature and the formation of heat islands are well-known effects of urbanization. In the Tokyo area there are a number of heat islands. The lowest temperatures are found beneath the canopy of urban forests and in ponds, lakes, rivers and the sea. The heat island pattern is maintained in the atmosphere above the buildings up to 1,000 m (Mitsudera *et al.* 1972).

Rivers

A hydrological cycle in a river basin (the Oguri River) in the western part of Tokyo was examined using rain gauges, gauges for recording ground-water-level fluctuation, and a discharge-recording gauge in the watershed area (about 25 km^2). The area of forests, paddy-fields and grasslands in the basin decreased, and the residential and the impervious areas increased with urbanization. When compared with typical hydrographs for non-urban stretches of the Oguri River, the time between the beginning of rainfall and the run-off peak in a hydrograph, and that between the run-off peak and the nick point of a recession curve for the hydrograph, became shorter with urbanization. (The nick point of a recession curve for the hydrograph is the boundary point between the run-off and base flow (Ichikawa 1973).)

The same tendency is found along the largest river (the Tama River) in Tokyo (140 km long): the upper stretches (about one-third of the river) are virtually unpolluted. However, in the middle and lower stretches, residential waste-water and treated sewage water run into the river. Such widely distributed water pollution in the Tama River has been recognized since 1960. Food and textile companies were established on this river and these resulted in an increase in the population. The organic effluent increased. The BOD was less than 2 mgl^{-1} before 1965, but afterwards increased to 3–5 mgl^{-1} halfway up the river. The content of ammonium nitrogen was about 0.05 mgl^{-1} before 1960, but was 1.3–5.2 mgl^{-1} after 1965. A polysaprobic area, as determined by the biotic index of Beck-Tsuda (Tsuda *et al.* 1974; Hisai 1977), occurred in the lower stretches below the Maruko Bridge in 1963, but it had enlarged in area three times by 1975. Polluted water exceeding the self-purification capacity of the Tama River was always found to be discharged in the lower reaches of the river.

In the ponds and lakes of Tokyo, eutrophication proceeded more quickly than in natural lakes. Underground water, particularly the amount gushing from springs, was very much reduced by urbanization.

Soils

Soils as a part of the urban environment were evaluated from the standpoint of (1) human life and health, (2) landscape and (3) plant growth or food production (Yamane 1976). The soil in which trees grow in streets is weakly alkaline down to 1 m in depth, and has much available phosphorus originating in the surrounding concrete. The surface horizon, rich in humus, is removed or mixed with the lower horizons or foreign materials. The carbon content is low, and the phosphorus-absorption coefficient tends also to be low (Hamada 1973). In the Meiji Shrine Forest (planted woodland established 100 years ago), the surface horizon was shallower than we expected due to human interference, but otherwise the soil profile and microflora were very much like those of a natural soil.

CHANGES IN BIOTIC FACTORS DUE TO URBANIZATION

Plants

There are forested areas preserved in the heart of Tokyo, such as the woods dominated by *Castanopsis cuspidata* Schottky var. *sieboldii* Nakai in Shin-juku-Gyoen Park, Rikugien Park, the Nature Study Park and at the Gakushuin University. These urban woods were compared with natural *C.cuspidata* forests in rural areas. The total number of constituent tree species of these natural forests is usually about 50; however, in the urban forest the number is around 30. In the urban environment the stratification becomes simpler, with a poorly developed herbaceous layer. Seral species found naturally in secondary forests and forest margins, such as *Quercus serrata* Thunb., *Mallotus japonicus* Müll. Arg. and *Pleioblastus chino* Makino, invade urban woods (Okutomi *et al.* 1973). *Aucuba japonica* Thunb. and *Trachicarpus excelsa* Wendl. grow abnormally as an undergrowth (Suzuki & Yano 1973).

Since 1950 a census has been taken of the existence and health of trees of more than 5 cm in diameter at breast height in the Nature Study Park in the heart of Tokyo. *Abies firma* Sieb. et Zucc. had already disappeared by 1950, and since then *Cryptomeria japonica* D. Don has decreased considerably (only

5% of trees still remaining), as has *Pinus densiflora* Sieb. et Zucc. and *Castanea crenata* Sieb. et Zucc., *Pinus thunbergii* Parl. is relatively tolerant to urbanization but *Castanopsis cuspidata* has shown the most vigorous growth (Mitsudera *et al.* 1972).

The sensitivity of tree species to SO_2 pollution has been studied in the laboratory. The result of the census in the Nature Study Park correlates with the sensitivity to SO_2 in the laboratory. Evergreen needle-leaved trees, with the exception of *Juniperus chinensis* L., are very sensitive to SO_2. Broad-leaved trees particularly *Castanopsis cuspidata* are generally more resistant. The 'degree of health' of trees is an index of existing conditions in urbanized areas. This can be judged from the leaf biomass and crown cover, the rate of shedding of branches, the longevity of leaves, the condition of the bark and the presence of epiphytic fungi and of young regenerating shoots from the trunk base (Okuda & Yano 1972; Kataoka & Numata 1975). An effective judgement of the health of trees can be made from the air using remote sensing with infrared film or by using a multi-band camera.

In the Nature Study Park there are 13 alien species among 718 native flowering plant species. However, this value is low compared with the ratio of aliens in the urban flora of Japan as a whole (10%). In islands like Japan the percentage of aliens in the flora is a good indicator of urbanization.

Certain Convolvulaceae are very sensitive to photochemical oxidants, particularly *Ipomoea triloba* L., *Pharbitis nil* Choisy and *Calystegia japonica* Choisy. The leaves of three varieties of *Pharbitis nil* are used as a phytometer for monitoring photochemical smog (Mitsudera *et al.* 1974).

As in western countries, lichens and bryophytes are used as indicators of air pollution and urbanization. *Parmelia tinctorum* Nyl., an epiphytic lichen, is used to assess the amount of SO_2 pollution. Its distribution area roughly coincides with the area where the annual mean concentration of SO_2 is less than 0.02 ppm. The coverage of *P.tinctorum* thalli on tombstones is a particularly useful measure (Kurokawa 1973, 1974). A 'bryometer', using mosses (e.g. *Bryum argenteum* Hedw.) or liverworts (e.g. *Marchantia polymorpha* L.) exposed to polluted air in a growth chamber compared with that in a carbon-filtered growth chamber, is also useful as a kind of phytometer (Taoda 1977).

Animals

The disappearance of animals from the heart of Tokyo was traced using questionnaires. From the results, isopleths of the disappearance of the firefly, dragonfly, grasshopper, hare, bat, mole, weasel and fox were drawn (Shinada & Tomioka 1972; Chiba 1974). The avifauna in urban woods in Tokyo has fallen by half over the last 20 years or so. The decreasing numbers of common birds of urbanized areas, such as the tree sparrow, crow (*Corvus levaillanti*

Bonaparte), great tit, bamboo partridge and domestic pigeon, demonstrate the deterioration of environmental quality. For example, the number of territories of the great tit has decreased, and the area of each territory has enlarged (Sakurai 1972). The vigour of the great tit (breeding and singing, singing only and no singing) is related to the rate of loss of forested areas (Sakurai 1973).

The chrysomerid beetle fauna was studied as a zoological indicator of urban ecosystems. The number of species in urban woods in Tokyo is about 200, which is one-third of the total species in Japan. Species of chrysomerid beetles depend on plants, therefore changes in the composition and structure of vegetation (particularly of the forest margins, grasslands and wet meadows), the influence of air pollution and of pesticide sprays are particularly important. Ruderal plants, weeds and ornamentals such as *Azalea*, are important for overwintering of chrysomerid eggs. The larvae live in plant tissue, and their mortality is lowered owing to the decrease in their natural enemies (carnivorous insects, spiders, amphibia, reptiles, birds and mammals). There are a number of urban specialists, and the percentage of these in the chrysomerid beetle fauna may be used as an environmental indicator. The percentage is, for example, 64.7 in Shinjuku Gyoen Park, 77.7 in Meiji Shrine, 88.9 in Ueno Park, 100 in Rikugien Park but only 35.0 in the Nature Study Park (Ohno 1974).

The numbers of Joro gumo (*Nephila clavata* L. Koch), a common spider, is also an indicator of the quality of forested areas. For example, the number of individuals per 1000 m^2 was 2.7 in Rikugien Park, 9.7 in the Meiji Shrine and 19.9 in the Nature Study Park. This number depends on the stratification of the forest and the numbers of prey insects (Ohno 1976). Urban coccids show a high tolerance to air pollution, and environmental stress due to urbanization has more severe effects on their natural enemies than on the coccids. Thus the proportion of urban coccids in the total coccid fauna is a good indicator of urbanization (Kawai 1977).

In the Tama River, benthic animals were collected and compared in the upper and lower reaches. The biomass of the intolerant (oligosaprobic) species was greater in the upper reaches; however, that of the tolerant (α-mesosaprobic, β-mesosaprobic or polysaprobic) species was greater in the lower reaches below the Haijima Bridge. Some benthic animals increase in polluted water; however, many insects such as mayflies, stone flies, caddis flies and so on disappear, and their biomass decreases due to heavy water pollution. The Tama River is at present too heavily polluted for many benthic animals, especially insects, to live in, except in the upper reaches of the river (Hisai 1977).

In an urban forest the longevity of leaves of evergreen broad-leaved trees is reduced. One of the causes of this may be the activities of leaf-miners (*Nepticula* sp.) and a leaf-cutter (*Deporaus mannerheimi* Humel). The defoliation season is concentrated in the spring (April–May) in urban areas, while the normal peak of defoliation is in the summer (Hisai 1974, 1975; Yano 1974).

From the observation of insect pest populations, the differences in species composition of flies, mosquitoes, cockroaches and black-flies were observed different areas with different degrees of urbanization. Black-fly larvae were absent in most of the streams which were polluted by sewage; however, in irrigation ditches between paddy-fields, the larvae and pupae of black flies were found in small numbers. These insects may thus indicate a relatively unpolluted environment (Ogata & Tanaka 1977).

The ratio of the total number of bacteria to gram-negative bacteria may indicate suitability of soil conditions for bacterial growth, particularly moisture. Gram-negative bacteria are more sensitive to decreases in soil moisture than are gram-positive species. The NH_3-oxidizer counts were always higher in urban soil (Hamada 1973; Hamada *et al.* 1975).

CONCLUSION

Our knowledge of urban ecosystems is related to a comprehensive understanding of the integration of their structure, function and dynamics. The central idea of our study is a knowledge of the plant and animal communities and of the direct and indirect effects of man on them. The interrelations between the various communities, and the ways that effects on the population of one species may affect those of others, should not be neglected. In the Nature Study Park in the centre of Tokyo that we have been studying since 1950, various trees have died over the last 30 years, and the floristic composition of the vegetation has changed. Usually this phenomenon of deteriorating survival ratios of trees is said to be caused by air pollution and, as stated earlier, the concentration of SO_2 has increased since 1945. However, it is not wise to assume that the two phenomena, the deterioration of tree growth and the present SO_2 pollution, are necessarily directly related. This could represent an earlier cause and a later effect. There is a complex sequence of cause-and-effect relationships involved here. The survival ratio of a climax evergreen broad-leaved tree, *Castanopsis cuspidata* var. *sieboldii*, is rather high, but the condition of many trees is not always good. Their vigour is gradually declining due to defoliation by leaf-miners and other noxious insects which attack the trees in the spring every year. This abnormal and unseasonal defoliation accelerates the deterioration in the vigour of the trees. One of the causes of the outbreak of such noxious insects may be the disappearance of insectivorous birds in the area. The disappearance of some birds is caused by the effects of urbanization, such as noise, air pollution and loss of habitat, etc. Thus a network of interacting factors may bring about the poor growth of the trees.

REFERENCES*

* The main sources of cited papers are UEJ (*Studies in Urban Ecosystems*, Japanese version, edited by M. Numata), UEE (*Studies in Urban Ecosystems*, English version, edited by M. Numata) and TP (*Tokyo Project, Interdisciplinary Studies of Urban Ecosystems in the Metropolis of Tokyo*, in English, edited by M. Numata).

Chiba S. (1974) Environmental transitions and community of animals. *UEE (1974)*, 46–64.

Hamada R. (1973) Urban ecosystem and soil. *UEE (1973)*, 17–28.

Hamada R., Kiso S. & Muraoka M. (1975) A characterization of urban soil with total bacterial counts to gram negative counts ratio (TB/GNB) and soil perfusion. *UEE (1975)*, 80–86.

Hisai N. (1974) A study on the outbreak of *Nepticula* sp. in the urban ecosystem. *UEE (1974)*, 93–102.

Hisai N. (1975) Analysis of a fluctuation mechanism of *Nepticula* sp. population in urban areas in Japan. *UEE (1975)*, 66–71.

Hisai N. (1977) On the influence of the polluted water upon the benthic animals in the Tama River. *TP*, 199–204.

Ichikawa M. (1973, 74) Effects of urbanization on the hydrological cycle in the Oguri River Basin, western suburb of Tokyo. *UEE (1973)*, 11–16; *UEE (1974)*, 13–21.

Kataoka M. & Numata M. (1975) On the healthiness of trees in urban environments. *Miscellaneous Reports of the National Park for Nature Study*, 6, 21–29.

Kawai S. (1977) Changes of coccid-fauna with urbanization in Tokyo. *TP*, 148–172.

Kurokawa S. (1973) Preliminary studies on lichens of urban areas in Japan. *UEE (1973)*, 80–85.

Kurokawa S. (1974) A study on distribution of lichens in urban areas in Japan. *UEE (1974)*, 26–32.

Mitsudera M. (1979) Urban atmospheric environment along the bay-coast. In *Integrated Ecological Studies in Bay-Coast Cities* I (Ed. by M. Numata), pp. 23–29, Chiba.

Mitsudera M., Chiba S. & Sugawara T. (1973) Urban environmental atmosphere and changes in biotic communities. *UEE (1973)*, 1–10.

Mitsudera M., Chiba S. & Sugawara T. (1974) Changes in urban environmental atmosphere and transitions in biotic communities. *UEE (1974)*, 1–12.

Mitsudera M., Sugawara T. & Chiba S. (1972) Changes in urban environment and biotic communities. *UEJ (1972)*, 45–54.

Numata M. (1953) *Methodology of Ecology*. Kokon-Shoin, Tokyo.

Numata M. (1976) Methodology of urban ecosystem studies. In *Science for Better Environment*. Proceedings of the International Congress on the Human Environment (1975, Kyoto), pp. 221–228. HESC, Tokyo.

Numata M. (1977) The impact of urbanization on vegetation in Japan. In *Vegetation Science and Environmental Protection* (Ed. by A. Miyawaki & R. Tüxen), pp. 161–171. Maruzen, Tokyo.

Obara H., Hirata H. & Okuzaki M. (1977) An aspect of the existence of mammals in urban ecosystems. *TP*, 173–187.

Ogata K. & Tanaka I. (1977) Observations of the changes in insect pest population with the urbanization of Kawasaki City. *TP*, 138–147.

Ohno M. (1974) Distribution of chrysomerid beetles in the urban environment. *UEJ (1974)*, 93–128.

Ohno M. (1976) Distribution of spiders in the urban environment, particularly on *Nephila clavata*. *UEJ (1976)*, 135–154.

Okuda S. & Yano M. (1972) Successional changes of forest communities in the urban environment. *UEJ (1972)*, 1–11.

Okutomi K., Ageishi M. & Takahashi Y. (1973) Studies on the characteristics of urban vegetation, particularly on the composition and structure of urban forests. *UEJ (1973)*, 55–66.

Sakurai N. (1972) Annual variation of breeding birds in green spaces in the 23 wards of Tokyo. *UEJ (1972)*, 83–96.

Sakurai N. (1973) Varieties of birds that breed in the heart of Tokyo Metropolis and the breeding condition of Japanese great tit. *UEE (1973)*, 29–40.

Shinada Y. & Tomioka H. (1972) Studies on the dynamics of urban ecosystems, II. *UEJ (1972)*, 148–156.

Suzuki Y. & Yano M. (1973) Propagation of *Aucuba japonica* in urban forests. *UEJ (1973)*, 67–82.

Taoda H. (1977) Bryophytes in the urban ecosystem. *TP*, 99–117.

Tsuda M., Morishita I. & Marunouchi Y. (1974) Biological judgement of the water quality of the Tama River. In *Reports of the Biological Researches of the Tama, Asahi, Niyodo and Natori Rivers* (Ed. by M. Tsuda), pp. 6–17.

Yamane I. (1976) Soils in urban ecosystems. *UEJ (1976)*, 13–16.

Yano M. (1974) Influences exerted by the outbreak of two species of insect in *Shiia sieboldii* forests. *UEE (1974)*, 86–92.

15. PLANT CONTAMINATION CAUSED BY URBAN AND INDUSTRIAL EMISSIONS IN THE REGION OF CRACOW CITY (SOUTHERN POLAND)

K. GRODZIŃSKA

Institute of Botany,
Polish Academy of Sciences,
Lubicz 46, 31-512 Cracow, Poland

SUMMARY

The Niepołomice Forest, a large forest complex (11,000 ha), situated close to the biggest steel mill in Poland (annual production 7×10^6 tons of iron and steel) and Cracow city (700,000 inhabitants), was the object of study. This urban-industrial agglomeration emits, mainly directed towards the Niepołomice Forest, 170,000 tons of SO_2 and 130,000 tons of dust per year. The concentrations of sulphur and heavy metals (Cd, Ni, Pb, Zn, Fe) in the air, precipitation, plants and soils were determined. Significant correlations were found between the distance from pollution sources and (1) the heavy metal content in precipitation and plant materials, (2) the number of lichen species, and the degree of damage to lichen thalli, (3) the number of macrofungi, and the distribution of pathogenic fungi and (4) the degree of needle, crown and branch damage to pines. Using plant indicators, zones of the deterioration of the forest ecosystem were drawn up. Some practical recommendations for forest management in an urban-industrial agglomeration are given.

INTRODUCTION

The Niepołomice Forest (N.F.) is situated within the Cracow-Silesian industrial region (Southern Poland) 10–35 km to the east of the city of Cracow and a great metallurgic complex. This complex was built up in the 1950s and produces 7 million tons of iron and steel per year. Cracow's population is 700,000, and the city has several factories, power stations and heavy vehicle traffic.

The N.F. is a large forest complex (11,000 ha). Its southern part is mainly coniferous (pine and oak–pine) and the northern part consists of deciduous (oak–hornbeam) stands. Due to the direction of the prevailing wind in this region (from west to east), it is seriously affected by the pollutants emitted both by the metallurgic complex and the city.

The total annual emission in the Cracow agglomeration amounts to 170,000 tons of SO_2 and 150,000 tons of dust containing large quantities of toxic heavy metals (e.g. 170 tons of Pb, 7 tons of Cd, 18,000 tons of Fe).

At the beginning of the study it was expected that air pollution from the Cracow agglomeration during recent years would have caused deterioration of the N.F. ecosystem. This deterioration was examined in respect of changes in: (1) the concentration of sulphur and heavy metals in the air, precipitation, soils and plants; (2) the distribution of lichens and fungi—a group of plants sensitive to air pollution; and (3) the morphology of pine trees (damage to needles, branches and crowns).

MATERIALS AND METHODS

Most of the studies were conducted during 2 years (1977, 1978), on ten sites 0.5 ha. each, located along a west–east transect, at different distances from the emission sources. Three of these areas were located in a rich oak–hornbeam forest, while the remaining seven were in a poorer mixed oak–pine forest. The Białowieża Forest, one of the cleanest Polish National Parks (Grodzińska 1978), was used as a control.

The concentration of sulphur compounds and heavy metals was measured in the air (Kasina *et al.* 1980), in atmospheric precipitation (Zając 1980), in the soils (Grodzińska unpublished data), and in plant materials (Grodzińska & Berbeka 1980). Morphological damage of pine stands (Grabowski 1980) and the distribution of lichens (Kiszka 1980), macro-fungi (Komorowska 1980) and phytopathogenic fungi (Kućmierz 1980) were also studied.

The concentrations of SO_2 and aerosol particles were measured as daily means, and the chemical composition of dust was analysed in samples taken over 10 days. The SO_2 concentration was estimated by the West-Gaeke method, the dust concentration by a reflectometric method, the sulphate ion concentration by titration using thorin and the heavy metals by atomic absorption spectrophotometry.

Rain was collected monthly (April to October) in 10 plastic rain gauges placed at a height of 50 cm above the ground. The concentration of pollutants was measured in the filtered rain samples using the same methods described above.

Ten common plant species in the N.F. were chosen for chemical analyses, i.e. two trees (*Quercus robur* L., *Pinus sylvestris* L.), three shrubs (*Frangula alnus* Mill., *Salix caprea* L., *Vaccinium myrtillus* L.), two herbs (*Calamagrostis arundinacea* (L.) Roth., *Carex brizoides* L.), two mosses (*Pleurozium schreberi*

Mitt., *Hylocomium splendens* (Hedw.) Br. eur.) and one lichen (*Hypogymnia physodes* (L.) Nyl.).

Bark, wood, leaves and needles of the trees, small branches of the shrubs some 10 cm in length (shoots and roots for *Vaccinium myrtillus*), shoots and roots of the herbs, leaves of the mosses and thalli of the lichens were sampled, dried in an oven (80°C) and treated with mixed concentrated acids HNO_3 and $HClO_4$. The concentration of total sulphur in the plant materials was measured by means of the Butters, Chenery nephelometric method.

RESULTS

Air, precipitation and soil pollution by sulphur compounds and heavy metals

The average annual concentration of SO_2 in the air in the N.F. is 25 $\mu g\, m^{-3}$. It is 2.5 to 7 times higher in the cold period (October–March) than in the warm one (April–September). No spatial variation in the SO_2 concentration in the N.F. has been recorded (Kasina *et al.* 1980). The average annual concentration of dust is 46.2 $\mu g\, m^{-3}$, and it decreased with distance from the sources. The western part of the N.F. is, therefore, under the highest dust load. The concentration of sulphate aerosol in the N.F. amounts to 17.6 $\mu g\, m^{-3}$, and iron, zinc and lead concentrations are 0.63, 0.20 and 0.20 $\mu g\, m^{-3}$, respectively. All these aerosols show neither spatial nor seasonal variation in the N.F.

Airborne gases and particles are introduced to the ecosystem mainly by precipitation, which removes the pollutants from the airstream. The average total annual precipitation in the N.F. amounts to 729 mm, ranging from 10.2 to 134 mm in particular months. Tree crown interception is approximately 30%. The infiltration rate of precipitation depends upon the type of forest stand—it is higher in the oak–hornbeam forest (73%) than in the oak–pine one (66%) (Klein 1980).

Rain in the N.F. is highly polluted (Zając 1980). The average annual concentration of sulphate ions is 25 mg l^{-1} and it is twice as high in the forest stands beneath the tree canopy as in open stands (clear cutting). More sulphate ions are accumulated in the rain in deciduous forests (39 mg l^{-1}) than in oak–pine forests (29 mg l^{-1}). The average annual concentration of heavy metals in the rain in the N.F. is as follows: 0.13 mg l^{-1} Fe, 0.86 mg l^{-1} Zn and 0.02 mg l^{-1} Cu and Pb.

To judge from the composition of humus and the proportions of various forms of heavy metals and sulphur in the soils in the N.F. area, they have already undergone a partial transformation into industrisoils (Grodzińska unpublished data). When compared to the control samples taken from the Białowieża Forest, the soils are richer in bitumens, heavy metals and sulphur.

The humus horizons in the mixed oak–pine and the deciduous forest complexes in the N.F. contain, on average, twice as much Cd, three times more Pb, six times more Fe, two to three times more Zn, Cu and Mn in assimilable forms and two to four and a half times more sulphate (S-SO$_4$) than the control samples.

Plant pollution by sulphur compounds and heavy metals

The average concentration of heavy metals in all analysed plant materials in the N.F. is 2.5 μg g^{-1} for Cd, 8.7 for Ni, 9.5 for Cu, 30.2 for Pb, 96.2 for Zn and 936 for Fe (Grodzińska & Berbeka 1980). The concentration shows considerable spatial variation. The highest amounts of metals were found in the plants from the west, in proximity of the iron works and the Cracow agglomeration. There is a negative correlation between the concentration of metals and the distance from the emission sources: it is strongest for copper (r $-$0.52) and lead (r $-$0.51), and weakest for cadmium (r $-$0.44) and nickel (r $-$0.40). This correlation is particularly well demonstrated in pine needles, browse of *Salix caprea* and mosses (Fig. 15.1).

In general, larger amounts of heavy metals are accumulated in plants from habitats rich in nutrients (deciduous forest) than in plants growing in the poorer soils (mixed oak–pine forest). The average global pollution index for the analysed heavy metals is 6.4 for plants from oak–hornbeam forest and 6.0 for those from oak–pine forest. The most significant difference was found for nickel.

The concentration of heavy metals in the plant materials from the N.F. is about three times higher than in those from the Białowieża Forest. The global pollution index, which represents the average standardized contents of five heavy metals (Ni, Cu, Pb, Zn, Fe), reaches 5.2 in the N.F. and only 1.8 in the Białowieża Forest. The concentration of Fe, Ni and Pb in the N.F. exceeds that in the Białowieża Forest by a factor of 3.5, while the concentration of Cu and Zn is greater by a factor of 2.

The most effective accumulators of heavy metals are mosses, lichens and browse of *Salix caprea*, while the least effective is tree wood. The grasses and sedges accumulated considerably more heavy metals in their roots than in in their shoots, whereas the opposite was true for *Vaccinium myrtillus*. Trees accumulated heavy metals mainly in their bark, less in young twigs and leaves, and least in wood. Heavy metal concentration in pine needles increased with needle age.

Differences in metal accumulation were found. Considerable amounts of Ni were accumulated in grasses and sedges, Zn in the browse of *Salix caprea*, and Fe in tree bark.

The average sulphur concentration in the plants in the N.F. is 2,112 μg g^{-1}, and is not strongly correlated with the distance from sources (r $-$0.33).

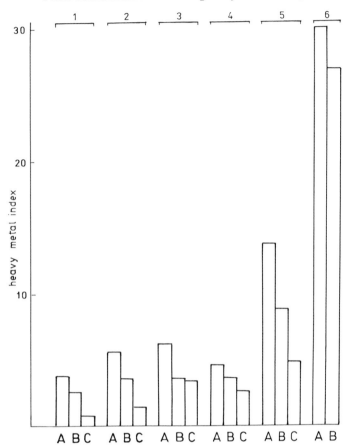

FIG. 15.1.   Heavy metal index of plants in the western (A) and central (B) parts of the Niepołomice Forest and in the Białowieża Forest (C). 1—pine needles, first fascicle; 2—pine needles, second fascicle; 3—*Vaccinium myrtillus*, shoots; 4—*V. myrtillus*, roots; 5—*Salix caprea* browse; 6—mosses.

The concentration of sulphur in the plants from the N.F. is twice as high as in those from the Białowieża Forest (Fig. 15.2).

Lichen distribution

The pollution of the forest ecosystem caused changes in the lichen flora of the N.F. (Kiszka 1964, 1977, 1980). Species-richness of the lichen flora has decreased by 10% over the last 20 years (Kiszka 1977). *Parmeliopsis aleurites* (Ach.) Lett., *Pertusaria amara* (Ach.) Nyl., *Parmelia caperata* (L.) Ach., *Cetraria islandica* (L.) Ach., species very sensitive to air pollution, have

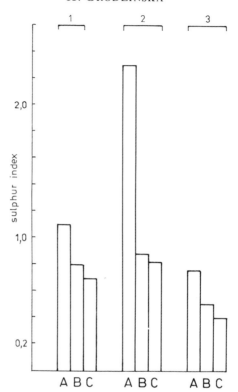

FIG. 15.2. Sulphur index of plants in the western (A) and central (B) parts of the Niepołomice Forest and in the Białowieża Forest (C). 1—pine needles, first fascicle; 2—pine needles, second fascicle; 3—*Salix caprea* browse.

disappeared from the western part of the N.F., while their frequency in the central and eastern parts has decreased considerably. There has also been a decrease in lichen cover of tree trunks and an increase in algal cover. Morphological changes in the thallus and the formation of soredia in lichens from the western part of the N.F. were observed. Finally, the expansion of pollution-tolerant species (e.g. *Lecanora conizaeoides*) was found in the western part of the N.F.

Four deterioration zones, based on lichen surveys (Kiszka 1977, 1980), have been recognized in the N.F. (Fig. 15.3). The western part of the forest complex and the eastern margin of the forest show the worst deterioration, whereas the central part is less affected by the air pollution.

Distribution of macro-fungi and phytopathogenic fungi

Industrial emissions have also caused changes in the mycoflora of the N.F.

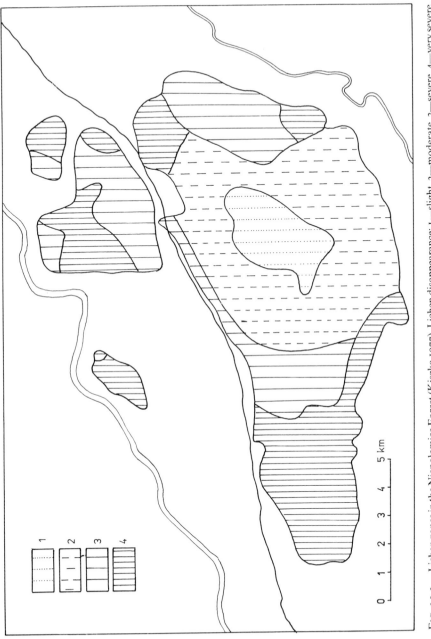

FIG. 15.3. Lichen zones in the Niepołomice Forest (Kiszka 1977). Lichen disappearance: 1—slight, 2—moderate, 3—severe, 4—very severe.

(Komorowska 1980). Mycorrhizal fungi showed the strongest response to the pollution. Some species showed a decreased distribution and production of fruit bodies (e.g. *Armillariella mellea* (Vahl. ex Fr.) Karst.), whereas others increased their distribution (e.g. *Heterobasidion annosum* (Fr.) Bref., *Naematoloma fasciculare* (Huds. ex Fr.) P. Karst.); edible fungi (e.g. *Boletus edulis* (Bull. ex Fr.)) have almost disappeared. There is a relationship between the number of species of macro-fungi and the distance from the pollution sources: 51 species were recorded in the western part (10 km from the ironwork) and 104 species in the central part of this forest complex (20 km distant).

Among the phytopathogenic fungi, species of the Erysiphales, mostly in the conidial stage, occur infrequently in the study area. The rust, *Melampsoridium betulinum* Kleb., in spite of the commonness of its host, occurs rarely (Kućmierz 1980). On the other hand, *Lophodermium pinastri* Chev. and *Sclerophoma pityophylla* Höhn, important pathogens of pine needles, are common. Their frequency increases with the age of the needles. On the young fascicles (first and second age group), *Lophodermium* appears in the conidial stage only, but on the older ones (third age group) it has asci and ascospores (Kućmierz, unpublished data). Pine needles taken from the control area are only rarely infected with *Lophodermium*, and then only with the conidial stage on the oldest needles.

Morphological damage of pine stands

Pine, a dominant tree species, shows deformed needles, twigs and crowns in the N.F. (Grabowski 1980). Zones of severe, moderately intense and moderately typical damage were recognized in the N.F., based on these deformations. The zone of severe damage accounts for 47% of the total area, moderately intense damage affects a further 47%, while moderately typical damage is confined to merely 6% of the area (Fig. 15.4). There are no pines in the N.F. completely devoid of damage.

DISCUSSION

The pollution of the air, precipitation, soil and plants in the N.F. is several times higher than in the control areas, for example national parks in Białowieża or the Tatra Mts (Kasina *et al.* 1980; Grodzińska *et al.* unpublished data; Grodzińska & Berbeka 1980; Jelesnianska-Krzemien unpublished data), but still lower than in the Silesian industrial region (Każmierczakowa 1975; Warteresiewicz 1979; Makomaska 1978; Jelesnianska-Krzemien unpublished data).

In the 1960s, variation in the SO_2 concentration in the N.F. was apparent, the western part being much more polluted than the others (Kasina 1971).

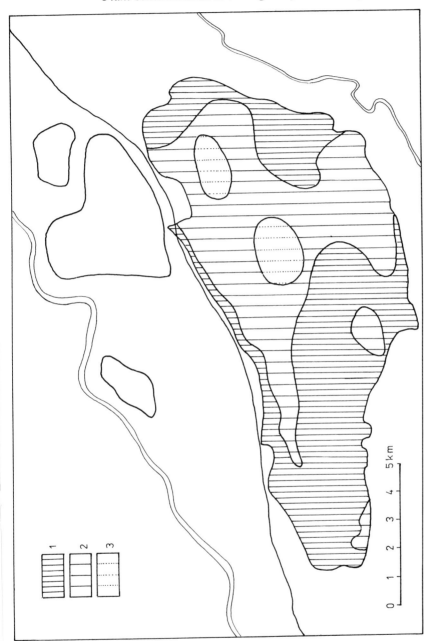

Fig. 15.4. Zones of damages to pine trees in the Niepołomice Forest (Grabowski 1980). 1—severe, 2—moderately intensive, 3—moderately typical.

Grodziński W. & Lesiński J.A. (Ed.) (1978) *Ecological principles for rebuilding the region of Niepołomice Forest* (in Polish), Krakow.

Jop K. (1979) Quality evaluation of roe deer antlers from industrial regions in Southern Poland. *Acta theriologica*, **24**, 23–34.

Kasina S. (1971) Distribution of atmospheric pollution in the region of the Puszcza Niepołomicka (Niepołomickie Wilderness) (in Polish). *Ochrona Powietrza*, **5**, 5–8.

Kasina S., Kwiek J., Lewińska J., Rapacz J., Walat W. & Zgud K. (1980) Air pollution in the Niepołomice Forest. In *Acidification of forest environments (Niepołomice Forest) caused by SO₂ emissions from steel mills* (Ed. by K. Grodzińska). Final report. Grant PL-FS-75, FG-PO-355/JB-22. Krakow.

Kaźmierczakowa R. (1975) Correlation between the amount of industrial dust fall and the lead and zinc accumulation in some plant species. *Bulletin de l'Academie Polonaise des Sciences*, Cl.II, **23**, 611–621.

Kiszka J. (1964) The lichens of the Sandomierz Lowland, Part I. Lichens of Niepołomice Forest district. *Fragmenta floristica et geobotanica*, **10**, 527–564.

Kiszka J. (1977) The effect of town and industry emissions on the lichen flora of Cracow and the Niepołomice Forest (in Polish). *Prace monograficzne WSP w Krakowie*, **19**, 1–133.

Kiszka J. (1980) Lichens. In *Acidification of forest environments (Niepołomice Forest) caused by SO₂ emisions from steel mills* (Ed. by K. Grodzińska). Final report. Grant PL-FS-75, FG-PO-355/JB-22. Krakow.

Klein J. (1980) Infiltration of precipitation and light penetration to the bottom of various forest communities. *Ibid.*

Komorowska H. (1980) Mushrooms. *Ibid.*

Kućmierz J. (1980) Microscopic phytopathogenic fungi. *Ibid.*

Maczek W. (1977) Photosynthesis production of *Pinus sylvestris* L. in the Niepołomice Forest within the range of industrial emission. *Bulletin de l'Academie Polonaise des Sciences*, Cl.II, **25**, 683–695.

Makomaska M. (1978) Heavy metals contamination of pinewoods in the Niepołomice Forest (Southern Poland). *Bulletin de l'Academie Polonaise des Sciences*, Cl.II, **26**, 679–685.

Rapacz J. & Bartosik J. (1976) Expansion of air pollution in a forest area exemplified by the Lenin steel mill and Niepołomice Forest region (in Polish). *Biuletyn IKS* **3**, 24–26.

Rich V. (1979) Down in a Polish forest, something is stirring. *Nature, London*, **277**, 9.

Sawicka-Kapusta K. (1979) Roe deer antlers as bioindicators of environmental pollution in Southern Poland. *Environmental Pollution*, **19**, 283–293.

Warteresiewicz M. (1979) Effect of air pollution by sulphur dioxide on some plant species in the Upper Silesian industrial region (in Polish). *Archiwum Ochrony Srodowiska*, **1**, 95–166.

Zając P.K. (1980) Rain pollution. In *Acidification of forest environments (Niepołomice Forest) caused by SO₂ emissions from steel mills* (Ed. by K. Grodzińska). Final report. Grant PL-FS-75, FG-PO-355/JB-22, Krakow.

16. ACCUMULATION OF HEAVY METALS BY CERTAIN TREE SPECIES

JAN GRESZTA

Institute of Botany,
Polish Academy of Science,
Lubicz 46, 31-512 Cracow, Poland

SUMMARY

The effects of lead–copper and cadmium–lead–zinc dusts from smelters on the growth of deciduous and coniferous trees were estimated. The heavy metal content of seedlings was also determined, and a relationship between dust content of the soil and plant heavy-metal content was established.

INTRODUCTION AND METHODOLOGY

An increase of substances injurious to vegetation which inhibit growth and, in extreme cases, can eliminate individuals or species, thereby affecting ecosystems as a whole, has been observed in recent years in urban and industrial complexes. Such effects cause particular difficulties for agricultural, forestry and recreational areas.

The purpose of this study was to determine to what extent certain heavy metals (Cu, Zn, Pb and Cd) and other components of dusts from electrofilters installed on copper and zinc smelting works are injurious to seedlings of basic forest tree species. The following factors were determined: the chemical composition of the dusts from the electrofilters, the influence of introduced dusts on soil and on the growth of seedlings, and the sensitivity of certain tree species to increasing amounts of heavy metals in the soil.

In order to study the effects on plants, experimental plots (150×200 cm) were established, 12 being subjected to lead–copper dusts and 12 being subjected to cadmium–lead–zinc dusts. The dusts used were thoroughly mixed with soil to a depth of 30 cm in the following percentages: 0 (control plot), 1, 3, 5, 8 and 10.

The dust-treated areas were then planted with 30 2-year-old seedlings of each of the following species: *Pinus sylvestris* L., *P.nigra* Arnold, *Picea abies* (L.) Karsten, *Abies alba* Miller, *Larix decidua* Miller, *Quercus robur* L., *Fagus sylvatica* L. *Alnus glutinosa* (L.) Gaertner and *Acer pseudoplatanus* L. Every 2 weeks the seedlings were monitored and the following factors recorded:

survival rate, root growth, shoot growth, and size, shape and colour of leaves (including necroses). The studies, which extended over two successive growing periods, aimed at establishing (1) a maximum value here called 'threshold of broken resistance', at which the level of introduced dusts caused a death rate of over 20% of the seedlings during the first growing period and (2) a maximum value here called 'threshold of sensitivity', at which level observable damage was caused to the plants.

Both types of dust used in the experiment differed qualitatively and quantitatively: (a) lead–copper dusts containing about 16.5% copper, the same amount of silica, about 7.5% lead and smaller quantities of calcium, magnesium, iron, zinc and potassium, and (b) cadmium–lead–zinc dusts containing about 56% zinc, over 15% lead, and a considerable amount of cadmium, with other components occurring in quantities ranging from 0.01 to

TABLE 16.1.   *Growth of coniferous trees on plots treated with lead–copper and cadmium–lead–zinc dusts.*

		Lead–copper dust		Cadmium–lead–zinc dust	
			Growth		Growth
			mean increment		mean increment
	Dust % in		ratio of affected		ratio of affected
	top soil	Number of dead	seedlings to	Number of dead	seedlings to
Species	layer	trees in %	the control	trees in %	the control
Abies	control	0.0	100.0	0.0	100.0
alba	1	3.4	84.9	3.4	70.0
	3	30.0	75.3	16.7	51.2
	5	66.7	63.0	16.7	40.0
	8	70.0	45.2	36.7	35.0
	10	70.0	43.7	50.0	20.0
Picea	control	0.0	100.0	0.0	100.0
excelsa	1	0.0	110.5	3.4	93.0
	3	0.0	100.7	13.3	73.0
	5	6.7	80.3	40.0	48.7
	8	23.3	61.8	70.0	47.8
	10	30.0	58.6	90.0	23.4
Pinus	control	0.0	100.0	0.0	100.0
sylvestris	1	6.7	119.6	0.0	159.4
	3	16.7	124.2	3.4	172.7
	5	20.0	118.0	6.7	159.4
	8	23.3	111.5	33.3	123.6
	10	30.0	97.1	95.3	36.4
Larix	control	0.0	100.0	0.0	100.0
decidua	1	10.0	104.0	6.7	102.7
	3	13.3	108.0	23.3	88.2
	5	20.0	99.8	40.0	87.4
	8	23.3	97.8	56.7	84.3
	10	30.0	76.7	80.0	24.0

1.90%. An analysis of the ionic content of the water-soluble components of the dusts, i.e. occurring in a form easily assimilated by plants, was carried out.

The introduction of the dusts changed the soil pH by only 0.5. Treatment with the lead–copper dusts was followed by a slight acidification of the soil, whereas the cadmium–lead–zinc dusts had the reverse effect.

RESULTS

A summary of seedling growth measurements and heavy metal determinations is presented in Tables 16.1–16.3.

Of the tree species studied, conifers, particularly *Abies alba*, proved to be the least resistant to lead–copper dusts, as little as 1% in the soil causing the

TABLE 16.2. *Growth of some deciduous tree species on plots treated with lead–copper and cadmium–lead–zinc dusts.*

Species	Dust % in top soil layer	Lead–copper dust		Cadmium–lead–zinc dust	
		Number of dead trees in %	Growth mean increment ratio of seedlings treated to the control	Number of dead trees in %	Growth mean increment ratio of seedlings treated to the control
Alnus	control	0.0	100.0	0.0	100.0
glutinosa	1	0.0	129.6	0.0	79.1
	3	0.0	109.6	10.0	64.2
	5	0.0	97.5	13.3	43.7
	8	0.0	77.5	33.3	30.6
	10	3.3	52.1	50.0	27.7
Fagus	control	13.3	100.0	0.0	100.0
sylvatica	1	10.0	84.2	3.3	92.0
	3	6.7	73.6	20.0	74.3
	5	3.3	70.5	30.0	67.2
	8	0.0	54.8	50.0	65.4
	10	0.0	44.1	90.0	56.6
Quercus	control	0.0	100.0	0.0	100.0
robur	1	0.0	137.3	0.0	100.0
	3	0.0	117.9	0.0	83.0
	5	0.0	92.5	3.3	64.0
	8	3.3	85.1	6.7	64.3
	10	3.3	61.9	23.3	51.8
Acer	control	0.0	100.0	0.0	100.0
pseudoplatanus	1	6.7	67.0	13.3	82.1
	3	10.0	62.2	23.3	43.8
	5	30.0	48.1	53.3	21.9
	8	30.0	45.9	63.3	20.8
	10	50.0	13.2	87.6	16.7

TABLE 16.3.   *Contents of Cu, Zn, Pb, and Cd (in ppm) in seedlings of different tree species according to amounts of lead–copper and cadmium–lead–zinc dusts introduced into soil.*

Species	Dust contents in soil in per cent	Lead–copper dusts				Cadmium–lead–zinc dusts			
		Cu	Zn	Pb	Cd	Cu	Zn	Pb	Cd
Abies	0	6	54	8	0.5	9	58	8	0.3
alba	1	71	75	67	0.7	14	132	53	2.1
	3	201	147	113	1.3	18	250	80	4.0
	5	361	167	121	1.4	25	355	123	8.1
	8	434	318	302	1.2	26	357	128	8.1
	10	453	316	740	1.4	30	394	225	13.1
Picea	0	8	44	7	0.3	7	49	10	0·7
abies	1	169	160	108	0.4	13	208	142	3.4
	3	272	174	218	0.6	14	351	259	5.7
	5	295	191	334	0.7	21	457	383	7.1
	8	409	242	406	0.8	26	513	357	8.6
	10	478	225	403	0.9	34	650	549	13.7
Pinus	0	8	41	7	0.6	10	46	7	0.4
sylvestris	1	50	74	87	0.4	11	182	55	2.3
	3	63	104	190	1.1	10	235	70	3.0
	5	96	187	227	1.0	17	270	133	5.8
	8	231	189	271	1.3	15	357	140	6.2
	10	354	228	283	2.4	19	385	164	12.8
Larix	0	7	38	2	0.2	7	41	4	0.3
decidua	1	25	46	20	0.2	6	82	28	1.8
	3	50	86	41	0.1	8	106	58	2.6
	5	111	106	98	0.1	8	106	70	2.8
	8	168	150	184	0.3	9	121	84	3.9
	10	193	126	250	0.3	8	288	105	6.5
Alnus	0	11	47	12	0.5	12	47	10	0.4
glutinosa	1	72	102	65	1.6	14	142	36	1.1
	3	83	124	88	2.1	13	154	70	3.4
	5	112	136	278	2.0	16	262	229	6.8
	8	136	134	318	2.9	19	654	194	10.5
	10	431	157	596	2.3	23	776	256	12.1
Fagus	0	8	71	12	0.4	10	79	13	0.4
sylvatica	1	75	84	73	0.7	10	93	82	4.3
	3	263	95	278	1.1	17	116	221	3.9
	5	856	102	713	1.9	19	211	480	4.7
	8	1469	139	909	2.5	21	626	620	6.8
	10	1777	165	1303	3.0	24	781	746	16.1
Quercus	0	8	40	15	0.7	10	46	19	0.2
robur	1	88	83	76	0.4	12	230	127	1.2
	3	141	108	128	0.7	12	233	128	6.2
	5	175	113	235	1.0	11	201	160	5.7
	8	230	142	338	1.0	13	367	197	10.1
	10	259	207	433	1.2	14	628	265	28.1

death of seedlings in the first growing period. A 5% and 10% admixture of the dusts caused the death of 20% and 63% of the seedlings, respectively. These values increased in the second growing period. In the case of broad-leaved species, the lowest death rate of the seedlings was observed for *Quercus robur* and *Alnus glutinosa*. The reaction of the seedlings of all the tree species to the cadmium–lead–zinc dusts was much greater. *Quercus robur* proved to be the most resistant to this dust. From these experiments it is impossible to determine a degree of toxicity of individual elements.

To determine the increase in the content of the heavy metals in the seedlings, the content of copper, zinc, lead and cadmium in particular parts of the plants from the dust-treated areas was compared with the content of these metals in the seedlings planted on the control site. In the latter, relatively little difference was observed in the content of the trace elements. However, the experiments do show how the quantity of heavy metals accumulated by plants depends upon the dose and type of dusts introduced into the soil. Furthermore, it can be seen that a larger quantity of heavy metals accumulated by the seedlings did not always cause damage or death. For example, the seedlings grown in the soil treated with the cadmium–lead–zinc dust accumulated much smaller amounts of the heavy metals than the ones grown on the plots treated with the lead–copper dust. Nevertheless, the degree of damage and the mortality rate of the former was much higher than that of the latter.

A strict dependence was also observed between the dose of the element introduced into the soil and its content in the plants. Such plants may, therefore, be used as indicators of the degree of environmental contamination.

The above-mentioned experiments are of great practical significance for the planning of protection zones around industrial works.

ACKNOWLEDGEMENT

This work was partially supported by Grant No. FG-PO-329 from U.S. Department of Agriculture, and in part from project No. 10.2.

TABLE 18.3.   *Acute injury: percentage of total leaf length destroyed in grass populations from polluted sites (Helmshore and Askern) and clean-site/bred cultivars after fumigation with 5,320 µg m^{-3}* SO$_2$ for 6 h.*

Populations	Polluted-site plants %	Clean-site plants/bred cultivars %	P =
Lolium perenne (Askern)	46.6	46.1	NS
L.perenne (Helmshore/cv. S23)	20.3	33.5	< 0.001
Dactylis glomerata (Askern)	2.2	12.5	< 0.001
D.glomerata (Helmshore/cv. S37)	24.2	41.4	< 0.001
Festuca rubra (Askern)	11·2	26·3	< 0.05
F.rubra (Helmshore/cv. Engina)	3.5	9.0	< 0.001
Holcus lanatus (Askern)	0.8	3.0	< 0.01
H.lanatus (Helmshore/Ascot)	0.8	1.6	NS
Phleum bertolonii (Helmshore/cv. S50)	49·3	60.4	NS

* 9,610 µg m^{-3} for *Dactylis glomerata*.

RATE OF SELECTION FOR TOLERANCE: PHILIPS PARK POPULATIONS

The smokeless-fuel plant at Askern was established in 1926 and thus selection for SO$_2$ tolerance must have taken place within a period of 50 years. At Helmshore, SO$_2$ pollution has probably been present since the early nineteenth century and it is not possible to establish the time-scale there for selection of tolerance in any of the species except *Phleum bertolonii*: in this case tolerance has appeared during the 24 years since cv. S50 seed was sown.

The minimum time for selection for tolerance under current British urban SO$_2$ levels was investigated at Philips Park. Populations of *Lolium perenne* cv. S23, *L.multiflorum* cv. RVP, *Phleum pratense* cv. S48, *Poa pratensis* L. cv. Baron, and *Festuca rubra* cv. Engina were sampled randomly in 1976, 1978, 1979 and 1980 from experimental monoculture plots established in 1975 by the Sports Turf Research Institute of Bingley, Yorkshire (Ayazloo *et al.* 1980). On each occasion the plants were subjected to acute SO$_2$ fumigations, together with similar plants grown from seed of the cultivars which were

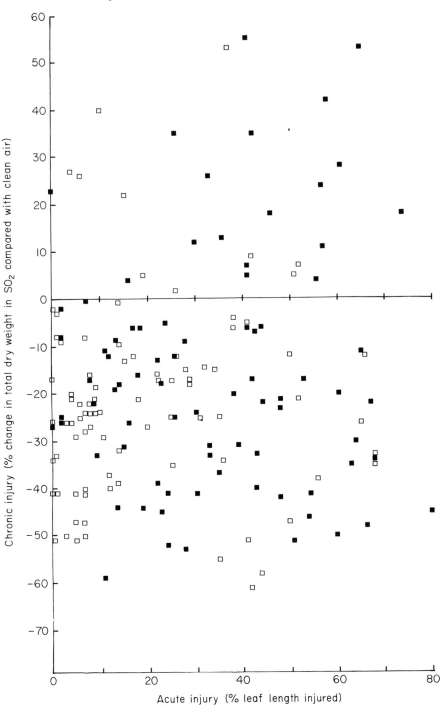

FIG. 18.1.   The relationship between acute and chronic SO$_2$ injury in *Lolium perenne* cv. S23 and Helmshore plants. ■ cv. S23 (r = 0.077; n = 89); □ Helmshore (r = 0.016; n = 89).

TABLE 18.4.   Percentage of total leaf length injured after acute SO_2 fumigations of grass species collected from plots in Philips Park, Manchester, established in 1975, in comparison with plants grown from the original seed.

| Species | Date of collection | | | | | | | | | | | |
| | 1976 | | | 1978 | | | 1979 | | | 1980 | | |
	Original seed	Plots	P=	Original seed	Plots	P=	Original seed	Plots	P=	Original seed	Plots	P=
Lolium perenne cv. S23	20.5	18.5	NS	23.5	20.1	NS	9.4	4.3	<0.01	42.7	33.5	0.05
L.multiflorum cv. RVP	50.7	52.5	NS	48.0	44.7	NS	20.0	12.0	NS	55.2	64.3	NS
Phleum pratense cv. S48	59.8	61.4	NS	67.0	62.5	NS	5.8	9.0	NS	67.3	55.0	<0.05
Poa pratensis cv. Baron	6.1	5.8	NS	9.4	8.8	NS	3.2	5.1	NS	44.5	35.0	NS
Festuca rubra cv. Engina	4.5	4.4	NS	4.4	3.9	NS	4.1	8.1	NS	24.5	20.2	NS

originally sown in the plots. No chronic fumigations were carried out because of logistical problems in screening the large number of plants used in this investigation. During the first 3 years from sowing no significant differences were seen between the two populations of any species, but in the 1979 collection *Lolium perenne* showed a greater tolerance in the plot plants than those grown from the original seed; this was maintained in the 1980 collection, when selection for tolerance was also detected in *Phleum pratense* (Table 18.4). Thus it appears that evolution of tolerance to acute injury can take place in a grass sward within 4–5 years, under the selective pressure of the SO_2 concentrations characteristic of a British city at the present time (150–200 μg m^{-3} winter mean).

CONCLUSIONS

It is apparent that selection for SO_2 tolerance is widespread in polluted urban and rural sites and can occur remarkably rapidly even in the presence of the lower SO_2 levels prevailing since the reduction in emissions from domestic fires, following clean-air legislation. The present work underlines the difficulties inherent in the extrapolation of the results of fumigation experiments to the field. Within a grass sward there is intense intraspecific competition and relatively small environmental pressures may have a marked selective influence. Thus in urban areas it appears that the adverse impact of SO_2 on amenity grasslands may be reduced by a shift towards tolerance within grass populations. However, in many, but not all, cases, the tolerant plants are overall less productive than the SO_2-sensitive individuals. Consequently, it is desirable for SO_2-tolerant genotypes to be incorporated into breeding programmes for the development of high yielding turfgrass cultivars suitable for parks and sports fields in polluted urban areas.

ACKNOWLEDGMENTS

M.A. and G.B.W. were supported on studentships provided by the Iranian authorities and the Ministry of Agriculture, Fisheries and Food, respectively. We thank Mr R.W. Laycock and Mr J.P. Shildrick of the Sports Turf Research Institute for permission to sample the plots at Philips Park.

REFERENCES

Ashenden T.W. (1979) The effects of long-term exposures to SO_2 and NO_2 pollution on the growth of *Dactylis glomerata* L. and *Poa pratensis* L. *Environmental Pollution*, **18**, 249–258.

Ashenden T.W. & Williams I.A.D. (1980) Growth reduction in *Lolium multiflorum* Lam. and *Phleum pratense* L. as a result of SO₂ and NO₂ pollution. *Environmental Pollution (Series A)*, **21**, 131–139.

Ayazloo M. (1979) Tolerance to sulphur dioxide in British grass species. Ph.D. Thesis. Imperial College, University of London, U.K.

Ayazloo M., Bell J.N.B. & Laycock R.W. (1980) The relative susceptibility of six turfgrass cultivars to acute sulphur dioxide injury. *The Journal of the Sports Turf Research Institute*, **6**, 85–90.

Bell J.N.B. & Clough W.S. (1973) Depression of yield in ryegrass exposed to sulphur dioxide. *Nature (London)*, **241**, 47–49.

Bell J.N.B. & Mudd C.H. (1976) Sulphur dioxide resistance in plants: A case study of *Lolium perenne*. In *Effects of Air Pollutants on Plants* (Ed. by T.A. Mansfield), pp. 87–103. Society for Experimental Biology Seminar Series, vol. 1. Cambridge University Press, Cambridge.

Bell J.N.B., Rutter A.J. & Relton J. (1979) Studies on the effects of low levels of sulphur dioxide on the growth of *Lolium perenne* L. *The New Phytologist*, **83**, 627–643.

Bleasdale J.K.A. (1973) Effects of coal-smoke pollution gases on the growth of ryegrass (*Lolium perenne* L.). *Environmental Pollution*, **5**, 275–285.

Canaway P.M. (1980) Wear. In *Amenity Grassland: An Ecological Perspective* (Ed. by I.H. Rorison & R. Hunt), pp. 137–152. John Wiley & Sons, Chichester.

Crittenden P.D. & Read D.J. (1978) The effects of air pollution on plant growth with special reference to sulphur dioxide. II. Growth studies with *Lolium perenne* L. *The New Phytologist*, **80**, 49–62.

Crittenden P.D. & Read D.J. (1979) The effects of air pollution on plant growth with special reference to sulphur dioxide. III. Growth studies with *Lolium multiflorum* Lam. and *Dactylis glomerata* L. *The New Phytologist*, **83**, 645–651.

Davies T. (1980) Grasses more sensitive to SO₂ pollution in conditions of low irradiance and short days. *Nature (London)*, **284**, 483–485.

Horsman D.C., Roberts T.M. & Bradshaw A.D. (1978) Evolution of sulphur dioxide tolerance in perennial ryegrass. *Nature (London)*, **276**, 493–494.

Horsman D.C., Roberts T.M. & Bradshaw A.D. (1979) Studies on the effect of sulphur dioxide on perennial ryegrass (*Lolium perenne* L.). II. Evolution of sulphur dioxide tolerance. *Journal of Experimental Botany*, **116**, 495–501.

Horsman D.C., Roberts T.M., Lambert M. & Bradshaw A.D. (1979) Studies on the effect of sulphur dioxide on perennial ryegrass (*Lolium perenne* L.). I. Characteristics of fumigation system and preliminary experiments. *Journal of Experimental Botany*, **30**, 485–493.

Taylor G.E. & Murdy W.H. (1975) Population differentiation of an annual plant species, *Geranium carolinianum*, in response to sulfur dioxide. *Botanical Gazette*, **136**, 212–215.

19. LICHEN ECOLOGY OF CHANGING URBAN ENVIRONMENTS

M. R. D. SEAWARD

School of Environmental Science,
University of Bradford,
Bradford, West Yorkshire, BD7 1DP, U.K.

SUMMARY

The ecological performance of certain saxicolous lichen species in urban environments are evaluated under conditions of rising and falling air-pollution levels, particularly sulphur dioxide. The substrate is found to be of crucial importance for the success of urban lichens, especially in respect of the establishment of propagules. The influx of propagules, and the spread, growth and competitive ability of their thalli in ameliorating urban environments, where sulphur dioxide is no longer the major factor affecting these ecological and developmental processes, are also examined. The growth rates of cohorts for the first 3 years following initial establishment were found to be significantly higher than those of the next 4 years; these rates remained remarkably constant over a 10-year period of detailed time and space analyses.

INTRODUCTION

Despite dramatic improvements brought about by the implementation of the Clean Air Acts of 1956 and 1968 in the U.K., the urban atmosphere is still laden with contaminants in the form of gases (e.g. SO_2, CO, CO_2, NO_x, hydrocarbons), aerosols, dusts, heavy metals, etc. These pollutants are mainly contained within particular climatic conditions generated by built-up areas, known as the 'urban climate', the physical and chemical components of which may act independently or synergistically to create conditions detrimental to lichens.

LICHENS IN THE URBAN ENVIRONMENT

The 'urban climate' reduces species diversity, and those lichen species remaining tend to have a high reproductive capacity and a tenacious hold on

181

the substrates they colonize. The mosaic or pattern of lichen communities, which would relieve the severity of many urban landscapes, is rarely attained; buildings, walls, monuments, etc., are dominated by a few species which can often create a monovegetation. The mellowing effect produced by a mosaic of lichens on bricks, tiles and stonework of rural buildings cannot be reproduced in urban areas due to the higher air-pollution levels, mainly sulphur dioxide, to which these plants are extremely sensitive.

Similarly, the monotonous verdure, created by one or two species of algae (*Pleurococcus* spp.) and/or lichens (*Lecanora conizaeoides* Nyl. ex Cromb., *Lepraria incana* (L.) Ach.), which coats the trunks of trees in urban areas (other than the very centres of conurbations, where no epiphytes can survive) is symptomatic of a low species diversity and a high reproductive capacity of a few toxitolerant organisms in a vitiated atmosphere.

The major detrimental factor influencing lichen distribution in urban areas is undoubtedly sulphur dioxide, but other pollutants, extremes of temperatures and water supply and substrate availability also play an important role. The decline in the lichen flora along transects running into urban areas has been investigated in many cities throughout the world. These studies have been directed mainly towards epiphytic and, to a lesser extent saxicolous, lichens.

Terricolous lichens in urban areas have not been studied to the same extent; undisturbed terricolous habitats are few, having been ousted by brick, concrete, tarmacadam and actively maintained gardens. Such derelict land as exists is unsuitable for lichen colonization due to the instability and/or mineral deficiency or toxicity of the substrate—the whole being exacerbated by pollutants derived from air, water and substrate. However, interesting, albeit species-poor, lichen communities are occasionally to be found on industrial spoil heaps (including those derived from heavy-metal industries). Some species survive in pockets of poor heathlands engulfed by urban expansion, but the decline in the lichen flora in such habitats (cf. Laundon 1958, 1973) can be dramatic over short periods of time. More luxuriant lawns and grasslands in suburban areas occasionally afford protection to *Peltigera spuria* (Ach.) DC. and several *Cladonia* spp. *C.fimbriata* (L.) Fr. is frequent on a diverse range of soil types, mosses and stonework in cemeteries, rock gardens, derelict sites, etc., in suburban areas.

By far the most important habitats for lichens in urban environments involve a wide variety of saxicolous substrates, the majority of which are dressed stone and other man-made materials, and possess distinctive chemical and physical properties. These properties and the major factors operating on the cryptogamic flora of such habitats are summarized in Seaward (1979a).

Urban churchyards often provide important habitats for lichens: a variety of stonework, imported and unpolished form, affords a range of substrates (mainly calcareous) suitable for relatively diverse lichen assemblages. According to Laundon (1970), 65% of the species of the London lichen flora are found in such habitats. A few species may survive in suburban churchyards as relicts from earlier times of more rural surroundings and lower levels of air pollution, yet are absent from nearby cemeteries of more recent origin.

The inner limit for the distribution of many species is quite clearly defined; the ecological factors operating in these critical areas at or immediately preceding a particular date must be critical for the lichen's performance, or even for its existence (Brightman & Seaward 1977). When investigating incipient changes in the inner distribution limits of lichens in urban areas, care should be taken in interpreting which of those species survive in microclimatic niches by chance establishment, which are relicts and which have reponded to atmospheric improvement following the implementation of clean-air legislation.

Many man-made saxicolous substrates have proved advantageous to lichen colonization and are, therefore, very significant in urban lichen distribution analyses; those of particular lichenological importance include concrete, mortar and asbestos-cement, and to a lesser extent brick and tarmacadam.

The distribution is mainly governed by mortar-work, although zonations can be detected where environmental gradients such as shade are pronounced. Zonations may also develop from point or line sources due to local effects such as nutrient enrichment from excreta on bird-perches, water (often as nutrient streaks) from copings, etc., of a different chemical composition to the major building material on which they are found, and metal-enriched drips or streaks caused by run-off from overhead wires or iron and zinc roofing pins, bolts and washers (Seaward 1974).

On free-standing walls the most diverse lichen floras are to be found on mortar and coping stones. Calcareous substrates are more favourable than non-calcareous substrates to lichen colonization. The high pH of such substrates as mortar and asbestos-cement provides a buffering effect on the toxicity of the urban climate. It would appear, therefore, that a man-influenced climate with an artificially low pH has to be counteracted by a substrate with an artificially high pH if lichens are to succeed in an urban environment. This is borne out by field observations: distinctive lichen distributions in urban areas can be correlated with the pH of the saxicolous substrate available and the ambient air-pollution level (Seaward 1976a).

LICHENS AND CLIMATIC AMELIORATION

Lecanora muralis (Schreb.) Rabenh. has inner limits according to substrate preference which can be mapped periodically to determine its rate of spread (or otherwise) and hence the ambient air-pollution level (Seaward 1976a,

1980; Brightman & Seaward 1977). During the period 1970–80, the spread of *L.muralis* towards the centre of Leeds on asbestos-cement, concrete and mortar was *c*. 150 m per annum; thus the appropriate reductions in mean daily sulphur dioxide concentration could be predicted along transects from the city centre, although it must be borne in mind that these reductions are not absolute to specific dates since reinvasion by lichen propagules is not immediate.

L.muralis has spread into the urban desert of the West Yorkshire conurbation at a rate of *c*. 9 km² per annum over the past 8 years, mainly through its ability to exploit man-made calcareous substrates and thus extend its geographical and ecological ranges in urban areas. Computational models for both existing field data and to predict the response of *L.muralis* to ameliorating conditions within this conurbation have been produced (Henderson-Sellers & Seaward 1979).

Surprisingly little is known of lichen dispersal and colonization. The suitability of the substrate is certainly critical in the establishment and development of the propagules, and its physico-chemical properties are no doubt more complex, and therefore more influential, in the early stages of thallial growth in polluted environments. Furthermore, a reduction in sulphur dioxide pollution will affect these properties, and newly introduced substrates may have an advantage over existing ones in terms of propagule establishment.

The rate at which lichens reinvade cleaned-up areas is enormously variable. Successful establishment and germination may well be influenced by complex factors, such as rainfall acidity. The observation that lichens have been more successful in growing on saxicolous than corticolous substrates in the reinvasion of urban environments lends support to this hypothesis.

The time-lag between pollution levels dropping below an identifiable threshold and the reinvasion by propagules of such substrates has to be credibly established before any effective use can be made of lichen maps for monitoring a fall in sulphur dioxide. Lichens take several years to respond to ameliorating conditions, whereas a sudden increase in pollution produces a much more rapid effect. Computer simulations, based on relatively long-range field data, have therefore been employed to compare the rates of reinvasion of *L.muralis* under different time-sequence regimes whilst holding a constant threshold of 120 μg m⁻³ sulphur dioxide (Henderson-Sellers & Seaward 1979). This work has shown that a time-lag of *c*. 5 years seems to be most realistic. Further simulations to consider variations in sulphur dioxide threshold and colonization criteria, employing the 5-year time-lag, have been undertaken, and it has been possible to produce computational models to predict the response of *L.muralis* to ameliorating conditions within the West Yorkshire conurbation. The results underline the fact that the sulphur dioxide level alone is no longer the major factor affecting lichen distribution within urban areas implementing clean-air legislation.

Since the implementation of the Clean Air Acts, the range of sulphur dioxide concentrations has declined considerably; under such conditions it is difficult to identify a direct relationship between environmental factors, particularly the ambient pollution levels, and the success of lichens. Recently collected data are, for example, rather poor at demonstrating any relationship between species diversity and air-pollution level (Seaward 1976b, 1979b).

At numerous sites in Leeds where the presence of *L.muralis* was restricted to asbestos-cement roofing at the beginning of the investigation, it had spread to cement-tile roofing at a later date indicating a reduction in mean daily sulphur dioxide concentration of *c.* 10 μg m^{-3} per annum over a 10-year period. Its rate and mode of spread at one of these sites is being carefully monitored: detailed mapping of thalli has been undertaken annually from 1970 to 1980. Some preliminary information relating to this space and time analysis is provided in Seaward (1980).

Detailed analysis of propagule influx and thallial growth measurements over the 10-year period at this site has furnished interesting data. For instance, by extrapolation of the growth lines (Fig. 19.1) to zero it is possible to determine an approximate time of establishment for each of the seven cohorts (i.e. new thalli detected in February of a particular year). Cohorts A, B and C (i.e. first measured in 1971, 1972 and 1973, respectively) vary in extrapolated establishment times (November–April), but cohorts D, E, F and G (i.e. first measured in 1974, 1975, 1976 and 1977, respectively) show consistency in their estimated times of establishment: all are within the month of May, for the years 1972, 1973, 1974 and 1975, respectively, when significant reductions in air-pollution concentrations relative to the winter period are to be encountered (cf. establishment times estimated for cohorts A–C).

Other striking differences between cohorts A–C and cohorts D–G are apparent from the analyses. Although the data show an influx of propagules at a constant rate throughout the 7-year period, there is little aggregation within the first 3 years (cohorts A–C) but there is an increase in aggregation thereafter (cohorts D–G), indicating spread from existing thalli and/or the exploitation of certain preferred sites. Furthermore, the growth performances of cohorts A–C (cf. Seaward 1976a, Fig. 4) are very dissimilar to those of cohorts D–G (Figs 19.1 & 19.2), the thalli of the former having an annual increase in diameter within the range 3.68–4.01 mm (av. 3.87) and the latter within the range 2.29–2.67 mm (av. 2.50).

It is difficult to make valid hypotheses from the above observations; nevertheless, some tentative conjectures may reasonably be made. Although *L.muralis* is a successful lichen in urban environments and has a relatively rapid growth rate, it seems likely that in the long term it would be unsuccessful in competition with other slower-growing species. Nevertheless, it is remark-

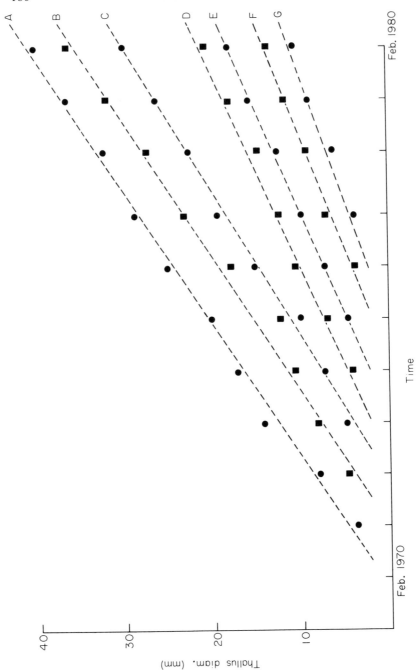

FIG. 19.1   Mean growth of successive cohorts of *Lecanora muralis* thalli during the period 1970–80.

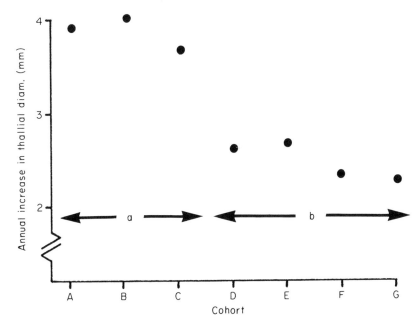

FIG. 19.2.   Growth rates of seven cohorts of *Lecanora muralis*; a = random colonization: influx of propagules from air spora only for first 2 years (cohorts A and B) and
mainly from this source for third year (cohort C); b = period of increasing aggregation:
propagules possibly from established adjacent thalli as well as influx of propagules from
a distance.

able that during the 10-year analysis, cohorts A–C constantly maintained a
higher growth rate, whereas cohorts D–G constantly maintained a lower
growth rate, despite a gradual fall in the sulphur dioxide level throughout the
entire period and climatic variation from year to year.

Since the roofing tiles were known to be more than 40 years old, any
change in the physico-chemical nature of the substrate, as a result of the
reduction in air pollution, would be negligible. However, the competition
effect of the pioneer colonizers exploiting the more favourable sites may have
some bearing on pattern and growth rates of thalli, and the possibility of a
chemical suppression of growth by initial over secondary colonizers cannot be
discounted.

Concrete and cement are particularly valuable as substrates for urban
lichens. *Lecanora dispersa* (Pers.) Sommerf.—*Candelariella aurella* (Hoffm.)
Zahlbr. communities rapidly colonize fresh concrete and cement: within 4–5
years this species-poor and air-pollution-tolerant pioneer phase can occupy
80–85% of the substrate. The growth of *Lecanora dispersa* on urban concrete
surfaces corresponds to a positive logistic curve up to *c.* 13 years following

initial colonization; at this stage an optimum density of the species is attained whereby 70–85% of the substrate is covered (Ayrton & Seaward unpublished data). Increased inter-, and possibly intra-, specific competition after this period, no doubt associated with acidification of the substrate (from pH 8.0 to 4.5) brought about by air pollution, results in a gradual decline in the population of *L.dispersa*.

Several other lichen species are known to be highly successful in urban areas; most of these species are equally successful elsewhere, but some species which formerly had narrower ecological requirements and/or more restricted distributions appear to be highly successful, probably favoured to some extent by reduced competition, on variant substrates subjected to new atmospheric regimes (Seaward 1980). The following species fall into one or the other of these categories: *Bacidia chlorococca* (Stiz.) Lett., *Caloplaca decipiens* (Arnold) Jatta, *Candelariella medians* (Nyl.) A.L. Sm., *Lecanora conizaeoides, L.muralis, Stereocaulon pileatum* Ach. and *Xanthoria elegans* (Link) Th. Fr.

Lichens have been employed almost exclusively to monitor the extent or spread of air pollution, particularly sulphur dioxide, and bioindicational scales, based on species diversity and/or simple phytosociological analyses, have been developed for this purpose. Although the lichen flora of urban areas is poor, the few species to be found can be related to a mean annual or winter sulphur dioxide level: in conditions of stable and relatively high sulphur dioxide air pollution there is a clearly defined negative relationship between species diversity and the concentration of the pollutant.

This paper has shown that it is possible not only to monitor air-pollution concentrations by means of a critical appraisal of the ecological performance of a single lichen species, but also, and perhaps more importantly in view of current clean-air policies, to monitor ameliorating environments.

ACKNOWLEDGEMENTS

I wish to express my gratitude to Dr P.B. Topham and Mr J.E.P. Currall for their valuable criticism of the draft manuscript.

REFERENCES

Brightman F.H. & Seaward M.R.D. (1977) Lichens of man-made substrates. In *Lichen Ecology* (Ed. by M.R.D. Seaward), pp. 253–293. Academic Press, London & New York.

Henderson-Sellers A. & Seaward M.R.D. (1979) Monitoring lichen reinvasion of ameliorating environments. *Environmental Pollution*, **19**, 207–213.

Laundon J.R. (1958) The lichen vegetation of Bookham Common. *London Naturalist*, **37**, 66–79.

Laundon J.R. (1970) London's lichens. *London Naturalist*, **49**, 20–69.

Laundon J.R. (1973) Changes in the lichen flora of Bookham Common with increased air pollution and other factors. *London Naturalist*, **52**, 82–93.

Seaward M.R.D. (1974) Some observations on heavy metal toxicity and tolerance in lichens. *Lichenologist*, **6**, 158–164.

Seaward M.R.D. (1976a) Performance of *Lecanora muralis* in an urban environment. In *Lichenology: Progress and Problems* (Ed. by D.H. Brown, D.L. Hawksworth & R.H. Bailey), pp. 323–357. Academic Press, London & New York.

Seaward M.R.D. (1976b) Lichens in air polluted environments: Multivariate analysis of the factors involved. In *Proceedings of the Kuopio Meeting on Plant Damages Caused by Air Pollution* (Ed. by L. Kärenlampi), pp. 57–63. University of Kuopio, Finland.

Seaward M.R.D. (1979a) Lower plants and the urban landscape. *Urban Ecology*, **4**, 217–225.

Seaward M.R.D. (1979b) Lichens as monitors of environments with decreasing sulphur dioxide levels. In *International Symposium on Sulphur Emissions and the Environment*, pp. 255–258. Society of Chemical Industry, London.

Seaward M.R.D. (1980) The use of lichens as bioindicators of ameliorating environments. In *Bioindikation auf der Ebene der Individuen* (Ed. by R. Schubert & J. Schuh), pp. 17–23. Martin-Luther-Universität Halle-Wittenberg, DDR.

20. EFFECTS OF AIR POLLUTION ON CORTICOLOUS MICROARTHROPODS IN THE URBAN DISTRICT OF CHARLEROI (BELGIUM)

H. M. ANDRE AND PH. LEBRUN

Université Catholique de Louvain,
Laboratoire d'Ecologie animale,
Place de la Croix du Sud 5,
B-1348 Louvain-La-Neuve, Belgium

SUMMARY

The effects of air pollution on corticolous microarthropods populations are analysed in three sites of the urban district of Charleroi. Estimated also is the diversity of arthropod populations. Results from this study are compared with observations from previous surveys in two other areas. Lastly, the use of corticolous mite populations as bioindicators of air pollution and the behaviour of diversity indices are discussed.

INTRODUCTION

While many investigations have been devoted to lichen mapping and sensitivity to sulphur dioxide (SO_2) and other pollutants, few works deal with the effects of air pollution on arthropods. Melanism in moths and coccinelids has been described and discussed (Bishop *et al.* 1975; Muggleton *et al.* 1975). Some species were tested in the laboratory (Lebrun *et al.* 1977, 1978; Kuribayashi 1977a, b) and the influence of urban emission on aphid enzymes was analysed by Richter (1980). Przybylski (1974) and Wiackowski (1978) have described the effects of aerial sulphur compounds on insect abundance. Communities of soil oribatid mites affected by industrial emissions were observed by Vaněk (1967). Lastly, corticolous arthropod populations and/or communities have been studied by Kudela and Wolf (1964), Gilbert (1971), Lebrun (1976), and André (1977). This study is a continuation of the two last quoted references.

histograms of Gamasida predators with both Collembola and Oribatida are similar in shape (Fig. 21.1). Thus, low densities or absence of Gamasida predators seem to be due to the extremely low number of their potential prey.

Acari Oribatida are scarce in the highly perturbed zones (0.70 individuals $\times$ $10^3 m^{-2}$ at the Fontainebleau site and 0.30 individuals $\times$ $10^3 m^{-2}$ at the Montmorency site (first row)). Though the densities increase in the less perturbed zones, their values do not exceed half of that of the control zones (Table 21.1).

Brachychthoniidae Oribatida seem to be particularly sensitive to human trampling. They are absent from the highly degraded zones, and scarce in the less perturbed ones (Fig. 21.2 and Table 21.1). In Fontainebleau forest, in a given area, densities observed at the litter accumulation points (11.5 ± 1.9 individuals $\times 10^3$ m^{-2}), are much higher than where there is no litter accumulation (0.38 ± 0.38 individuals $\times 10^3$ m^{-2}). Indeed, here some samples contain no Brachychthoniidae, even when the edaphic parameters of this area are normal.

It is interesting to note therefore, that at the trampled sites, the total abundance of the microarthropod community is clearly correlated with the amount of litter ($r = 0.80$, $\alpha \leqslant 0.001$, for Montmorency and $r = 0.55$, $\alpha \leqslant 0.01$ for Fontainebleau). This observation may be explained by the fact that trampling leads to a redistribution of litter. Thus the high degradation points correspond to a low quantity of litter and the accumulation points correspond to a less perturbed edaphic structure. The amount of litter seems, therefore, to be linked to soil activity.

DISCUSSION

The study of microarthropods as biological indicators of soil damage induced by trampling is interesting on two counts.

First, the structure of the microarthropod community is linked to the degree of perturbation of the edaphic system. Moreover, the microarthropods seem to be more sensitive indicators than certain physical or chemical parameters of the soil. Indeed, whereas in the visited sites the level of organic matter, porosity and litter layers are normal, the density of Brachychthoniidae is reduced, and some species have disappeared.

Some categories of microarthropods, such as Brachychthoniidae or Uropoda, disappear under the effect of trampling; others, such as Collembola, Oribatida and Gamasida predators, are present at a low density. However, the best indicator is certainly the whole microarthropod community.

The study of the Montmorency forest shows that in the vicinity of the small road, in spite of the fact that litter seems normal, the perturbations induced by random trampling are as pronounced as those in the recreation areas of Fontainebleau forest.

Thus for the management of forests near urban areas it is necessary to define the threshold of trampling beyond which degradation becomes irreversible. A study of the microarthropod community can be helpful for this purpose.

The present investigation suggests clearly that this threshold corresponds to a situation in which the points with minor degradation are distributed in a spatial mosaic, with litter accumulation points.

It would be interesting to verify whether the edaphic community may be reconstituted from the litter accumulation points.

REFERENCES

Berthet P. & Gerard G. (1970) Note sur l'estimation de la densité de populations édaphiques. *Actes du Colloque de Paris*, UNESCO, PBI, 189–192.

Garay I., Cancela da Fonseca J.P. & Blandin P. (1981) The effects of trampling on the fauna of a forest floor. I. Microarthropods. In *Acts of VII International Soil Zoology Colloquium* (Soil fauna as related to land use practices), 200–212.

Lebrun P. (1977) Incidences écologiques des pesticides sur la faune du sol. *Pédologie*, **27**, 67–91.

Zyromska-Rudzka H. (1977) Changes in Oribatid mite community after chemical fertilizer application in a meadow. In *Soil Organisms as Components of Ecosystems*, Ecol. Bull. (Stockholm), **25**, 133–137.

22. INFLUENCE OF VEGETATION AND LAND-USE ON VAPORIZATION AND GROUND-WATER RECHARGE IN WEST BERLIN

H. M. BRECHTEL
Hessische Forstliche Versuchsanstalt
Institut für Forsthydrologie-Postfach 1308,
3510 Hann. Munden 1, West Germany

SUMMARY

How land is used and managed has a very definite effect on the local water budget. Particularly in areas on permeable soils where a significant amount of surface run-off cannot occur, the natural ground-water recharge depends to a large extent on the specific vaporization conditions which in turn can be influenced by human activities. The extent of this influence can be demonstrated for the densely populated area of West Berlin, where the local ground-water yield should be of major interest for future land-use planning. According to available values of annual vaporization from different land surfaces for a year of normal precipitation, the natural ground-water recharge was estimated separately for the following groups of land surfaces: 1, densely sealed with buildings; 2, sparsely covered with buildings; 3, sparse vegetation; 4, shrub-like vegetation; 5, meadows; 6, agricultural fields; 7, forests; and 8, peat land and water surface areas.

INTRODUCTION

How much of the local precipitation evaporates from land surfaces, becomes surface run-off or is absorbed by the soil, being available for transpiration by plants, or finally remains for ground-water recharge and for usable water supply, is not only dependent on the natural site conditions, but is also affected markedly by the specific hydrological influences of different plant cover and land-use practices (Colman 1953; Sopper & Lull 1967; Brechtel & v. Hoyningen-Huene 1979). This fact, which is the basis for the management of areas for water yield, is not only significant in reference to planning and development of local water resources (Krems 1975) but is also an important aspect for assessments of ecological changes caused by human activities.

In order to demonstrate the degree to which urbanization for instance, can modify the hydrological conditions of an area, an attempt was made to estimate the amount of vaporization and ground-water recharge for the densely populated land of West Berlin in total, and separately for areas of different land use.

METHODS

In areas with non-indurated sediments, where under natural conditions no significant surface run-off occurs, the ground-water recharge from local precipitation can be quantified by determination of the annual amount of vaporization as it is influenced by precipitation and climate, soil type and depth of water-table, plant cover and land use (Dyck & Chardabellas 1969; Josopait & Lillich 1975; Armbruster & Kohm 1976). Using these factors the ground-water recharge in West Berlin was estimated for a year with normal precipitation. The average meteorological values for the period 1931–60 were used, as determined at the Berlin-Dahlem weather station. As shown by Schlaak (1963, 1972), this station represents fairly well the climatic conditions of the total area under consideration. The data correspond very closely with observations reported from the airport recording station at Frankfurt. For the same time period the average monthly values of precipitation, relative humidity, wind-speed, air temperature and duration of sunshine were comparable. Thus the conditions for potential vaporization in the Berlin area are very similar to those in Frankfurt in the Rhine-Main Valley, as shown by calculations using the procedure published by Albrecht (1962), Thornthwaite (1948) and Penman (1954). Even the conditions concerning precipitation intensities are without significant difference in both areas. This was concluded by comparing the average number of days with precipitation of 0.1, 1.0, 2.5 and 10.0 mm per day, during the total year as well as during the four seasons.

On the basis of site mapping and the findings reported by Blume *et al.* (1975), it can be concluded that a sandy soil not influenced by ground-water is typical of local conditions in Berlin.

The kind of plant cover and land-use was determined from data published by Statistisches Landesamt Berlin (1974) and from documents on the local forest administration (Landesforstamt Berlin).

The main difficulty found was in sorting the numerous kinds of area-units of different land-use into categories for which values of annual vaporization from long-term water-balance measurements are available. Finally, it was decided to categorize land surfaces into the following eight groups:

1. Densely sealed with buildings, including all industrial and urban area without any infiltration.
2. Sparsely covered with buildings, representing the village type areas of the city, where some infiltration occurs.

3. Sparse vegetation, including areas like railway verges, fallow land, storage yards, undeveloped building sites, etc.
4. Shrub vegetation, representing parks, cemeteries, gardens and tree nurseries.
5. Meadows, including as well as true meadows, areas of grassland such as sportsgrounds and airfields.
6. Arable fields.
7. Forests.
8. Water surface areas, including peatlands.

To estimate the mean annual vaporization from the above eight types of land surface, the results of water-balance investigations, shown in Figure 22.1 were used. In addition to the minimum, average and maximum lines, published by Baumgartner (1967) summarizing all available information from Central Europe, a number of more recent findings of Liebscher (1970), Wesche (1970), Klausing and Salay (1974), Lützke and Simon (1975) and others have also been taken into consideration. The values for water surface are calculated for Frankfurt and Berlin, using the procedure of Penman (1954). The values used were selected for research areas with similar site conditions to West Berlin. The criteria for this selection were sandy soil, average annual precipitation 550–650 mm and average air temperature during the growing season 15–17°C (—○— in Fig. 22.1). For broad-leaf and conifer forest the corresponding values of mean annual vaporization were calculated for Berlin, using the results from long-term water-balance measurements made in the Forest Hydrological Research Area of Frankfurt (Brechtel 1973). On the basis of this procedure, values for the average annual vaporization were derived, which are probably suitable for Berlin as far as bare soil, fields, grass, broad-leaf and conifer forest and water surface are concerned (in Fig. 22.1: 40, 65, 75, 89, 90, 116% of the precipitation, respectively).

However, values of vaporization for the land surfaces are: 1, densely sealed; 2, sparsely covered; 3, sparse vegetation; and 4, shrub vegetation were still to be determined. In category 1 the value of 40% from bare soil was reduced to 20% taking into account information from Plate (1976). For category 2 a value of 70%, being the average between arable fields and grassland, was assumed. For category 3 a value of 52% was calculated, being an average of bare soil and arable fields. In a similar way for category 4 a value of 85% was estimated, which lies between grassland and forest.

RESULTS

Using the above-mentioned percentage values for annual vaporization from the eight categories of land surface in West Berlin in relation to the normal

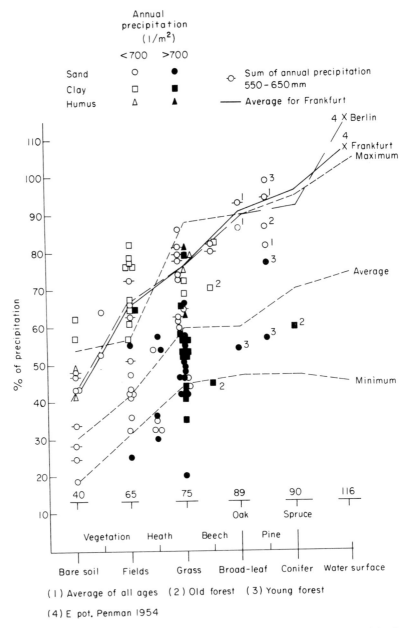

FIG. 22.1. Average annual vaporization of different vegetation cover and land surfaces as a percent of annual precipitation. The values for water surface are calculated for Frankfurt and Berlin, using the procedure of Penman (1954).

annual sum of precipitation of 581 l m^{-2}, the amount of average annual vaporization and ground-water recharge was calculated. The results are presented in Table 22.1.

For the total area of West Berlin, the average of vaporization is 418 l m^{-2} (72%); about 41 l m^{-2} can be assumed to be surface run-off, making the ground water recharge 122 l m^{-2}, which is 21% of the annual precipitation. Lillich *et al.* (1973) found very similar results on sandy soil in the area of Hanover. For the year 1968, they determined a ground-water recharge of 146 l m^{-2} for an annual precipitation of 659 l m^{-2} (i.e. 22% of the precipitation).

There are many conclusions to be drawn from the data listed in Table 22.1

TABLE 22.1. *Vaporization and ground-water recharge in West Berlin, calculated for the normal annual sum of precipitation (P) of 581 l m^{-2} (Berlin-Dahlem ϕ 1931–60). For details of land surface categories see text.*

Land surface category	Area km^2	Vaporization % of P.	Vaporization l m^{-2}	Ground-water recharge l m^{-2}	Ground-water recharge % of P.
Densely sealed	48.60	20	116	0*	0
Sparse vegetation	26.21	52	302	279	48
Arable fields	20.28	65	378	203	35
Sparsely covered	188.66	70	407	174	30
Meadows	24.33	75	436	145	25
Shrub vegetation	74.83	85	494	87	15
Forests	65.12	89	517	64	11
Water surface	32.03	116	673	0	0
Total area of West Berlin	480.06	72	418	122†	21

* about 465 l m^{-2} surface run-off.
† plus about 41 l m^{-2} surface run-off.

relating both to the water yield aspects and to the ecological conditions. In this short contribution only a few highlights can be summarized.

The land surface category 'densely sealed with buildings', which covers with 48.6 km^2 (about 10% of the total area), does not contribute a significant amount to ground-water recharge. The vaporization at 20% is the lowest of all categories, but it occurs only during and shortly after precipitation events. All the water not evaporated becomes surface run-off and must be considered to be at least a local loss. In these particular areas the recharge of soil with water for evapo-transpiration, which also cools and moistens the air during dry periods, is badly needed.

The category 'water surface' which covers 32 km^2 (about 7% of West Berlin) must also be excluded from the area with ground-water recharge, as the amount of vaporization is higher than the precipitation falling on it. Unlike the sealed areas, however, the water surfaces in West Berlin are useful in contributing to the ground-water by infiltration, and most important they bring about recreational and climatic improvements.

Of the remaining six categories with infiltration of local precipitation, the urban categories, 'sparse vegetation', 'sparsely covered with buildings' and 'shrub vegetation' are by far the most significant for ground-water recharge. They cover about 60% of the area and contribute about 80% of the ground-water recharge. Sealing of such areas would reduce the ground-water recharge to an amount of $87-279 \text{ l m}^{-2}$.

The categories of land surface mostly outside the urban area, 'arable fields' 'meadows' and 'forests', cover in total only about 23% of West Berlin and contribute about 20% to the annual ground-water recharge. The sealing of such areas would cause a reduction of ground-water recharge of $64-203 \text{ l m}^{-2}$. But of much greater importance is the fact that this uncommon small rural area outside the city is of enormous environmental significance for the people of Berlin. This is especially true for the forests, covering a total area of 65 km² (almost 14% of West Berlin). The remaining forest stands in West Berlin are of vital importance for recreation and sports, improvements in the local climate, control of noise and air pollution, and also in providing the best natural protection of ground-water quality.

Under specific local conditions in West Berlin, the most important hydrological management possibilities for increasing the local ground-water yield are not based on measures designed to reduce vaporization losses, but mainly on the conservation, restoration and improvement of infiltration and seepage capacities. Careful consideration must be given to the maintenance or improvement of water quality under the impact of human activities in the urban areas of West Berlin. The estimation of natural ground-water recharge made in this paper of different land-use categories points especially to the large amount of water lost by surface run-off, when precipitation reaches roofs, pavements and other impervious surfaces in the city area.

REFERENCES

Albrecht F. (1962) Die Berechnung der natürlichen Verdunstung (Evapotranspiration) der Erdoberfläche aus klimatologischen Daten. *Berichte des Deutschen Wetterdienstes*, Bd. 11, Nr. 83, Offenbach.

Armbruster J. & Kohm J. (1976) Auswertung der Lysimetermessungen der badischen Oberrheinebene. *Wasser und Boden*, 44, 302–306.

Baumgartner A. (1967) Energetic bases for differential vaporization from forest and agricultural lands. In *International Symposium on Forest Hydrology, Proceedings* (Ed. by W. Sopper and H.W. Lull), 381–389, Pergamon Press/Vieweg und Sohn GmbH, Braunschweig.

Blume H.P., Dummler H. & Roper H.P. (1975) Boden und Gewasser Westberlins. *Landwirtschaftliche Forschung, Sonderheft*, 31, 234–239.

Brechtel H.M. (1973) Ein methodischer Beitrag zur Quantifizierung des Einflusses von Waldbeständen verschiedener Baumarten und Altersklassen auf die Grundwasserneubildung in der Rhein-Main-Ebene. *Zeitschrift der Deutschen Geologischen Gesellschaft*, **124**, 593–605.

Brechtel H.M. & v. Hoyningen-Huene J. (1979) Einfluß der Verdunstung verschiedener Vegetationsdecken auf den Gebietswasserhaushalt. *Schriftenreihe des Deutschen Verbandes für Wasserwirtschaft und Kulturbau*, **40**, 172–223.

Colman E.A. (1953) Vegetation and Watershed Management. In *An Appraisal of Vegetation Management in Relation to Water Supply, Flood Control, and Soil Erosion*. The Ronald Press Company, New York.

Dyck S. & Chardabellas P. (1969) Wege zur Ermittlung der nutzbaren Grundwasserreserven. *Berichte Geologische Gesellschaft DDR*, **8**, 245–262.

Josopait V. & Lillich W. (1975) Die Ermittlung der Grundwasserneubildung sowie ihre Kartendarstellung im Maßstab 1:200,000 unter Verwendung von geologischen und bodenkundlichen Karten. *Deutsche Gewässerkundliche Mitteilungen*, **5**, 132–136.

Klausing O. & Salay G. (1974) Die Abhängigkeit der Grundwasserneubildung von Vegetation und Bewirtschaftung. *Allgemeine Forstzeitschrift*, **29**, 1091–1094.

Krems F. (1975) Die Grundwassersituation in Berlin (West) und die Auswirkungen von Grundwasserabsenkungen im Rahmen von Baumaßnahmen auf den Grundwasserhaushalt. *Zeitschrift der Deutschen Geologischen Gesellschaft*, **126**, 215–222.

Liebscher H.-J. (1970) Grundwasserneubildung und Verdunstung unter verschiedenen Niederschlags-, Boden- und Bewuchsverhältnissen. *Die Wasserwirtschaft*, **60**, 168–173.

Lillich W., Kuckelkorn K.F. & Hofmann W. (1973) Untersuchungen zum Grundwasserhaushalt im repräsentativen Lockergestein-Gebiet Fuhrberger Feld bei Hannover—Bilanzjahre 1967 und 1968. *Beiheft geologisches Jahrbuch*, **107**.

Lützke R. & Simon K.-H. (1975) Zur Bilanzierung des Wasserhaushalts von Waldbeständen auf Sandstandorten der DDR. *Beiträge für die Forstwirtschaft*, **1**, 5–12.

Penman H.L. (1954) Evaporation over parts of Europe. Publication No. 37 de l'Association Internationale d'Hydrologie, Assemblée Générale de Rome, Rome, 168–176.

Plate E.J. (1976) Auswirkung der Urbanisierung auf den Wasserhaushalt. *Die Wasserwirtschaft*, **66**, 1–8.

Schlaak P. (1963) Die Wirkung der bebauten und bewaldeten Gebiete auf das Klima des Stadtgebietes von Berlin. *Allgemeine Forstzeitschrift*, **18**, 455–458.

Schlaak P. (1972) Mittere und extreme Niederschlagsverhaltnisse in Berlin. Beilage zur Berliner Wetterkarte 13.1.1972, FU Berlin.

Sopper W.E. & Lull H.W. (Ed.) (1967) *International Symposium on Forest Hydrology*. Proceedings of a Seminar held at University Park, Pennsylvania, Aug.29–Sept.10, 1965. Pergamon Press/Vieweg u. Sohn GmbH, Braunschweig.

Statistisches Landesamt Berlin (1974) *Statistisches Jahrbuch Berlin 1974*. Kulturbuch-Verlag, Berlin.

Thornthwaite D.W. (1948) An approach toward a rational classification of climate. *Geographical Review*, **38**, 85–94.

Wesche J. (1970) Weitere Ergebnisse aus Bodenwasserhaushalts-Messungen in der Dahlemer Lysimeteranlage (2. Bericht, Versuchabschnitt 1964–67). *Zeitschrift für Kulturtechnik und Flurbereinigung*, **11**, 229–248.

cambisols on glacial sands, is situated in Berlin-Gatow (mean annual temperature 8.8°C, mean annual rainfall 660 mm). It is partitioned into small embanked allotments of 0.25 ha, which are flooded several times annually with mechanically purified waste-water.

Formerly (until 1945), between 3,000 and 5,000 mm of water were added to the allotments per year, but this has been reduced in recent years, and since 1977 3–5 applications of between 100–400 mm have been made depending on the soil properties and manner of agricultural use.

The allotments have underground drainage pipes at 1.20 m depth, 6 m apart. In order to understand the effects of such waste-water irrigation on the properties of a loamy luvisol, oxidation potentials were measured with platinum/calomel electrodes and water potentials were measured with tensiometers on a weekly basis, at depths of 5, 25, 50, 100, 150 cm and 25, 50, 75, 100, 125 cm, respectively. During flooding, measurements were made at intervals of between 15 minutes and 4 hours. Soil solutions were extracted using 30 cm-long filter tubes (ceramic: Diapor G 8, 4 cm diameter) and NO_3-N, NH_4-N, organic N and C, Mn, Zn and P contents were determined. Auger samples were also taken from boreholes in between irrigations for chemical analysis using saturation extracts. Rainwater and waste-water were also analysed.

Other soil properties determined were: total porosity and pore size distribution (determination of 100 cm^3 samples through desorption with a high- and low-pressure apparatus); hydraulic conductivity under saturated and unsaturated conditions (Becher 1971); texture following $Na_4P_2O_7$ dispersion; organic nitrogen (Kjeldahl) and NH_4-N, NO_3-N and NO_2-N following extraction with 1% K Al$(SO_4)_2$; and heavy metal content following extraction with 0.05 M EDTA at pH 7 (for methods see Schlichting & Blume 1967).

RESULTS

The luvisol is characterized by a humic sandy topsoil (Ap+Al), a clay-enriched subsoil (Bt) and a calcareous parent material (C) (Fig. 23.1). Hence the topsoil contains relatively few pore spaces of medium size and has a moderately available water capacity. The subsoil has few large pore spaces. Under natural forest vegetation conditions this luvisol would be moist in winter and spring and sometimes dry in summer when water availability may limit the growth of shallow-rooting plants.

The conditions have changed drastically since the supply of waste-water (Fig. 23.2). Soil drying (as measured by an increase in volume of air and a decrease in the available water content during the spring due to evapotranspiration) is periodically interrupted by the waste-water irrigation and during

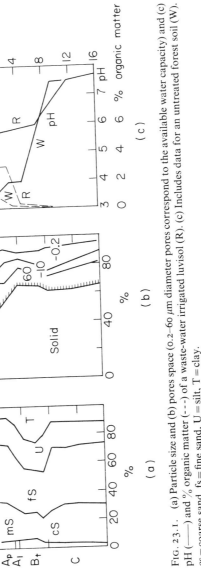

FIG. 23.2. (a) Amount of precipitation and waste-water applied (figures on columns), (b) water tension, (c) available water content and (d) air content of a luvisol, 1978–79. The dotted line indicates the water front.

FIG. 23.1. (a) Particle size and (b) pores space (0.2–60 μm diameter pores correspond to the available water capacity) and (c) pH (——) and % organic matter (- - -) of a waste-water irrigated luvisol (R). (c) Includes data for an untreated forest soil (W). cs = coarse sand, fs = fine sand, U = silt, T = clay.

continuation of ammonification of the nitrogen-rich organic compounds under snow cover and there is no loss through plant uptake (Fig. 23.7).

There is an increase in the content of water-soluble P as well as mobile Zn, particularly in the topsoil because of the high pH values there whereas Mn, through low redox potential values (< 350 mV), mobilizes and is displaced from the root zone with the gravitational movement of water (Fig. 23.5).

The non-oxidized dissolved organic substances (Fig. 23.6) do not contribute an extra displacement of Mn and Zn due to organic complex formation by low redox potential values. Manganese precipitates as $MnCO_3$ on reaching the calcareous C horizon, but Zn precipitates only partly, and therefore reaches the ground-water to a greater extent than Mn. However, the

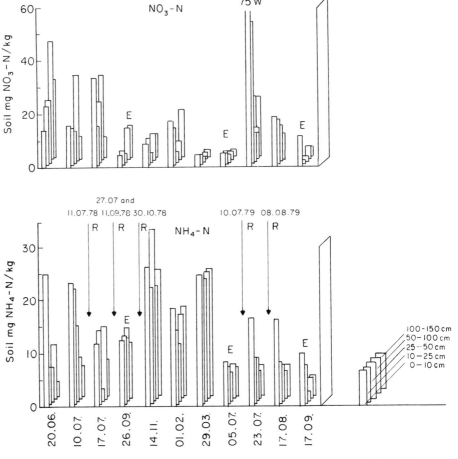

FIG. 23.7. NH_4-N and NO_3-N contents and their distribution in a luvisol with waste-water irrigation from June 1978 to Sept. 1979. (R = irrigation, E = harvest).

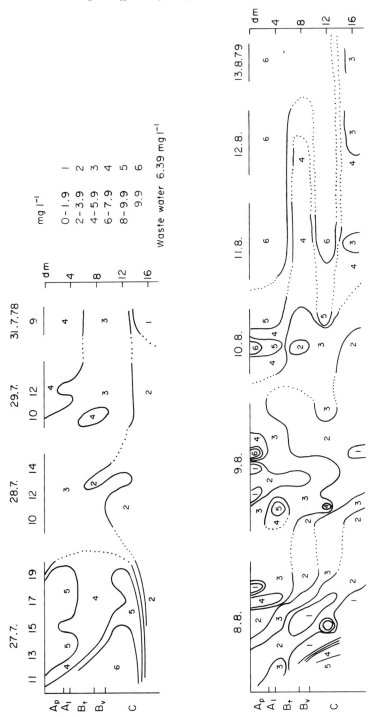

Fig. 23.8.   Water-soluble phosphorus in a luvisol after two waste-water irrigations.

TABLE 23.2. *Possible profile balance of a luvisol under a forest and a waste-water field in Berlin (total contents in g m^{-2}; calculation depth 120 cm).*

place		Element content			
		Mn	Zn	P	N
forest	initial	443	86	678	1
0–120 cm	present	461	94	630	511
	loss/gain	+18	+8	−48	+511
waste-water	initial	390	75	570	1
field	present	322	151	1082	1006
0–120	loss/gain	−68	+76	+512	+1006
loss/gain due to					
waste-water irrigation		−86	+68	+560	+495

Zn concentration in percolating water is clearly below the given upper limit (Scheffer-Schachtschabel 1976) for drinking water.

Mobilization, displacement and fixing of phosphorus, apart from its dependence on pH and redox, are related to the degree of water saturation of the soil (Alaily 1979). Phosphorus displaced from the topsoil precipitates in the calcareous C horizon as calcium phosphate (Fig. 23.8) and, therefore, it does not reach the ground-water. Table 23.2 shows the increase and decrease of some elements in irrigated soil to a depth of 120 cm as compared to a forest location (for methods see Blume *et al* 1980).

DISCUSSION

The purification of waste-water using the filtering effect of the soil brings about great changes in the physical and chemical characteristics of the soil as a habitat for plants. The waste-water irrigation on a luvisol effects an increase in the nitrogen and phosphorus content of soil, in addition to the more obvious increase in water availability. Under good aeration conditions the Dauco-Arrhenatheretum and the Lolio-Cynosuretum which are normally present in these fields are replaced by plant communities like the Urtica-Malvetum, the Bromo-Hordeetum or the Lolio-Plantaginetum, which are found on soils with high N and P availability and which tolerate short-term water-logging. These plant communities can also tolerate the decrease in Mn and increase in Zn contents (Weigmann *et al* 1977). However, maize showed symptoms of Zn toxicity in the form of chorotic leaves when grown on arable land in the neighbourhood. *Sambucus nigra* L. communities replace the Tilio-Carpinetum which may reflect both the improved nutrient conditions and also a tolerance of long-term waterlogging conditions in deep-rooted plants. The luvisol also showed remarkable earthworm and mouse populations which were able to survive up to 200 mm flooding, but which decreased strongly during intensive waste-water treatments.

A discontinuous irrigation system deserves strong consideration in order to keep up the optimal filtering effect of the soil. The quantity of waste-water and the time of application should be so selected that oxidizing conditions are regularly present in the soil so that element loss is minimized (also see Baumann & Bramm 1976; Miner & Hazen 1977).

REFERENCES

Alaily, F. (1979) P-Dynamik in Böden während der Verrieselung von Siedlungsabwässern. *Mitteilungen des Deutschen Bodenkunde Gesellschaft*, **29**, 917–921.

Baumann H. & Bramm A. (1976) Einflüsse der Abwasserbehandlung auf oberflächennahes Grundwasser. *Mitteilungen des Deutschen Bodenkunde Gesellschaft*, **23**, 191–199.

Becher H.H. (1971) Ein Verfahren zur Messung der ungesättigten Wasserleitfähigkeit. *Zeitschrift für Pflanzenernährung und Bodenkunde*, **128**, 1–12.

Blume H.-P., Horn R., Alaily F., Jayakody A.N. & Meshref H. (1980) Sandy cambisol functioning as a filter through long term irrigation with waste-waters. *Soil Science*, **130**, 186–192.

Fester J. (1964) Untersuchungen über den Einfluß unterschiedlicher Abwasserlandbehandlung auf die Eutrophierung der Gewässer. *Zeitschrift für Kulturtechnik und Flurbereinigung*, **5**, 390–403.

Miner J.R. & Hazen T.E. (1977) Transportation and application of organic wastes to land. In *Soils for management of organic wastes and waste waters* (Ed. by M. Stelly), pp. 319–428, Soil Science Society of America, Madison.

Scheffer F. & Schachtschabel P. (1976) *Lehrbuch der Bodenkunde. 9. Auflage.* Ferdinand Enke Verlag, Stuttgart.

Schlichting E. & Blume H.-P. (1967) *Bodenkundliches Praktikum.* Paul Parey, Berlin.

Weigmann G. et al. (1977) Auswirkungen unterschiedlicher Nutzungsintensität auf Ökosysteme am Beispiel Gatow/Kladow. *Hochschulforschung Technische Universität Berlin*, **2/3**, 294–322.

24. ECOLOGICAL ASPECTS OF THE URBANIZATION OF A CANAL

JOHN G. KELCEY

Milton Keynes Development Corporation,
Wavendon Tower, Wavendon, Milton Keynes, U.K.

SUMMARY

Milton Keynes, which is situated in 9,000 ha of rural North Buckinghamshire, England, was designated a new city in 1967 to accommodate 250,000 people by the end of this century.

The Development Corporation's ecological policy includes a programme of monitoring the effects of urbanization on the major ecosystems that existed at the time of designation. The main objective of the first phase is to obtain base-line data against which change can be measured.

The ecological monitoring of the 20 km of the Grand Union Canal that runs through the city is described. Surveys of the vegetation include the bryophytes, aquatic macrophytes, the terrestrial vegetation and the boundary hedge. Surveys of the freshwater invertebrates, dragonflies and fish have been carried out and are summarized together with the results of the vegetation surveys.

INTRODUCTION

Little is known about the urban ecosystems of the British Isles or about the effect of urbanization on man-made and semi-natural ecosystems.

Milton Keynes, North Buckinghamshire, England was designated a new city in 1967 to accommodate about 250,000 people. At the time of designation Milton Keynes comprised the small urban areas of Bletchley, Wolverton and Stony Stratford together with 13 hamlets with a total population of 44,250; it is now (1980) about 91,000. Most of the remaining land was intensively farmed arable land with some pasture. The land-use within 2 km of the Canal in 1968, 1979 and as it will be when the city is complete in the 1990's is shown in Figure 24.1. In addition to providing advice and information for its planning, design and management operations, the Corporation's ecological policy includes a programme of monitoring the effects of urbanization on the major ecosystems that existed at the time of designation. The canal ecosystem is a complex association of terrestrial and aquatic habitats; this paper summarizes

231

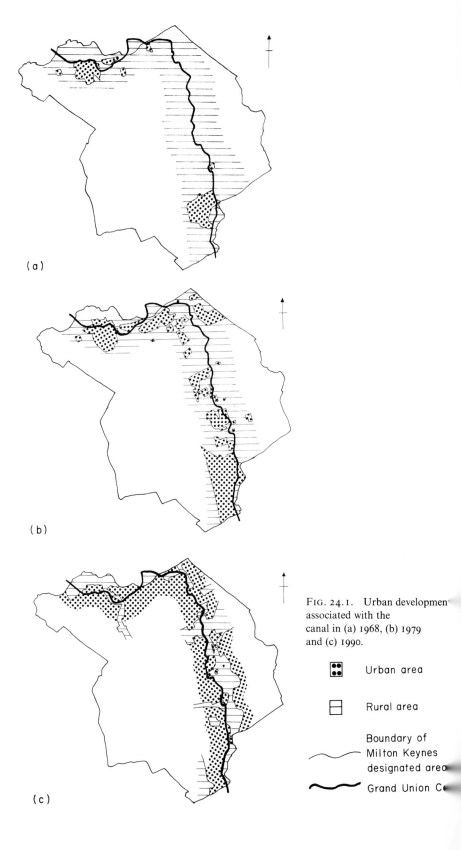

Fig. 24.1. Urban development associated with the canal in (a) 1968, (b) 1979 and (c) 1990.

Urban area

Rural area

Boundary of Milton Keynes designated area

Grand Union Canal

the results that have so far been obtained in relation to the aquatic aspects of the Grand Union Canal in Milton Keynes. The major objective of the monitoring programme is to obtain base-line information against which change can be measured.

HISTORY

The main period of canal construction in England started about 1755 and continued until 1805, during which period about 3,000 km of canal were built. In some cases they were improved river channels but the majority were dug out of the landscape. The Grand Union Canal, which is one of the latter, connects Birmingham to London and was opened to traffic in 1801 but further widening occurred in the 1930s. It was nationalized in 1948 and is now under the control of the British Waterways Board. Use by commercial traffic stopped in 1963.

ECOLOGICAL MONITORING

The canal monitoring programme has covered most ecological aspects of the canal including zooplankton, freshwater invertebrates, dragonflies, fish and flowering plants. The six sites of wildlife importance are being monitored (see Fig. 24.2). These sites were selected subjectively. In addition, 19 100 m monitoring sites have been established at intersections of the national grid, 26 in the city and three 'controls' outside the city, one in the north, one in the centre and one to the south (see Fig. 24.2). The latter sites have been used for surveys of the physical characteristics, the freshwater invertebrates and the vegetation (including biomass studies). However, it has not been practical to use the sites for monitoring all groups of organisms.

PLANTS AND ANIMALS

Flowering plants

Lists have been made of the flowering plants occurring in both the sites of wildlife importance and the monitoring sites. Both sides of the canal were included in the surveys and the relative abundance was recorded. A total of 246 species was recorded in the sites of wildlife importance. Ninety species, 45 of which are aquatic, occurred in 80% of the sites whilst 60 were confined to only one site. Two hundred and three species were recorded in the monitoring sites, of which 23 occurred in 80% of the sites, and 52 species being confined to

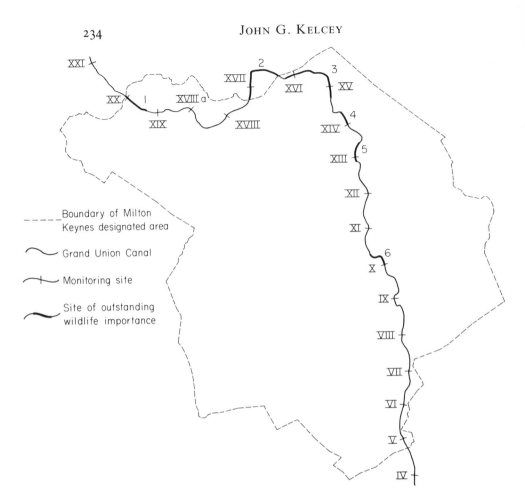

FIG. 24.2. Monitoring sites and sites of outstanding wildlife importance.

only one site. Whilst no nationally or regionally rare or unusual species were found, a number are of local importance, for example *Butomus umbellatus*,* *Sagittaria sagittifolia* and *Acorus calamus*. In August 1980 a survey of the emergent floating-leafed and submerged macrophytes was carried out.† The distribution and abundance of these plants was assessed at 17 designated monitoring sites, each 100 m long. Abundance of emergent species was assessed using cover estimates but the abundance of submerged species required a more complex technique. The method used involved sampling with a standard grapnel at 10 random points within each site.

Twenty-nine species were recorded (two algae, three bryophytes and 24

* Nomenclature for flowering plants follows Clapham, Tutin and Warburg (1962).
† Reports of the primary surveys are available from the author.

higher plants), the majority of which are typical of eutrophic slow-moving water bodies in southern England. Emergent vegetation was richer and denser in the central region, from Walton to Tongwell, than in northern or southern regions where the canal passes through older urban centres. At three of these latter sites there was no emergent vegetation present. No single species was dominant, but *Juncus effusus, Sagittaria saggitifolia* and *Sparganium erectum* were all common. The submerged vegetation was generally dominated by *Elodea canadensis* from the most southern site to Linford in the north. However, the remainder of the canal from Stantonbury to Wolverton contained little *Elodea*, the dominant species being *Potamogeton pectinatus* or mosses. Biomass varied erratically from site to site, although very high values only occurred in the central region.

Freshwater invertebrates

A survey of the freshwater invertebrates has been carried out, which included the zooplankton, the nektonic and benthic invertebrates and the sessile organisms attached to plants, stones and walls. Sampling was carried out at two points at each of the 100 m monitoring sites, one close to the towpath bank, the other close to the opposite bank.

The following sampling procedure was carried out at each point:

1. Plankton samples: Two samples were taken at each site with a vertical haul of a plankton net (26.5 cm in diameter). One sample was taken about 1.5 m from the towpath bank, the other about 0.5 m from the non-towpath bank.
2. Benthos: The benthos in the soft mud about 2 m from the towpath bank was sampled using an Eckman Grab (area 225 cm^2) and the organisms isolated by sieving the sediment.
3. The larger nektonic organisms were sampled using five sweeps of a pond net (mouth area 500 cm^2)
4. Sessile organisms on plants, stone and retaining walls were collected for 15 minutes.

The results showed that the fauna was typical of that found in hard, moderately eutrophic, slow-flowing water with abundant weed and a muddy substrate.

The type of edge affects the invertebrate fauna because it determines the development of the aquatic vegetation. The species richness of sections with piled edges being reduced compared with those with gently sloping natural edges, which generally support a good marginal vegetation.

The species diversity (using the Shannon-Weiner information statistic (see Fig. 24.3), the number of caddis and mayfly species (see Fig. 24.4), and the ratio of the number of insect species: number of non-arthropod species were thought to be useful parameters against which to measure change as well as

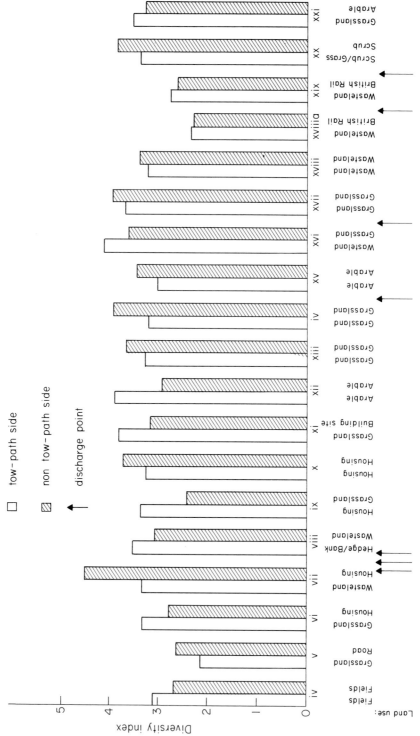

FIG. 24.3. Diversity indices of the monitoring sites.

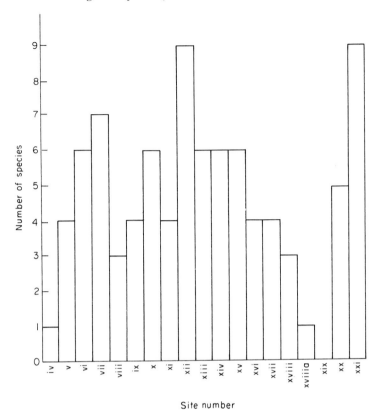

Fig. 24.4.   Distribution of caddis and mayfly species on the Grand Union Canal.

being useful in assessing the degree of pollution. The results indicated that in general the canal is not badly polluted. However, sections through the existing urban areas in the north and south of the city were shown to be of poorer quality than the remainder.

The mayfly *Caenis horaria* (L.) and the total number of mayfly and caddis fly species (Figs 24.5 and 24.4, respectively), all of which are sensitive to pollution show a marked decline at certain sites, whilst *Tubifex* which are tolerant of pollution show an increase at the same sites (see Fig. 24.6).

The diversity indices (see Fig. 24.3) suggest that the adjacent land-use is not a significant factor in determining the diversity of the site.

Dragonflies

A survey of the odonata of Milton Keynes, including the canal, was carried out in 1979; it showed that seven of the 14 species recorded in Milton Keynes breed in the canal, including *Aeshna grandis* L. and *A.mixta* Latreille. The most important areas for odonata are the small bays that are used for turning boats round and which, because of lack of use, have become colonized by submerged, floating-leafed and emergent vegetation. The canal is the only breeding site in the city for *Libellula quadrimaculata* L.

Fish

Electro-fishing surveys of the canal were carried out in the autumns of 1974 and 1979. Samples (100 m in length) were taken every 2 km.

The number and biomass for both years are given in Table 24.1 Nine species were caught in 1974 and 13 in 1979, but the canal remained dominated by perch, roach and bream. Between the surveys the number of fish had

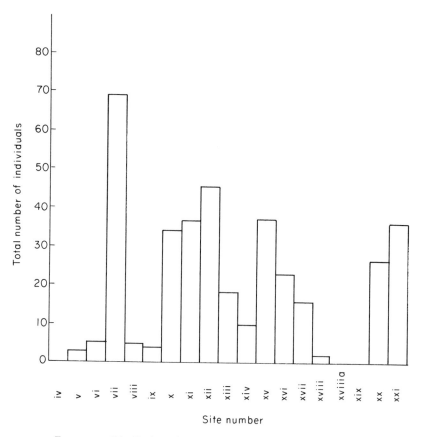

FIG. 24.5. Distribution of *Caenis honoraria* on the Grand Union Canal.

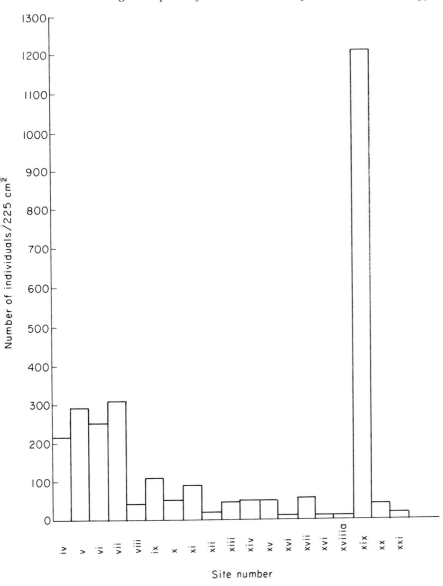

FIG. 24.6 Distribution of Tubificidae in the Grand Union Canal.

increased by 7% and the biomass by 20%. However, these increases were not uniform throughout the canal.

In an attempt to gain information about the status of fish in the canal over a longer period, information was extracted from press reports of fishing

TABLE 24.1. *Numbers of fish and total weight, kg (biomass) in Grand Union Canal.*

Species	Total nos.		Total weight (kg)	
	1974	1979	1974	1979
Bream (*Abramis brama* L.)	2,000	6,557	156.16	1,419.4
Common carp (*Cyprinus carpio* L.)	—	547	—	2,714.0
Crucian carp (*Carassius carassius* L.)	—	1,093	—	79.6
Bullhead (*Cottus gobio* L.)	580	2,551	6.38	30.2
Dace (*Leuciscus leuciscus* L.)	280	2,551	3.40	58.3
Gudgeon (*Gobio gobio* L.)	11,660	5,466	194.37	94.3
Perch (*Perca fluviatilis* L.)	14,660	34,436	246.14	730.4
Pike (*Esox lucius* L.)	1,540	364	483.5	161.1
Roach (*Rutilis rutilis* L.)	100,240	91,828	3,290.8	2,354.4
Rudd (*Scardinius erythrophthalmus* L.)	200	547	8.20	28.9
Ruffe (*Gymnocephalus cernua* L.)	8,800	11,843	155.06	205.6
Stone loach (*Noemacheilus barbatulus* L.)	—	1,640	—	14.4
Tench (*Tinca tinca* L.)	—	3,280	—	290.0
Total	151,620	162,705	4,544.09	5,455.7*
Percentage change	+7.31%		+20.0%*	

* Without carp weight.

TABLE 24.2. *Total weight, number of catches and mean weight per catch 1969–79*

Season	Total weight (kg)	No. of catches reported	Mean weight/ catch (kg)
1969–70	94.96	73	1.30
1970–71	60.11	52	1.16
1971–72	129.76	77	1.69
1972–73	89.75	43	2.09
1973–74	54.07	41	1.32
1974–75	105.46	118	0.89
1975–76	96.27	130	0.74
1976–77	255.42	172	1.48
1977–78	200.32	174	1.15
1978–79	178.42	145	1.23

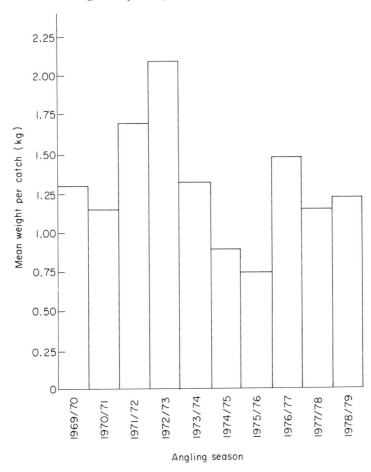

FIG. 24.7.   Mean weight of fish per catch per year (1969–79).

matches held during the 10-year period 1969–79. The results are shown in Table 24.2 and Figure 24.7 and show no consistent trend in mean weight per catch, but a marked increase in the number of fish caught. In January 1972 the canal was stocked with 30,500 fish (15,000 roach (*Rutilis rutilis* L.), 12,500 bream (*Abramis brama* L.) and 3,000 common carp (*Cyprinus carpio* L.)) following a breach in December 1971 that resulted in the loss of 8.5 km of water and a large quantity of fish.

CONCLUSION

So far there has been little development in the canal corridor and, therefore, urbanization has had little effect on the plant and animal communities. The whole of the canal through Milton Keynes is Class I (rivers unpolluted and recovering from pollution) on the Department of the Environment's water quality classification scheme.

Except for the phytoplankton the base-line monitoring studies have been completed. Unless there is a special reason for doing so it will not be necessary to repeat them for at least 5 years. For example, the 1974 fish survey was repeated in 1979 as part of an 'environmental impact analysis' for a proposed marina development.

Remote sensing, a very useful, but in Britain an under-used (and unappreciated), tool, may become increasingly important in environmental monitoring. The Grand Union Canal is included in the general aerial survey that the Corporation commissions every 2 years. It was specially flown in 1979 at a scale of 1:2500 using false-colour infra-red imagery, the data being particularly valuable for the impact study for the proposed marina development and for monitoring the effects of the marina when it is built.

Whether urbanization will be as detrimental to the existing plant and animal communities as is often predicted remains to be seen. Much will rest on the social responsibility of the human community as it does on the planning, design and management operations.

ACKNOWLEDGEMENTS

I wish to thank Anne Robinson for help in the preparation of this paper, and L. Baldock, K. Grimshaw, R.J. Halliday, P. Lackie, A. Newton, D.M. Parker, A. Tasker and M. Yoxon for undertaking the fieldwork and desk studies.

REFERENCE

Clapham A.R., Tutin T.G. & Warburg E.F. (1962) Flora of the British Isles (2nd Ed). Cambridge University Press.

25. ECOLOGICAL EFFECTS OF URBANIZATION ON LAKE PONTCHARTRAIN, LOUISIANA, BETWEEN 1953 AND 1978, WITH IMPLICATIONS FOR MANAGEMENT

JAMES H. STONE, LEONARD M. BAHR, JR.,
JOHN W. DAY, JR. AND REZNEAT M. DARNELL*

*Coastal Ecology Laboratory, Center for Wetland Resources,
Louisiana State University,
Baton Rouge, LA 70803*

SUMMARY

Lake Pontchartrain, a shallow, oligohaline estuary, is located in the Mississippi River deltaic plain of southeastern Louisiana. The 1631 km^2 lake is fringed by 2.5×10^6 km^2 of forest swamp and by 3.1×10^5 km^2 of fresh-to-brackish marsh. Greater New Orleans, with about 1.2 million people, occupies the south shore.

Lake and watershed activities include: urbanization, industrialization (especially refineries and petrochemicals), agriculture, hurricane leveeing, flood discharges, fossil-shell dredging, oil and gas development, commercial and sports fish harvest and extensive recreation.

Between the 1950s and 1978 upstream peak flood discharge increased by 29%; mean Secchi disc depths decreased by 53%; total phosphorus loading increased by 72%; marsh and grassbed areas decreased about 60% and 25%, respectively; nekton production possibly declined 5%; and species composition changed. Management alternatives include treatment of all discharge water or discharge into the Mississippi River and prohibition (or limiting) of shell dredging and of development in wetlands.

INTRODUCTION AND PURPOSE

During 1978–79 Louisiana State University made a year-long study of selected ecological components and processes of Lake Pontchartrain, its

* Department of Oceanography, College of Geoscience, Texas A&M University, College Station, TX 77843.

surrounding wetlands and selected land uses in its watershed (Stone 1980).
During 1953–55 Tulane University (Suttkus *et al.* 1953–55) had conducted a
somewhat similar study of the lake.

This paper compares these two time periods by analysing land use,
hydrological, nutrient, and turbidity changes, and species composition. Some
management alternatives are given.

LAND USE AND VEGETATION CHANGES

The 18,969 km^2 Lake Pontchartrain catchment is located in southeastern
Louisiana and southwestern Mississippi (Fig. 25.1). Six per cent of the area is
urban; 22%, agriculture; 40%, upland forest; 16%, total water; and 16%,
wetland (Turner & Bond 1980a). About 30% of Louisiana's population is in
Greater New Orleans and Greater Baton Rouge (1.2×10^6 and 3.5×10^5
people, respectively), the catchment's two largest population centres. Agriculture, pulp and papermaking, water transportation, flood protection, commercial and sports fishing, food processing, seafoods, aluminium production,
petroleum refining and petrochemical production dominate the watershed's
industries. However, the latter two activities are larger than the others by at
least an order of magnitude. Over $5 billion has been invested in the industries
within coastal Louisiana since World War II (LACCMR 1973). These
investments are especially evident along the Mississippi River corridor from
Baton Rouge to New Orleans, where there are 10 oil refineries, with a
combined production capacity of 1.5×10^6 barrels per day, and 38 petrochemical plants, with a combined production capacity of 43.1×10^9 pounds of
ethylene per year. In addition, these industries are expected to increase 89%
and 73%, respectively, during the next 10 years.

Most of the original vegetation was forest, and less than 60% now remains.
Pine and cottonwood are the dominant tree species, but oak hardwoods are a
major component. Softwoods, however, have increased in proportion to
hardwoods since 1950. During the same period, agricultural land between
Baton Rouge and New Orleans has trebled, and urban areas have also
increased significantly (Turner & Bond 1980a). Marshes have been reduced by
half through the expansion of New Orleans westward, along the south shore.
During the same period, the distribution of two dominant species of
submerged macrophytes in grassbeds along the lake's shoreline declined by
about 25%. These grassbeds occupy an area of about 730 ha, primarily along
the northeastern shore, and are considered a critical and unique habitat of the
lake (Turner *et al.* 1980). Forest swamps have been subjected to cypress
harvest techniques as well as to various hydrological changes (Cramer & Day
1980).

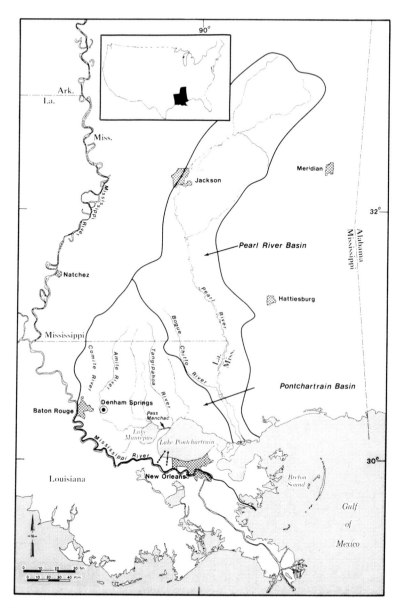

FIG. 25.1.   Lake Pontchartrain catchment with adjoining Pearl River catchment. Vertical lines near lower left corner of Lake Pontchartrain are approximate locations of transect stations for nutrients.

HYDROLOGICAL CHANGES

Two significant hydrological changes in the Lake Pontchartrain watershed in the last 25 years are:

1. An increase discharge rate and flood frequency of upland (near Baton Rouge) flood water, and
2. An increase in the discharge of the run-off water from Greater New Orleans into Lake Pontchartrain.

TABLE 25.1. *Percent change in peak river discharges and number of annual floods at selected stations in Lake Pontchartrain catchment (Turner & Bond 1980b).*

Station	Percent change in peak river discharge (1951–60 vs. 1961–70)	Number of annual floods (1951–60)	(1961–70)	(1971–78)
1. Comite River at Olive Branch, La. (control area)	−2	2.4	2.6	2.6
2. Amite River at Darlington, La. (control area)	−6	1.6	2.2	2.6
3. Comite River at Comite, La. (study area)	+23	3.8	3.9	5.3*
4. Amite River at Denham Springs, La. (study area)	+4	1.2	1.8	1.7

* Significant at $P = 0.05$.

Table 25.1 presents changes in peak flood discharges and number of annual floods at several river stations near Baton Rouge. The Comite River at Comite, La., location shows a 23% increase in peak flood discharge over the last 20 years; the other stations show very little change (6% or less). The Comite station shows a significant increase over the others in flood frequency: 5.3 floods per year compared to a mean of 2.3 for the other stations. The Comite station provides drainage for most of Baton Rouge, an urban area that shows, on the average, more land use changes than the other upland areas. The total volume of water reaching Lake Pontchartrain from upland Baton Rouge has not changed, but upland run-off waters now enter and flush the downstream lakes more quickly. For example, we estimate that the maximum flushing rate of Lake Maurepas (west of and connected to Lake Pontchartrain by Pass Manchac) has increased by about 30% which, in turn, may affect between 2–10% of Lake Pontchartrain waters (Turner & Bond 1980b).

NUTRIENTS

As might be expected, waters from upland Greater Baton Rouge and the run-off water from Greater New Orleans contain substantial amounts of nutrients. We estimate that phosphorus loading into the lake between 1953 and 1978 has increased by 72% (Table 25.2). Table 25.2 also presents phosphorus and nitrogen concentrations at stations along transects from a south shoreline marsh into lake Pontchartrain proper. Both of these nutrients were substantially higher in the marsh canals and bayous than in the lake. These particular canals and bayous drain discharge water from the marsh and nearby urban and industrial components of New Orleans. Nutrient levels in waters off Pass Manchac, which carries Lake Maurepas run-off into Lake Pontchartrain, are also significantly higher than in the lake (Tarver & Savoie 1976). Phytoplankton was significantly more abundant in areas with high

TABLE 25.2. *Phosphorus loading (A) into Lake Pontchartrain, Louisiana and nutrient concentrations at selected stations (B).*

A. Phosphorus loading rates into Lake Pontchartrain, Louisiana (modified from Craig *et al.* 1972)

Year	$Pg \cdot m^2 \cdot yr^{-1}$
1900	0.64
1920	0.70
1940	0.83
1950	0.94
1960	1.05
1970	1.23
1980	1.62
1990	1.72
2000	1.93

B. Nutrient concentrations and related data along marsh transects into shoreline stations of Lake Pontchartrain (see Fig. 25.1 for approximate transect locations (Cramer & Day 1980)

Location	TON mg l^{-1}	P mg l^{-1}
Marsh (Crossbayou Canal)	2.01	1.63
Marsh (Bayou La Branche)	1.46	1.15
Marsh (Walker Canal)	0.96	0.32
Marsh (Bayou Piquant)	0.69	0.31
Lake (off Bayou La Branche)	0.59	0.14
Lake (off Walker Canal)	0.63	0.16
$\bar{x}$'s Marsh Stations	1.28	0.85
$\bar{x}$'s Lake Stations	0.61	0.15

TON = Total organic nitrogen. P = Phosphorus.

nutrient levels (Stone *et al.* 1980). A trophic state analysis classifies Lake
Pontchartrain as meso-to-oligotrophic; the above marsh areas (and probably
Lake Maurepas) are hypereutrophic (Witzig & Day 1980).

TURBIDITY

Figure 25.2 plots mean Secchi disc depths for Lake Pontchartrain during

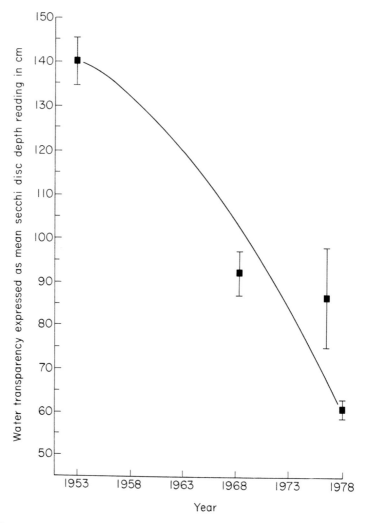

FIG. 25.2. Secchi disc depth (cm) and standard errors for specified time periods in
Lake Pontchartrain, Louisiana.

several time periods. The mean depth shows a decrease of 53% between 1953–55 and 1978. Secchi disc depths are subject to variations because of observers' error, wind and weather conditions. Our initial analysis however, indicates no systematic differences of wind speeds among the years.

SPECIES COMPOSITION

Both the 1953 and 1978 surveys of Lake Pontchartrain analysed phytoplankton, zooplankton, selected benthos and nekton. A preliminary comparison of these data is given in Table 25.3 using the Sorensen similarity index (Sorensen

TABLE 25.3. *Comparison of selected species in Lake Pontchartrain, Louisiana, between 1953–55 and 1978 from surveys of Lake Pontchartrain by Darnell unpublished, Stone et al. (1980), Bahr et al. (1980) and Thompson and Verret (1980).*

Taxa	No. of taxa 1953–55	No. of taxa 1978	Sorenson (1948) % similarity
1. Phytoplankton genera	68	60	16
Blue-greens	9	12	48
Greens	12	37	16
2. Zooplankton (micro)	53	47	16
3. Benthos	78	20	20
4. Nekton	110	85	87

1948). Considerable differences are evident between the taxa of 1953 and 1978. For example, there is more than 80% difference in the species composition of phytoplankton, zooplankton and benthos between 1953–55 and 1978. Nekton species, however, show a 87% similarity. Former differences may reflect differences in sampling procedures, whereas the nekton data probably indicate similar procedures (Stone 1980; Suttkus *et al*, 1953–55). Also, the Sorensen index is not without problems (Fager 1963). None the less, we tentatively conclude that pronounced changes have occurred in the species composition of Lake Pontchartrain between 1953 and 1978. More detailed analyses are necessary to make a complete assessment.

DISCUSSION

The Lake Pontchartrain ecosystem has three major features:

1. A decline in the area of wetlands, with indications of stress on some of the remaining wetlands.
2. Increased amounts of nutrients entering the lake, its surrounding marshes, and forest swamps, and
3. Decreasing water clarity in the lake proper.

A conceptual model was used for computer simulations of the Lake Pontchartrain ecosystem (Stone & Deegan 1980). Biomass and production data were determined for six trophic levels according to a simulation for 1953 turbidity levels and one for 1978 levels. Phytoplankton standing crop and production show the greatest reduction, i.e. 38%; the other trophic levels show reductions of from 4 to 12%. The transfer of energy from benthos to nekton does not appear to be very efficient.

The nutrients are probably interacting with and being chelated by suspended material in water column. The net effect is to reduce phytosynthesis, selected plant species and, eventually, fish productio. We believe the decrease in water clarity is caused primarily by shell-dredging operations in the lake. We estimate that the operations could stir up 25% of the lake's sediments at any one time (Bahr et al. 1980). Winds probably stir up bottom sediments 15% of the time (Swenson 1980). However, both of these estimates are somewhat speculative.

MANAGEMENT ALTERNATIVES

We believe that dredging operations and untreated discharge waters over the past 25 years have adversely affected the Lake Pontchartrain ecosystem. To prevent further adverse effects, those responsible for managing the natural resources of the area should restrict or suspend shell dredging. We also recommend that all water being discharged into the lake be treated or, if that is impossible, that it be discharged into the Mississippi River instead of into the lake. Development on the remaining wetland areas should also be prohibited.

REFERENCES

Bahr L.M. Jr., Sikora J.P. & Sikora W.B. (1980) Macrobenthic survey of Lake Pontchartrain, Louisiana, 1978. In *Environmental Analysis of Lake Pontchartrain, Louisiana, Its Surrounding Wetlands, and Selected Land Uses* (Ed. by J.H. Stone) pp. 659–710. CEL, CWR, LSU, BR, LA 70803. Prepared for U.S. Army Engineer District, New Orleans. Contract No. DACW29-77-C-0253.

Craig N.J., Day J.W. Jr., Kemp P., Seaton A., Smith W.G. & Turner R.E. (1977) *Cumulative Impact Studies in the Louisiana Coastal Zone: Eutrophication and Land Loss.* Final report to Louisiana department of transportation and development. Center for wetland resources, Louisiana State University, Baton Rouge, LA 70803. 157 pp.

Cramer G.W. & Day J.W. Jr. (1980) Productivity of the swamps and marshes surrounding Lake Pontchartrain, Louisiana. In *Environmental Analysis of Lake Pontchartrain, Louisiana, Its Surrounding Wetlands, and Selected Land Uses* (Ed. by J.H. Stone) pp. 593–646. CEL, CWR, LSU, BR, LA 70803. Prepared for U.S. Army Engineer District, New Orleans. Contract No. DACW29-77-C-0253.

Dow D.D. & Turner R.E. (1980) Structure and function of the phytoplankton community in Lake Pontchartrain, Louisiana. In *Environmental Analysis of Lake Pontchartrain, Louisiana, Its*

Surrounding Wetlands, and Selected Land Uses (Ed. by J.H. Stone) pp.321–435. CEL, CWR, LSU, BR, LA 70803. Prepared for U.S. Army Engineer District, New Orleans. Contract No. DACW29-77-C-0253.

Fager E.W. (1963) Communities of organisms. In *The Sea* (Ed. by M.N. Hill), pp. 415–437. Interscience Publishers, New York.

Louisiana Advisory Commission on Coastal and Marine Resources (LACCMR) (1973) *Louisiana Wetlands Prospectus.* Conclusions, recommendations and proposals of the Louisiana Advisory Commission on coastal and marine resources. 346 pp.

Sorensen T. (1948) A method of stabilizing groups of equivalent amplitude in plant sociology based on the similarity of species content and its application to analyses of the vegetation on the Danish commons. *Biologiske Skrifter* **5**, 1–34.

Stoessell R.K. (1980) Nutrient and carbon geochemistry in Lake Pontchartrain, Louisiana. In *Environmental Analysis of Lake Pontchartrain, Louisiana, Its Surrounding Wetlands, and Selected Land Uses* (Ed. by J.H. Stone) pp. 217–320. CEL, CWR, LSU, BR, LA 70803. Prepared for U.S. Army Engineer District, New Orleans. Contract No. DACW29-77-C-0253.

Stone J.H. (Ed.) (1980) *Environmental Analysis of Lake Pontchartrain, Louisiana, Its Surrounding Wetlands, and Selected Land Uses.* Coastal Ecology Laboratory, Center for Wetland Resources, Louisiana State University, Baton Rouge, LA 70803. Prepared for U.S. Army Engineers, New Orleans. Contract No. DACW29-77-C-0253. 1199 pp.

Stone J.H. & Deegan L.A. (1980) Preliminary modeling of the Lake Pontchartrain ecosystem by computer simulations. In *Environmental Analysis of Lake Pontchartrain, Louisiana, Its Surrounding Wetlands, and Selected Land Uses* (Ed. by J.H. Stone), pp. 1–20. CEL, CWR, LSU, BR, LA 70803. Prepared for U.S. Army Engineer District, New Orleans. Contract No. DACW29-77-C-0253.

Stone J.H., Drummond N.A., Cook L.L., Theriot E.C. & Lindstedt D.M. (1980) The distribution and abundance of plankton of Lake Pontchartrain, Louisiana, 1978. In *Environmental Analysis of Lake Pontchartrain, Louisiana, Its Surrounding Wetlands, and Selected Land Uses* (Ed. by J.H. Stone), pp. 437–592. CEL, CWR, LSU, BR, LA 70803. Prepared for U.S. Army Engineer District, New Orleans. Contract No. DACW29-77-C-0253.

Suttkus R.D., Darnell R.M. & Darnell J.H. (1953–55) *Biological Study of Lake Pontchartrain.* Annual reports to the Louisiana Wild Life and Fisheries Commission, 1953–1954. Tulane University Zoology Department, New Orleans, LA. 59 pp.

Swenson E. (1980) General hydrography of Lake Pontchartrain, Louisiana. In *Environmental Analysis of Lake Pontchartrain, Louisiana, Its Surrounding Wetlands, and Selected Land Uses* (Ed. by J.H. Stone) pp. 57–156. CEL, CWR, LSU, BR, LA 70803. Prepared for U.S. Army Engineer District, New Orleans. Contract No. DACW29-77-C-0253.

Tarver J.W. & Savoie L.B. (1976) *An Inventory and Study of the Lake Pontchartrain–Lake Maurepas Estuarine Complex.* Technical Bulletin No. 19. Louisiana Wildlife and Fisheries Commission, Oyster, Water Bottoms and Seafoods Division, New Orleans, LA. 159 pp.

Thompson B.A. & Verret J.S. (1980) Nekton of Lake Pontchartrain, Louisiana, and its surrounding wetlands. In *Environmental Analysis of Lake Pontchartrain, Louisiana, Its Surrounding Wetlands, and Selected Land Uses* (Ed. by J.H. Stone), pp. 711–864. CEL, CWR, LSU, BR, LA 70803. Prepared for U.S. Army Engineer District, New Orleans. Contract No. DACW29-77-C-0253.

Turner R.E. & Bond J.R. (1980a) Recent land use changes in the Lake Pontchartrain watershed. In *Environmental Analysis of Lake Pontchartrain, Louisiana, Its Surrounding Wetlands, and Selected Land Uses* (Ed. by J.H. Stone), pp. 1173–1206. CEL, CWR, LSU, BR, LA 70803. Prepared for U.S. Army Engineer District, New Orleans. Contract No. DACW29-77-C-0253.

Turner R.E. & Bond J.R. (1980b) Urbanization, peak streamflow, and estuarine hydrology (Louisiana). Louisiana Academy of Sciences, *in press.*

Turner R.E., Darnell R.M. & Bond J.R. (1980) Changes in the submerged macrophytes of Lake Pontchartrain (Louisiana): 1954–1973. *Northeast Gulf Science*, Volume 4, *in press.*

Witzig A. & Day J.W. Jr. (1980) A trophic state analysis of lake Pontchartrain, Louisiana, and surrounding wetland tributaries. In *Environmental Analysis of Lake Pontchartrain, Louisiana, Its Surrounding Wetlands, and Selected Land Uses* (Ed. by J.H. Stone) pp. 21–38. CEL, CWR, LSU, BR, LA 70803. Prepared for U.S. Army Engineer District, New Orleans. Contract No. DACW29-77-C-0253.

III

THE ACQUISITION AND APPLICATION OF
ECOLOGICAL KNOWLEDGE
IN THE URBAN ENVIRONMENT

26. ECOLOGICAL CONTRIBUTIONS TO URBAN PLANNING

M. HORBERT, H.P. BLUME, H. ELVERS AND H. SUKOPP

Institut für Ökologie,
Technische Universität Berlin,
Rothenburgstrasse 12, Berlin 41

SUMMARY

Far-reaching ecological changes must be regarded as an essential feature of large regional conurbations. This is expressed in the relatively great influence they have on urban climate, air hygiene, soil flora and fauna. In this regard Berlin (West) is used as an example for the discussion of many ecological problems and questions, which are of considerable consequence to the urban planner and place many demands on him. On the basis of the various forms of utilization in the inner-city area previous knowledge gained about urban ecology is summarized and a catalogue of recommendations for improving the urban environment is drawn up.

INTRODUCTION

An essential feature of urban areas and a main criterion distinguishing them from other settlement forms is the concentration of population on a limited surface area. This is evident, physiognomically, in the concentration of building mass. High population densities are accompanied by far-reaching changes in the ecosphere.

Urban construction and economic activity result in the subdivision between built-up and partly built-up zones. Garden plots and refuse and rubble dumps, as well as waste-water irrigation fields, characterize the inner suburbs, whereas forest areas and large parks are characteristic of the outer suburbs (Fig. 26.1, Table 26.1). Consequences for the climate, soil, water bodies, relief, vegetation and animal life are to be expected as a result of the modification of the ecosphere.

In the following paper the climate, soil type and vegetation of the urban environment will be characterized with the help of examples. Then, an attempt will be made to draw conclusions for the development of problematical urban areas.

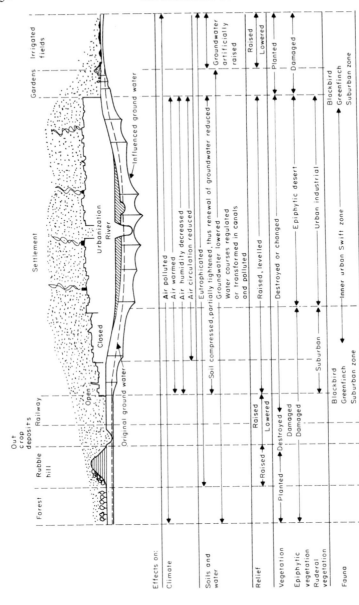

FIG. 26.1. Variations in the biosphere of urban areas (Reproduced by permission of Technische Universität Berlin).

TABLE 26.1. *Some floristic-vegetational characteristics of Zones 1–4 in Berlin (Sukopp* et al. *1979).*

Zone	Urbanization		Suburbs	
	Built-up	Partly built-up	Inner	Outer
	1	2	3	4
% Surface covered by vegetation	32	55	75	95
No. of vascular plants species km^{-2}	380	424	415	357
Rare species km^{-2}*	17	23	35	58
% Hemerochores†	49.8	46.9	43.4	28.5
% Archaeophytes‡	15.2	14.1	14.5	10.2
% Neophytes§	23.7	23.0	21.5	15.6

* Rare species—plants in Berlin with only 10 records.

† Hemerochores—plants introduced due to direct or indirect human action.

‡ Archaeophytes—species introduced up to the end of the Middle Ages.

§ Neophytes—species introduced after the year 1500.

URBAN CLIMATE

The essential cause for the formation of a characteristic climate in densely populated areas lies in the profound fluctuations in the local thermal balance. The marginal conditions which are responsible for the energy balance are fundamentally changed by the modification of the surface structure or the surface features and, last but not least, by the concentration of various substances in the atmosphere. This affects not only the radiation but also the conductivity of heat in the ground or in the atmosphere, and evaporation on the earth's surface.

Table 26.2 shows some compiled climate parameters which may be subject to change through the effects of very densely built-up housing in relation to the surrounding rural environment. In this summary, priority is given to air pollution occurring in the form of increased condensation and in gaseous concentrations. Tied up with air pollution is the formation of a haze layer. In the densely populated areas this has secondary effects on the climate of the city.

While the poorer light diffusion through the haze layer may be negligible, a reduction of direct solar radiation of 20–25% can be assumed. At the same time the near-ultraviolet radiation decreases during the summer by 5% and in winter by about 30%. The decreased warming caused by absorption is more than compensated for by the decreased outgoing radiation in the long-wave region.

TABLE 26.2. *Average changes of climate parameters in built-up areas (Horbert 1978).*

Climate parameters	Characteristics	In comparison to the surrounding area
Air pollution	Condensation	10 times more
	Gaseous pollution	5–25 times more
Solar radiation	Global solar radiation	15–20% less
	Ultraviolet radiation, winter	30% less
	„ „ summer	5% less
	Duration of sunshine	5–15% less
Air temperature	Annual mean average	0.5–1.5°C higher
	On clear days	2–6°C higher
Wind speed	Annual mean average	10–20% less
	Calm winds	5–20% more
Relative humidity	Winter	2% less
	Summer	8–10% less
Clouds	Overcast	5–10% more
	Fog (winter)	100% more
	„ (summer)	30% more
Precipitation	Total rainfall	5–10% more
	Less than 5 mm rainfall	10% more
	Daily snowfall	5% less

This so-called 'greenhouse' effect, coupled with the increased warming capacity of the buildings and the soils, produces a rise in the mean air temperature of around 0.5–1.5°C. The rise and modification of the air temperature maximum at midday is especially characteristic; likewise the considerable degree of cooling at night. The nightly difference in air temperature, in relation to the surroundings, can be especially high on clear nights. These values are, of course, dependent on the size of the green spaces within the city, but are also to a considerable degree subject to air turbulance between the city centre and the outskirts.

A further characteristic feature of the city climate is the decreased mean wind speed, ranging from 10–20% according to the topography of the building. This is also evident when the effects of increasingly calm winds are considered. The inversion weather conditions must, therefore, be regarded as problematic in urban districts, especially during statically stable weather. The urban districts are also drier than the surroundings in accordance with increased air temperature. The difference in the relative humidity is only 2% in winter, but it can be up to 8–10%, especially on clear days in summer. The total lack of vegetation, but also the rapid precipitation run-off, is of great importance here. Further facts deducible from Table 26.1 are the increased effects of convection and the poor ventilation in the city which allow for increasing cloud formation and precipitation.

The potential extent of climatic differentiation in the direct centre of areas of urban concentration will now be demonstrated, using the Tiergarten, Berlin and its heavily built-up surroundings as an example. This can also serve to illustrate the interactions between areas with extremely different structures, which in turn points up possibilities for climate improvement.

The landscape park Tiergarten, situated in the inner city of Berlin, with an area of 212 ha, is distinguished by a dispersed tree structure and more or less large grassy areas. It is bordered to the west by the densely built-up district of Charlottenburg, to the north by the dense old city district of Moabit, to the south by the historical neighbourhood of Schöneberg and to the east by the inner city of East Berlin.

Of the climatological parameters measured in these studies, air temperature was considered to be of special significance, since this variable, in particular, reacts with great sensitivity to anthropogenic influences such as construction density and the degree of surface sealing. Figure 26.2 shows the local temperature distribution in the form of isotherms, as the result of a measurement tour that was carried out on 30 March 1978, in the late evening, from 9:55 p.m. until 12:25 a.m. The dispersed cloud cover and relatively low wind speed of 1.7 m s^{-1} resulted in a very stable weather situation, i.e. one with poor air circulation.

Heat radiation in the area of the Tiergarten produces a great temperature reduction in comparison to the built-up surroundings, which retain larger heat reserves due to their building mass. Temperature differences of as much as 7°C were measured between the inner area of the Tiergarten, on the one hand, and the neighbouring urban areas to the southwest and, in particular, Moabit and Wedding to the north, on the other. As shown by separate measurements in the winter months, these values can be exceeded at that time of year. The wide streets within the Tiergarten lead to a subdivision of the old islands into several smaller areas. The traffic junction at the Grosser Stern and the Hofjägerallee cause local temperature increases of almost 2°C.

The relatively great temperature decline in inner-city green areas during the night hours is due to the vegetation structure which allows for unimpeded heat radiation. Thus, in the warm summer months, the Tiergarten in its present size is of a bioclimatic significance that should not be underestimated. However, the temperatures of the air layers near the ground, which are quite low in comparison with the surroundings, further stabilize the atmosphere near the ground under weather conditions with poor air circulation. The inner area of the Tiergarten is, therefore, particularly subject to emission pollution. High air pollution values are to be expected by early afternoon, especially in the winter months, due to the high traffic levels that prevail during these hours.

The influence of construction density can also be seen if the readings of a weather station in the Tiergarten (Gartenbauamt) are compared with those of a station in a heavily built-up area of Charlottenburg (Fasanenstrasse). Figure 26.3 shows the hourly temperature values for 7 April, 1978. These values are the result of poor air circulation with westerly winds. Whereas in Charlotten-

Fig. 26.2. Horizontal temperature distribution at the inner-city area of Berlin (West) 30.3.1978 23^{30}h

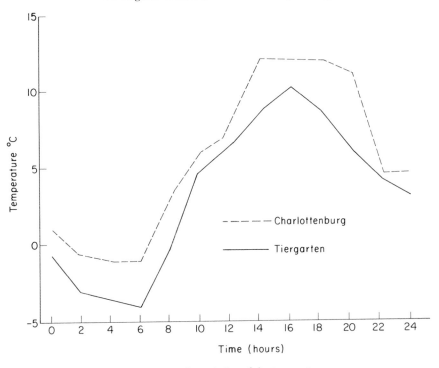

FIG. 26.3.   Daily variation of the temperature.

burg the values barely went below zero, a distinct decline below the freezing point is seen in the Tiergarten. The constant overheating of the heavily built-up district, particularly in the early evening hours, is quite evident.

In the course of temperature measurements in the Tiergarten, a more or less intensive interaction with the built-up surrounding areas was determined. Depending on the permeability of the surrounding construction, and whenever air circulation was not too weak, cooler air masses penetrated the overheated surrounding zones. However, the depth of penetration was greatly reduced with decreased air circulation.

Distinct horizontal gradients were also determined in connection with measurements of relative humidity corresponding to the dependence of the temperature on the construction density. In Figure 26.4 the distribution of relative humidity under poor air circulation conditions in the late evening hours of 2 June, 1978 is shown in the form of a surface diagram. Under prevailing southwest winds a very high relative humidity of almost 100% was recorded in the entire Tiergarten. The densely built-up areas of Schöneberg and Charlottenburg on the windward side appear to be much drier, with values of less than 75%. Southwesterly winds not only allow the dry air masses

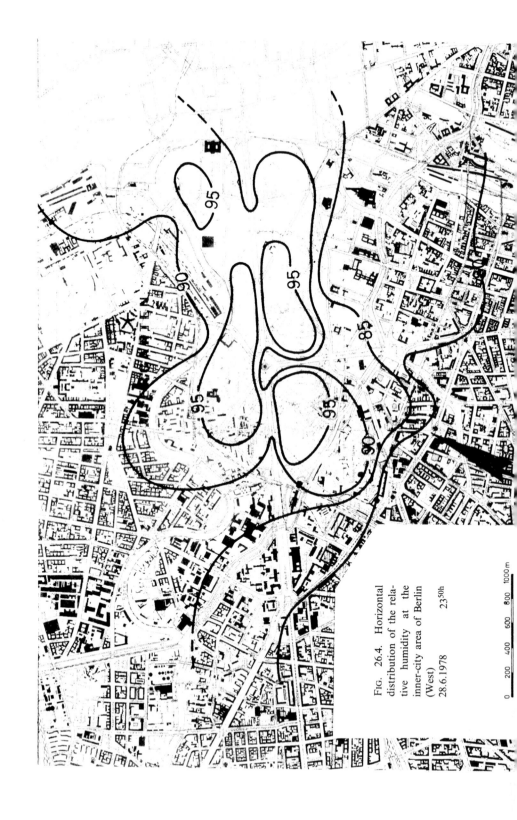

Fig. 26.4. Horizontal distribution of the relative humidity at the inner-city area of Berlin (West) 28.6.1978   23⁵⁰h

0   200   400   600   800   1000m

of the city to reach the fringes of the Tiergarten; they also permit them to be transported down the broad Hofjägerallee into the centre of the open areas of the park. Due to the definition of relative humidity the dependence that is seen here may be expected as a result of the great temperature differentiation in the area alone. On the other hand, vapour pressure (actual water vapour content of the atmosphere), which is of particular interest in this context, shows relatively little differentiation in the city areas. In general, however, at least during the day the actual water vapour of the air decreases with increasing surface sealing—even when good to moderate circulation conditions prevail.

In summary, the changes in air temperature, humidity and wind speed caused by a city climate can basically be correlated to the construction density, degree of sealing and the proportion of green areas in a particular city district. Altogether, seven surface types that are characteristic for the city area can be differentiated in the Tiergarten and its immediate and more distant surroundings:

Type 1, dense, inner city construction (mainly 4–6 storied block structure);
Type 2, dense, inner city construction with a limited amount of green areas (mainly city squares);
Type 3, mainly sealed or compacted areas with occasional construction (freight yards, harbour installations, trade and industrial areas, rubble-filled lands without vegetation);
Type 4, open construction type with high proportion of green areas (equal distribution of green areas and built-up areas, 3–4 storied row construction, in part block-edge construction with inner gardens);
Type 5, sealed surfaces in green areas (broad streets in parks and on the fringe of parks);
Type 6, green areas, mostly forest-covered (dense to disperse tree and shrub layer);
Type 7, mostly open green areas (large grass or fallow surfaces within parks or on the fringe of parks).

Figures 26.5 and 26.6 summarize the climate values recorded with the measuring vehicle in these seven groups, according to surface conditions and building structure. In the representation of air temperature, humidity, vapour pressure and wind speed, a qualitative differentiation according to the prevailing degree of air circulation was included.

With regard to air temperature Figure 26.5 may be interpreted as follows. A basic dependence of the temperature on the vegetation (e.g. forest), the degree of surface sealing (e.g. streets) and the particular construction density can be determined. These differences are, as can be expected, relatively slight under weather conditions with good air circulation. With increasing stability of the atmosphere near the ground the specific thermic structure of these areas becomes increasingly evident. Under conditions of poor air circulation an

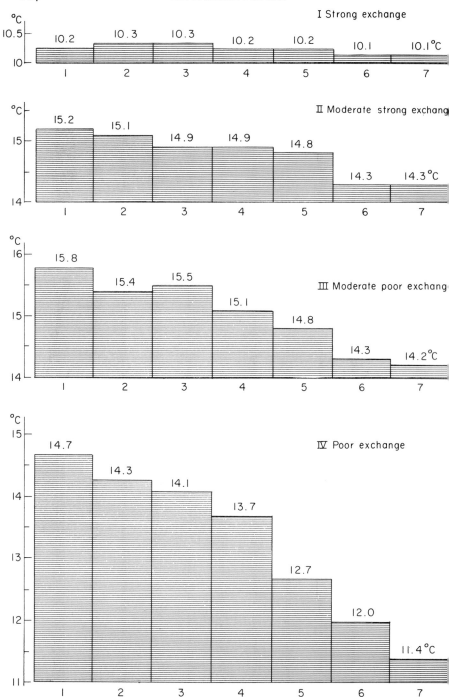

FIG. 26.5. Mean air temperature in °C in accordance with the weather situation (I–IV) and the relevant type of location (1–7).

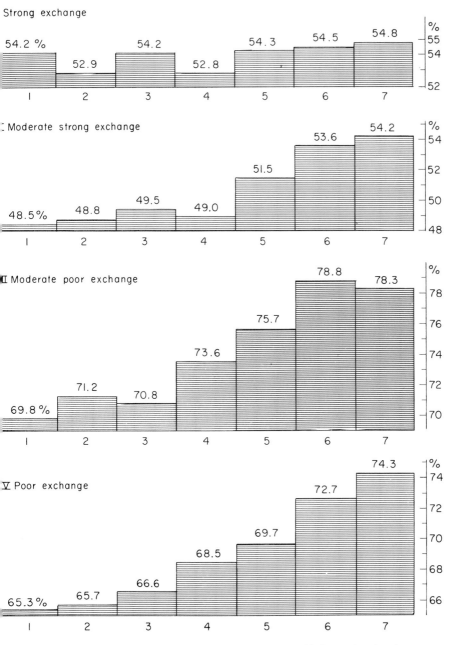

FIG. 26.6.   Mean relative humidity in percent in accordance with the weather situation
(I–IV) and the relevant type of location (1–7).

average temperature increase of 3.3°C in the built-up areas, as compared with the open spaces in the Tiergarten, was registered. As shown by individual studies overheating can reach much higher values in isolated areas. Residential areas with disperse construction, especially those with a high proportion of green areas, show much more favourable values.

In Figure 26.6 relative humidity, corresponding to the temperature, is shown in relation to the measurement site. Because of the definition of relative humidity the dependence on the characteristic surface type which is evident here was to be expected. A high density of construction and a high degree of sealing led to a large decline in humidity. In the case of vapour pressure a clear correlation to the particular surface type or to the prevailing weather conditions cannot be observed. Under moderate air circulation the water-vapour content of the air drops with an increase in the degree of sealing, as is to be expected. Under particularly stable weather conditions there is even a decrease in water-vapour content in the direction of open grass areas, probably caused by dew formation. In general, however, the differences between the individual surface types are very slight.

CITY SOILS

The natural function of soils as an environment for organisms, particularly root space for plants, is greatly limited in the cities. Here, soil serves chiefly as a base for buildings, industrial installations and streets and as a deposit for solid and liquid wastes (Blume *et al.* 1978). Thus, often only small areas remain for more natural uses in the form of parks, green strips along streets, garden plots and gardening businesses, athletic fields and cemeteries. On the other hand, the quality of life in a city depends decisively on these areas; only such natural soils make the development of green vegetation possible, which in turn guarantees stimulation, rest and good health. Furthermore, these soils serve as a filter for groundwater renewal, often a prerequisite for a sufficient supply of usable water for the city.

Even natural soils meet the demands made on them as plant habitats and water filter to quite varying degrees. They vary greatly in their penetrability for roots, water, heat, air and plant nutrient conditions, on the one hand, and in filter length (i.e., distance to groundwater) as well as filter quality (i.e., water permeability, absorption or degradation of pollutants), on the other. City soils are greatly modified with regard to these features, in particular to the first-mentioned group.

The use of groundwater generally lowers the water table, so that wet, poorly aerated soils which are cool in the spring have often become dry, well-aerated and warm environments. The construction of buildings and streets has led to compression and to mixing or covering of the soil with construction materials. The latter usually means a concentration of stones (in particular bricks and mortar pieces), alkalization with carbonates and nutrient enrichment, through discarded refuse. Since construction materials, after their use, and refuse remain for the most part in the city, the soils of inner city open areas are frequently composed, to a great extent, of such substrates (e.g. $\frac{1}{3}$ of the Tiergarten is composed of pararendzinas that have been formed in the past decades from a mixture of humus, valley soils and rubble).

In parks, overuse often leads to tread-compressed topsoil (which promotes air deficiency and water run-off after heavy rains), resulting in erosion of slopes. In many front yards and garden plots, loose, well-inhabited hortisols with a deep humus layer have been formed as a result of intensive care, i.e. frequent watering and fertilization.

Streets soils are often enriched by nutrients and made alkaline through refuse and construction materials and, at the same time, are subject to pollutants (especially lead) and de-icing salt. Furthermore, they are particularly compacted and, therefore, poorly aerated.

Specific changes can be found in connection with waste removal facilities; on and near refuse dumps, dump gases cause oxygen deficiencies over a period of decades and sometimes lead to toxic heavy-metal concentrations, as a result of reducing conditions.

VEGETATION AND FAUNA

With regard to the vegetation in the city landscape the following aspects will be discussed: trees in the settled areas; parks; gardens; inner-city waste lands; and roads, embankments and other road fringe areas.

There are more than 215,000 roadside trees in Berlin (West), but the total number of trees in gardens and parks in the settled areas is 10–15 times higher. Although the significance of gardens and parks with regard to climatic and air-hygienic effects has been recognized for a long time, very little is known about the woody plants of gardens, and only slightly more about those in parks.

Two types of settlements on otherwise open lands in Berlin (West) can be distinguished, i.e. forest settlements and park settlements. Forest settlements are chiefly characterized by the appearance of Scots pine, sand birch and European mountain ash. Park settlements contain valuable old stands of deciduous trees. Among the characteristic species are beech, box elder, sycamore, horse chestnut and oak.

The woody plant stands of many gardens are in danger of undergoing great changes in the future. Because of the space required and the leaf litter they cause, garden-owners today often avoid replanting long-lived, large-crowned deciduous trees. Instead, coniferous trees are favoured, although these suffer more from the urban climate than deciduous trees since they do not lose their leaves each year.

In terms of flora, Berlin (West) is divided into four zones (Table 26.1). Eight to eighteen bird species per km^2 breed in Zone 1; the number of species in Zone 2 is as many as 30. In Zones 3 and 4, 24 to 46 species per km^2 breed. Certain areas on the city's edge contain over 50 breeding species. Six to eight mammal species inhabit the heavily built-up city areas; in inner-city green areas 11 occur. The large Tiergarten park is the home of 22 mammal species.

The arrangement and use of parks is of significance for plant and animal life. Kunick (1978) studied the dependence of flora and vegetation on size, function, care and use intensity, as well as age and history of establishment, for 22 Berlin parks. In these parks, which differ in size and location in the city, the inventory of spontaneously occurring plants, i.e. those that in all probability were not intentionally cultivated on a particular site, was determined. It became evident that the absolute species number of large, intensively used parks was, on an average, twice as high as that of intensively used, smaller city parks. Some species groups occur almost only in large parks. These include, in particular, forest species, and also species typical of water and shore vegetation and of damp meadows and swamps. If they emerged from former hunting grounds of palace or estate parks or the like, these large inner-city parks also contain relics of relatively natural forest vegetation. They are often refuges for plant and animal species which have become rare in the rest of the city and which are in danger of becoming extinct. They can also function as dispersal centres for species which are just becoming established, as has been demonstrated for grass seed arrivals.

Green areas which reach far into the built-up zone represent, from a faunistic standpoint, refugees for bird species occurring otherwise only in forests in the surrounding areas. Furthermore, the typical mosaic-like structure of park and cemetery landscapes has produced a species composition which is characteristic for this type of landscape and unique in its combination. Even small (6 ha) inner-city cemeteries exhibit twice as many bird species (18) as their built-up surroundings.

More than 50 bird species are indigenous to the Pfaueninsel, Berlin's most beautiful and varied park with remnants of natural wilderness. This great number of species is significantly higher than that found in a comparable area in any Berlin forest. The specific species combination found here can hardly be matched by any other region of the middle-European cultivated landscape.

Waste land (ruderal areas) is colonized by new types of plant communities, which signify a new environment created by man. This vegetation also results in a specific fauna.

Rubble sites took up great areas of land after the destruction of the last war. Most soils of inner-city waste lands are thus composed of rubble layers which can reach several meters in depth. In the meantime, habitats with special features and special vegetation and fauna have developed on this anthropogenic material. On the carbonate-containing and dry ruderal sites, which predominate in the inner-city, colonizers such as Robinia, Tree of Heaven, Traveller's Joy (Clematis) and Butterfly Bush are to be found. Even with little vegetation cover the fallow chat, skylark and the tawny pipit breed here; so also, with progressing succession, do various species of *Sylvia* and the icterine warbler. On fresh-to-moist rubble sites, in contrast, indigenous woody plants such as the Norway Maple, Wych Elm or Elder dominate the scene. Under natural conditions these are typical components of deciduous forests rich in species and nutrients. Fruit trees often grow here, and the whitethroat, lesser whitethroat and willow warbler can be observed.

The species diversity of inner-city vacant lands is surprisingly high. For example, a block of land on Lützowplatz in Berlin-Tiergarten harbours 164 flowering plants and at least 250 arthropod species, of which the beetles alone make up 50 species and the flies another 50. Further studies may reveal that the species count is twice as high. The maintained lawns and shrubs of the adjacent Grosser Tiergarten contain only a quarter of these insects on a comparable area of land.

Whereas the area taken up by transportation routes is usually extremely unfavourable for vegetation, hard-to-reach remnant open areas often remain after the construction of streets, railroads and canals; for endangered species these remnant plots represent important retreat and dispersal centres. In Berlin approximately 400 species, i.e. 40% of the ferns and flowering plants of the city, grow on roadside verges.

The value of these sites and of their plant life can be illustrated by an example. The cross-breeding of a winter-resistant form of Bermuda-grass (*Cynodon dactylon* (L.) Pers.) from a Berlin roadside site has led to a new variety of Tifton 44, a cultivated plant of great economic importance. As a result of this cross-breeding it has been possible since 1978 to cultivate this plant much farther north than was previously possible (Sukopp *et al.* 1980).

CONSEQUENCES OF CLIMATE, SOIL AND VEGETATION STUDIES FOR URBAN PLANNING

The results of these and other studies carried out in Berlin can be applied to a certain extent to other urban areas. With respect to urban climates the following results are considered to be well founded:

—A decrease in temperature can be observed in inner-city open areas under all types of weather conditions. When stable air stratification prevails the temperature differences in comparison with the heavily built-up surroundings are rather large, particularly in the evening and night hours. The degree of temperature difference depends on the size of the site and on its vegetation structure.

—The danger of damage due to early and late frosts increases particularly for larger inner-city open areas that lack tree and shrub cover.

—An increase in relative humidity, corresponding to the recorded temperature values, has been determined for such sites. The increase in absolute humidity is, however, relatively low. In heat-radiating nights with poor air circulation, dew formation on the vegetation often extracts water vapour from the air layers near the ground.

—Windspeed is greatly reduced in green areas and parks. This effect is particularly noticeable under poor air circulation conditions, since the cold air masses near the ground result in a further stabilization of air stratification.

—Inner-city green areas are subject to quite high levels of pollution, and their establishment in areas with such emissions (e.g. streets and parking lots) should definitely be avoided. The interactions between green areas and their built-up surroundings depend not only on the prevailing wind and circulation conditions, but also on the size of the park and the density or permeability of the surrounding construction.

—Suitable air circulation corridors can effectively support climatic and air-hygienic interactions. Broad streets are, however, not ideal for this purpose. The high degree of surface sealing leads to overheating, and motor-vehicle traffic results in high air-pollution-emission concentrations in the transported air masses.

Taking these factors into account the following demands should be made, as far as the future development of the Tiergarten and its immediate surroundings are concerned, from the standpoint of climate and air hygiene:

The vegetation structure of the Tiergarten should be maintained in its present form, since the open lawns promote the production of cold air near the ground and its transport to the surrounding areas. Furthermore, the well-aerated tree and shrub patches are highly effective with respect to the deposition of air pollutants.

The high emission values caused by motor-vehicle traffic must be reduced if possible, in order to counteract a progressive restriction of the climatic and air-hygienic effectiveness of the Tiergarten. The planned Autobahn (expressway) through the Tiergarten, with a projected traffic load of 110,000 vehicles per day, would result in the exceeding of a number of critical environmental parameters (Horbert & Kirchgeorg 1980). Underground Autobahn construction, on the other hand, could significantly improve the present situation.

The existing transition area between the Tiergarten and its built-up surroundings must remain intact, if at all possible. If an expansion of the Tiergarten is not possible from the standpoint of urban planning, then the goal must be a disperse construction structure which is wind-permeable in the direction of the Tiergarten. Figure 26.7 illustrates how such demands can be taken into consideration in connection with future planning. The areas which are most stressed and those which are least endangered, as well as those areas which are essential for interaction between the two, are marked as such, along with their respective functions.

In urban areas the natural soil differences, together with the changes caused by a variety of uses, result in an extremely great variety of soil features and, therefore, in a wide spectrum of those features which are of importance for environmental and filter functions. This means that more demands are made on responsible city planners, who must reconcile the needs for residential, transportation, industrial and recreational sites, and must further-more guarantee a high level of clean groundwater. Exact knowledge of soil conditions, obtainable only from detailed mapping, is essential, but only rarely available. Using examples based on the situation in Berlin consequences for urban planning are as follows:

1. Exact information about the conditions on a particular site enables landscape offices, forest officials and garden-owners to choose suitable useful and ornamental plants (this is of particular importance for plantings on land-filled refuse dumps).
2. In larger parks and local recreational areas it may be profitable to minimize water use by choosing suitable plant types and plant densities, in order to secure a high groundwater yield.
3. The shores of lakes and streams are to be protected from soil eroson, since only well-colonized soils with a deep humus layer allow for an optimal purification of shore filtrates that renew the groundwater. This means curtailment of recreational use of water and an end to waste disposal, which leads to eutrophication.
4. The intensity of recreational use of parks should be directed in such a way that structurally unstable, erosion- or slide-prone slopes, are rarely fre-quented. Only then can soil life effectively combat tread-compression. Wherever necessary, heavily acidic sites (because of precipitation) should be limed in order to promote soil life (and improve the filter efficiency of the soil at the same time).
5. The use of de-icing salt in winter and the choice of roadside tree species should take into consideration whether the salt will be present in the root zone for a long period of time (depending on the soil and precipitation conditions) or will have left the main root zone of the trees before the beginning of the vegetation period.
6. Areas of intensive recreational use in parks (e.g. playgrounds) should be selected in such a way that the soils do not become waterlogged and that they allow the planting of durable grass varieties that are easy to care for and require little watering in dry periods.

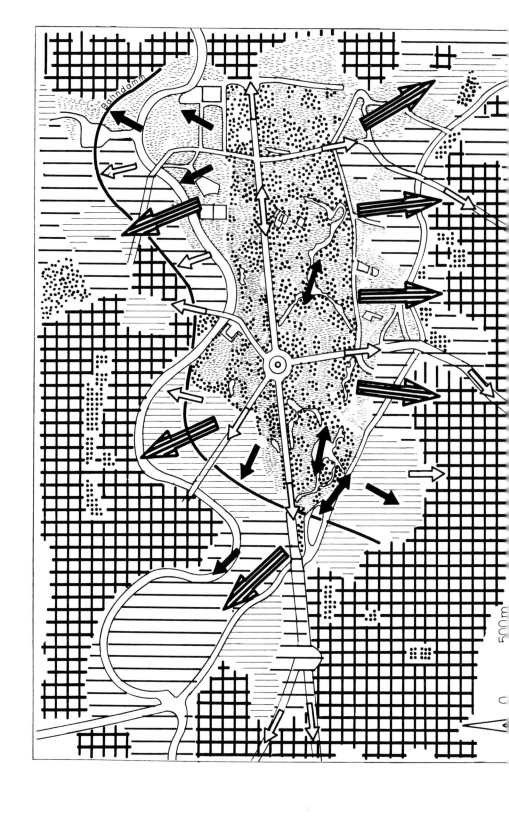

FIG. 26.7. Areas subject to climatic and air-hygienic stress and consequences for future planning

Stressed areas

Dense construction, poor air circulation, most subject to bioclimatic and air-hygienic stress (area type 1)

Avoidance of dense build-up in the surrounding areas, of street and railroad embankments, promotion of air circulation by open areas and opening of housing blocks

Disperse construction, high proportion of vegetation, moderate air circulation, moderately affected by emissions (depending on use of adjacent areas), bioclimatically less affected (area type 2)

Avoidance of further sealing and construction, establishment of air circulation pathways between parks and built-up areas

Mostly sealed surfaces, small proportion of vegetation, good air circulation, depending on use moderately to highly affected by emissions, bioclimatically stressed (area type 3)

Increase in the proportion of vegetation, establishment of air circulation pathways between parks and built-up areas

Less-stressed areas

Small green areas, reduce bioclimatic stress, but without far-reaching effects, affected by emissions (area type 2)

Open grass areas or mostly low vegetation, production of cold air, moderate to high air circulation, greatly affected by emissions, deposition of pollutants, reduced bioclimatic stress (area type 7)

Maintain climatic advantages with disperse vegetation structure and larger grass areas, avoidance of soil compression and sealing, no uses which lead to emissions

Mostly tree and shrub layer, reduce bioclimatic and air hygienic stress, greatly affected by emissions, protective climate (area type 6)

Water surfaces, reduced bioclimatic stress, moderate to high air circulation

Maintenance as air circulation pathways

Areas which promote circulation

Air circulation pathways (streets) between built-up and green areas, however with additional thermic and air-hygienic stress

Establishment of roadside vegetation belts for pollutant deposit and climate improvement

Air circulation pathways (lawns, water surfaces), most favourable form of air circulation within green areas or between green areas and built-up surroundings

Promotion of air circulation, avoidance of further construction built-up, dispersal of fringe construction, avoidance of emissions

additional air circulation pathways that are required

7. Waste deposit sites, in particular those for special refuse, should be chosen according to ecological criteria.

8. Plant litter and organic refuse should be composted for the purpose of recycling and improving soil life (which in turn promotes filtration and plant growth). Compost from roadside tree litter and other more contaminated refuse should, however, only be deposited on soils with a high absorption and filter capacity.

With regard to vegetation the following aspects must be taken into account:

1. In all parks, certain areas should remain uncared for, so that a forest-like vegetation with much undergrowth and a layer of herbaceous plants can emerge.

2. Meadows are, as landscapes, no less appealing than lawns, but are biologically much more valuable. For this reason the transformation of lawns into meadows should be undertaken.

3. Many park lakes are unfortunately totally paved with stone, so that a reed belt cannot develop. However, even shores without stabilization systems have at best only fragmentary reed patches. Floating and submerged plants are usually also missing. As a result of this the zoological interest is also limited, unless one considers the hordes of semi-domesticated mallard ducks and black-headed gulls to be a positive feature. This is, however, not possible, since their overpopulation leads to over-eutrophication, which limits or even destroys many other species. Park waters should, therefore, definitely be provided with reed belts and floating plants (through planting or by making spontaneous colonization possible). Moreover, a great reduction of the mallard and black-headed gull populations is needed, at least in a few selected waters.

As the examples have shown, city and nature are not contrary terms. The retreat of the biotic communities does not lead to a destruction of nature, but rather to its transformation. A variety of plants and animals is capable of living in the direct proximity of city dwellers. It is the goal of nature conservation to maintain these organisms for cultural, social, hygienic and ecological reasons. To this end, biotopes in settled areas, which are often small in size, must be systematically surveyed. The ecological conditions under which organisms exist there must be clarified. From this information, possibilities for the maintenance and care of such biotopes and concepts for planting vegetation in newly established green areas on similar sites can be developed.

A fundamental demand is to give space for vegetation to develop spontaneously, and for the fauna that accompanies it, wherever intensive management or sealing of surface area is not essential. In this manner the graduated, side-by-side existence of different vegetation formations can emerge, for example lawn–meadow–tall herbs–shrubs–forest stands, which provide an environment for a variety of organisms. Only those woody plants which achieve optimal growth under the climate and soil conditions prevailing here should be selected.

On the basis of these prerequisites it should be possible to achieve or create a varied environment that is adapted to urban living conditions, so that direct experiences with natural elements in the environment will become a part of daily life for city dwellers.

The basic concept of these suggestions for future use of the environment is one of moderate intensity. In the long run this concept can better guarantee ecological stability of the area than the establishment of areas with very intensive use (e.g. very intensive recreational use of open spaces in residential areas), which results in damaging effects on the ecological balance.

REFERENCES

Blume H.P., Horbert M., Horn R. & Sukopp H. (1978) Zur Ökologie der Grossstadt unter besonderer Berücksichtigung von Berlin (West). In *Verdichtungsgebiete und ihr Umland*. Deutscher Rat für Landespflege, **30**, 658–677.

Horbert M. (1978) Klimatische und Lufthygienische Aspekte der Stadt- und Landschafts-planung. *In Natur und Heimat*, **38**, 34–49.

Horbert M. & Kirchgeorg A. (1980) Klimatische und lufthygienische Aspekte zur Planung innerstädtischer Freiräume, dargestellt am Beispiel des Grossen Tiergartens in Berlin West. In *Stadtbauwelt*, Berlin, pp. 270–276.

Kunick W. (1978) Flora und Vegetation städtischer Parkanlagen. *Acta Botanica Slovaca Academia Scientia Slovacae A.* **3**, 455–461.

Sukopp H., Blume H.P. & Kunick W. (1979) The soil, flora and vegetation of Berlin's wastelands. In *Nature in Cities* (Ed. by Jan C. Laurie). Wiley, Chichester & New York.

Sukopp H., Elvers H., Runge M. & Schneider C. (1980) *Naturschutz in der Grossstadt*, Berlin.

27. THE ASSESSMENT OF URBAN DEVELOPMENT EFFECTS ON A TIDAL ECOSYSTEM

L. C. BRAAT AND S. W. F. VAN DER PLOEG
Institute for Environmental Studies,
Free University, Amsterdam,
The Netherlands

SUMMARY

The ecological submodel of an integrated environmental model for regional planning purposes is described. It is applied to an urban development plan by which a tidal ecosystem is turned into a partly urbanized lake.

Closing the estuary leads to desalinization and to an increase of phosphate concentration. Primary production will increase, marine and brackish species disappear and freshwater species and terrestrial plants appear after 10–15 years. Surface area and volume of the lake decrease as a result of the urban development. An additional increase of phosphate and chlorophyll concentrations is expected. Information content and regulating potential of the system decrease. Recreational use is enhanced. Increase of recreational activities leads to an extra increase of phosphate and chlorophyll levels, to a decrease of the surface area of littoral vegetation and to disturbance of vegetation and fauna community development.

INTRODUCTION

Urban planning is still often based on socio-economic objectives only. This frequently results in a complete destruction of the natural environment on the site to be developed. In recent years, however, more emphasis is being laid on a careful multidisciplinary planning of such developments, including recognition of ecological aspects of the site. In the Netherlands the National Physical Planning Agency is promoting such multidisciplinary planning.

A major problem in this approach is the incompatibility of socio-economic and ecological viewpoints. Therefore, the use of (international) standards for pollutants, surface area, energy flows, etc., might be advocated. This, however, inevitably includes a separate analysis of social and ecological features, respectively.

The model presented here aims to describe and forecast the most important effects of regional planning (see Arntzen *et al.* 1979; Arntzen & Braat 1980). The central problem is the coupling of economic, demographic, geographical and ecological structures and processes in such a way that effects of a specific plan can be traced throughout the whole system. This paper only deals with the ecological modelling of effects of urban developments on a tidal ecosystem.

MODEL REQUIREMENTS

Multidisciplinary modelling induces specific problems apart from the 'normal' problems in modelling. Consistency of such models can be realized by coupling variables per discipline into submodels which should be linked subsequently. Interactions between the submodels can be expressed in two ways:

1. *Dose–effect relationships.* However useful in a monodisciplinary model, dose–effect relationships between variables of different disciplines are hard to assess. In the present model this is tried by comparing parallel developments in different submodels.

2. *Feedback mechanisms.* These are often inverted dose–effect relationships, in which case they can be used as described above. Another type of feedback can be developed by including a decision step. Results of one run of the model can be evaluated by policy-makers whose choices can be fed back into the model.

Consistency in the approach of time and space is also required. As regards time, within our model all submodels are to simulate changes on a yearly basis for a period of 15 years (1980–95). For spatial interactions between submodels a separate *intermediate* has been developed, consisting of an aggregate of procedures, formulas and data sets (e.g. maps). In this submodel surface area, location and distance are described.

Finally, as regards the selection of variables for the ecological submodel, four criteria are most relevant:

1. Variables must be measurable within the space and time limits of the model;
2. Variables must pertain to important aspects of the functioning of the system;
3. Variables must reflect related changes in the other submodels;
4. Variables and their output levels must be, at least partly, understandable to the decision-maker.

THE URBAN DEVELOPMENT PLAN

The model is being constructed for an urban development in the south-western part of the Netherlands. The eastern part of the Oosterchelde estuary (surface area 2,100 ha) is to be enclosed in accordance with the Delta act. Cut off from salt water and tide, this area—called Markizaat lake—will ultimately desalinate. Three alternative developments of the future lake ecosystem are being considered:

1. A nature reserve with a fluctuating water level (surface area of the lake 1,050 ha, volume 13×10^6 m³);
2. A nature reserve with a fixed water level (1,050 ha; 13×10^6 m³);
3. A partially urbanized system consisting of the remainder of the lake (850 ha; 11×10^6 m³), a polder (300 ha) in which 10,000 houses are to be built and an urban lake (100 ha).

The former tidal flats around the lake, 1,090 ha in 1 and 2, 870 ha in 3, are included in the development plans.

The third alternative in particular will induce many socio-economic changes in the region which are being analysed in the demographic, economic and 'facilities' submodels. These analyses will not be discussed here; the results, however, constitute an important input for the ecological submodel.

METHODS OF ANALYSIS

The effects of the urban development plan are analysed in two ways. First, the direct effects of the urbanization are considered. Second, subsequent effects of increasing recreational activity are described. This second way in particular requires an integrated multidisciplinary approach, analysing demand for recreational facilities, related socio-economic activities and feedbacks from the ecosystem to recreationists ('attractivity'). Since these aspects of the plan have only partially been analysed yet, only some prominent effects are indicated in this paper.

The procedure used in analysing the effects of the plan is shown in Figure 27.1. In the *preliminary analysis* of the system, variables are chosen according to the criteria mentioned above and relationships between them are defined in either mathematical equations or qualitative descriptions.

Chloride and phosphate levels have been selected as abiotic water quality parameters, with regard to the desalinization and the primary production, respectively. A water balance equation and an equation for simulation of concentrations of chloride and phosphate have been developed. The following equation has been used:

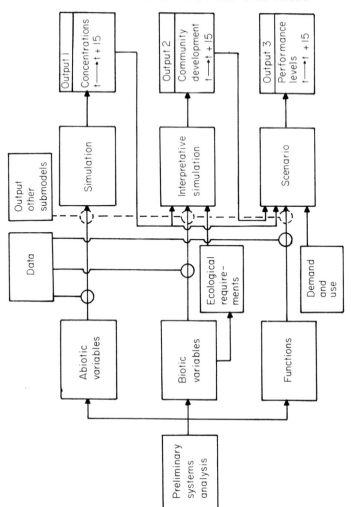

Fig. 27.1.　Procedure of the analysis.

$$c_t = \frac{c_{1,t-1} \cdot v_1 + \sum\limits_{i=1}^{n} c_{i,t-1} \cdot v_i}{v_1 + \sum\limits_{i=1}^{n} v_i}$$

in which c = concentration, i = input flows, v = volume and l = lake.

Complete mixing and a fixed volume of the lake are assumed. During desalinization chloride levels of some input flows decrease with decreasing chloride concentration in the lake. This effect is simulated by multiplying those inputs with a factor $c_{1,t}/c_{1,t-1}$

Biotic variables include abundance, primary production and species numbers of phytoplankton (see Bakker & Vegter 1978). Chlorophyll concentrations have been derived from phosphate level estimates (see De Jong *et al.* 1980). Surface areas of macrophyte vegetation zones in and along the lake are selected for the effects of polder construction and recreation.

Relationships between natural environments and society can be described in terms of functions which may be performed by the natural environment for society (see Braat *et al.* 1979). In this model changes and differences in the actual performance levels of these functions of the Markizaat lake are used as a third type of parameter indicating the effects of the urban development plan. These performance levels are to be estimated from the potential supply of means by the system and the potential demand from society. Supply can be estimated from the values of the various system variables. Demand is partly analysed in the economic and geographical submodels, and partly deduced from literature.

OUTPUT OF THE MODEL

Output 1, abiotic variables

The output of the simulations of chloride and phosphate concentrations is shown in Figure 27.2. In this stage of model development the graphs should be viewed as illustrations of the output only.

Recreational activity is not expected to influence the desalinization process. The phosphate input to the lake, however, is expected to increase with 5% at low recreation intensity (2,000 people/day for 3 summer months) and with 15% at high recreation intensity (7,000 people/day for 3 months), resulting in an increase of the phosphate level in the lake of 7% and 18%, respectively.

Output 2, biotic variables

The phosphate levels used by De Jong *et al.* (1980) in estimating chlorophyll

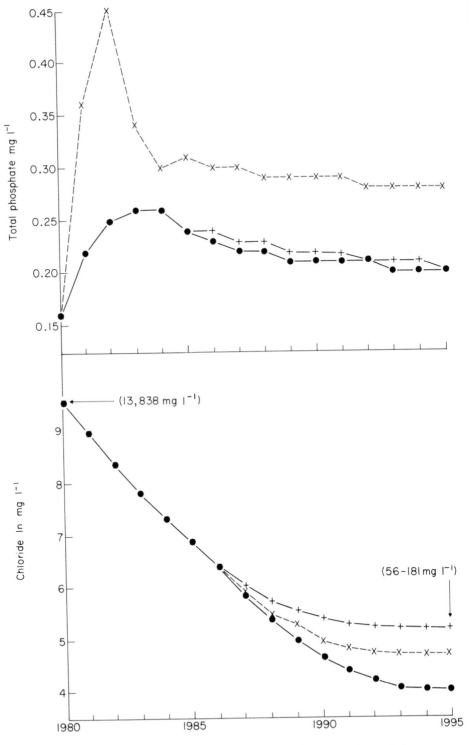

FIG. 27.2. Concentrations of chloride and phosphate in three development alternatives over a period of 15 years. ●——● = Nature reserve with fluctuating water level, +——+ = Nature reserve with fixed water level, ×——× = Urban development in the lake.

concentrations are 30–50% lower than the levels calculated in this study. This leads to expected chlorophyll concentrations of 20–30 mg m^{-3} in the nature reserve situation, and 27–45 mg m^{-3} in the urban development alternative, after 15 years.

The effects of desalinization are estimated by interpretation of data on plankton of two closed estuaries (10‰ and 16‰ chloride) and the Oosterschelde estuary (23‰ chloride) in Bakker and Vegter (1978). The Markizaat lake situation falls within the lower end of this salinity range in the first few years (1980–82) only. The abundance of marine phytoplankton cells in the Markizaat lake is thus expected to drop sharply after 1980, until extinction, while some brackish species may then show a short outburst, due to fading competition from marine species and lack of freshwater species. The latter will appear between 1985 and 1990 when the chloride concentration will have declined below 1‰.

Based on height above sea level, on former exposure to estuarine water and on water level of the lake, four macrophyte vegetation zones are expected to develop (see e.g. De Jong & De Kogel 1979; De Jong *et al.* 1980). The elevated parts of the shore will be covered by a brushwood of willows and alders. Around the waterline the halophile vegetation will be replaced by a vegetation dominated by *Phragmites australis* (Cav.) Trin. ex. Steud and *Typha angustifolia* L. After desalinization floating and submergent aquatic plants will invade the lake. The direct effect of polder construction will be a decrease in surface area for vegetation development. The urban development will cover about 20% of the enclosed area. About 25% of potential woodland and wet forest, 34% of the littoral vegetation and 10% of the floating and submerged aquatic plants will be lost.

The effects of water-based recreation include a decrease of primary production (via increase of turbulence), disturbance of aquatic and littoral vegetation development and of macrofauna (e.g. foraging and breeding waterfowl). Recreation along the shore causes a decrease in surface area of vegetation zones by constructing recreational facilities and by trampling. Presence of people and noise disturb the animals and, thereby, possibly cause their disappearance.

Output 3, functions of the system

A list of potential functions of natural systems (see Braat *et al.* 1979) has been checked with actual or potential performance of functions by the estuarine and future lake ecosystem. This procedure results in a provisional list of functions presented in Table 27.1. For most functions it is not yet possible to indicate changes quantitatively.

The functions which are important in economic life (Nos 1–6) are expected to have a higher performance level in the urban development alternative. The

Table 27.1   *Functions of the alternative Markizaat ecosystems.*

	Performance levels			Changes compared to A	
	A	B	C	B	C
1. Supply of fresh water	O	●●	●	+ +	+
2. Supply of sand	p	p	●	×	+
3. Commercial fisheries	●	O	O	−	−
4. Water control structure		●	●	+	+
5. Absorption of effluents	●●	●	●	−	−
6. Recreation on water and shores	●	●	●●●	×	+ +
7. Amenity as to wildlife	●	●●●	●●	+ +	+
8. Information from indicators	●●●	●●●	●	×	−
9. Research and education functions	●●●	●●●	●	×	−
10. Biological purification	●●●	●●	●	−	−
11. Stabilization (water retention and upland groundwater level)	O	●●	●	+ +	+

A = estuarine system, B = nature reserve lake, C = urbanized lake, O = not performed, p = potential performance, ● = low performance, ●● = medium performance, ●●● = high performance − = decrease, × = equal, + = increase, + + = large increase.

economically non-tangible functions (Nos 7–11) will generally lose importance if the lake is to be urbanized.

DISCUSSION

Nitrogen compounds and toxic substances will be added, as abiotic variables, as they may considerably affect structure and function of the lake ecosystem. Analysis of air pollution (data availability permitting), run via the intermediate submodel, will also reveal limits to possible community development. Chloride and phosphate concentrations largely determine the occurrence of species and the primary production. Therefore these concentrations, together with abundance and species numbers of organisms, are considered to be both consistent and representative variables.

The model is being built to fit existing data. As these are usually incomplete, the reliability of the output will necessarily be low, particularly when estimates, extrapolations and interpretations have to be done. However, the use of relatively simple key variables enables coupling of the submodels in such a way that the results are meaningful to decision-making processes. Examples are: the prediction over time of the effects of urban development and, subsequently, of increasing recreation pressure; suggestions for management as regards phosphate inputs and recreation control; the prediction of changes in function performance levels. The model only shows the results of different alternatives; the policymaker has to take the subjective decisions.

Finally, this paper only deals with a part of the regional analysis. Therefore, feedbacks and subsequent effects are scarce, outdoor recreation being a good example. The complete analysis will also deal with effects of air pollution and groundwater extraction. The model as a whole will show effects of the urban development plan in terms of changes in industrial productivity, employment rates, facilities infrastructure, etc., as well.

ACKNOWLEDGEMENTS

The authors acknowledge critical comments of their colleagues. The research is being funded by the National Physical Planning Agency of the Netherlands. We are indebted to Ms B.L.A. Jessurun for typing the manuscript.

REFERENCES

Arntzen J.W. & Braat L.C. (1980) *An Integrated Environmental Model for Regional Policy Analysis.* Paper submitted to the International Conference on Cybernetics and Society. Boston, October 1980.

Arntzen J.W., Braat L.C., Hordijk L. & Ploeg S.W.F. van der (1979) *Geïntegreerd MilieuModel, een theoretisch kader voor het toetsen van ruimtelijke plannen.* Instituut voor Milieuvraagstukken, publication 79/5. Amsterdam.

Bakker C. & Vegter F. (1978) General tendencies of phyto- and zooplankton development in two closed estuaries (Lake Veere and Lake Grevelingen) in relation to an open estuary (Eastern Scheldt). *Hydrobiological Bulletin,* **12**, 226–245.

Braat L.C., Ploeg S.W.F. van der & Bouma F. (1979) *Functions of the Natural Environment, an economic-ecological analysis.* Institute for Environmental Studies, publication 79/9. Amsterdam.

Jong D.J. de, Baaijens G.J., Bannink B.A. & Visser J. (1980) *Een afgesloten Markizaat van Bergen op Zoom.* Nota Deltadienst, Milieu en Inrichting, 80-08 Middelburg.

Jong D.J. de & Kogel T.J. de (1979) *Vegetatie-ontwikkeling op de slikken van Flakkee (1972–1978).* Nota Deltadienst, Milieu & Inrichting, 79–11 Middelburg.

28. APPLICATION OF PHYTOSOCIOLOGICAL MAPS TO URBAN PLANNING, WITH REFERENCE TO TWO SMALL TOWNS IN CENTRAL POLAND

ROMUALD OLACZEK
Institute of Environmental Biology,
University of Łódź, Poland

SUMMARY

Phytosociological maps are able to provide an input of ecological information into urban planning. The method of devising maps for urban planning is described, and the use of these in practice is discussed.

INTRODUCTION

The results presented here have been obtained at the instigation of the Country Planning Office in order to provide an ecological basis for the spatial development of certain towns (20–35,000 inhabitants) surrounded by agricultural land and forest, which are expected to expand rapidly in size. The discussion here is limited to two towns, Łowicz and Sieradz, for which the phytosociological maps have already been used by planners.

Łowicz (22,000 inhabitants), situated on a lowland plain beside the Bzura river, was formerly surrounded by swamps, but these have been drained and converted to meadows, fields and orchards. The town was founded before the eleventh century A.D., and the main period of growth was in the sixteenth century. The old town centre is in a good state of preservation, and contains Renaissance, Baroque and Classical architecture. The town will increase to 35,000 inhabitants. Its main industries are service, culture, tourism and food.

Sieradz (20,000 inhabitants) is an old town on an elevated plain, near the Warta river. A few Gothic, Renaissance and Baroque buildings are preserved. This town will increase quickly to 50,000 inhabitants, with expansion into the surrounding countryside.

METHODS

Ecologically homogeneous areas were recognized by observation of plant communities. The method used is based on Tüxen's (1956) concept of

the present time to find ways in which they may be treated at low cost to provide at least temporary, if not permanent, open space for the public. Inevitably, these sorts of areas do not attract much financial support. It is, therefore, important that any solution is as inexpensive as possible.

The obvious and commonly used solution is a vegetation cover which may consist of (a) grassland, (b) shrubs, (c) trees and (d) flower beds. For simplicity it may only consist of grass and trees. However, these sites might appear to be a very dificult environment for plants. It is the purpose of this paper to examine what are the restrictions to plant growth in urban derelict land and to suggest how they can be overcome.

THE NATURE OF THE ENVIRONMENT

Although urban climates as a whole may be different from rural climates, there is nothing particularly unusual about the climates of urban derelict areas. The special characteristics of their environment all relate to the soil. In most areas the original land surface will have been built over and the soil removed or buried. What is left after clearance is usually a wasteland of brick, stone, cement rubble and mortar from old buildings. Bricks, since they are made of clay, are likely to have high levels of potassium, magnesium and phosphorus; cement rubble and mortar will have high levels of calcium and magnesium; the mineral content of stone will be variable. There will normally be no nitrogen, except that derived from atmospheric deposition which can be relatively high in urban areas due to pollution—between 10 and 30 kg ha^{-1}. Chemical analyses of 'soils' in urban clearance areas reveal their curious composition—they are deficient only in nitrogen (Table 29.1).

Their physical characteristics are dominated by their raw mineral state, lack of organic matter and lack of structure. As a result they have a low pore space and a high bulk density (Table 29.2). Even after cultivation the surface consolidates rapidly and root growth may be impeded, although once plants are established they should be able to penetrate the underlying material with ease.

Nevertheless, the material appears to be by no means as hostile to plant

TABLE 29.1. *Chemical characteristics of soils in urban clearance areas compared with a garden soil (Bradshaw & Chadwick 1980).*

Site	pH	N (total %)	P	K	Ca
			(available μg g^{-1})		
Grove Street	7.2	0.05	36	220	3830
Tennyson Street	6.7	0.08	65	450	1070
Brunswick Road	7.0	0.05	19	290	8830
Garden soil	6.3	0.14	61	140	1030

TABLE 29.2. *Physical characteristics of eleven soils in urban clearance areas compared with a garden soil (data of J. Taylor).*

	Bulk density g cm^{-3}	Particle density g cm^{-3}	Pore space %
Mean	1.54	2.51	41.0
(Standard deviation)	(0.27)	(0.44)	(18.4)
Garden soil	1.11	2.33	52.5

growth as most derelict land materials. This is borne out by the readiness with which various weedy species, such as *Poa annua* L., *Hordeum murinum* L., *Senecio squalidus* L. and *Artemisia vulgaris* L., colonize. For successful plant establishment, cultivation should relieve the physical problems and high nitrogen fertilizer the nutrient problems. The nitrogen requirement may be large, bearing in mind that the nitrogen store in a normal soil/plant ecosystem is considerable. Recent work on derelict land (Dancer *et al.* 1977a; Roberts *et al.* 1981) has suggested that a minimum of 1,000 kg N ha^{-1} is necessary in the soil to provide an adequate supply of mineral nitrogen for plant uptake. A nitrogen content of .05% in a 20-cm rooting zone is equivalent to 1,000 kg N ha^{-1} so the nitrogen values in Table 29.1 look scarcely adequate.

EXPERIMENTAL ANALYSIS

Grass nutrition

A series of simple greenhouse and field experiments involving the application of various fertilizers to the soils from different urban clearance sites showed that the addition of fertilizer is all that is required to obtain good grass growth. This confirms the conclusions from the analytical evidence. There appears to be little variation in response between sites, at least between material from different areas in Liverpool (Table 29.3). As a result, grass swards have been

TABLE 29.3. *Dry weight yield (kg ha^{-1} including roots) of* Lolium perenne *and* Trifolium repens *on soils from six urban sites treated with 500 kg ha^{-1} of 17:17:17 (N, P_2O_5, K_2O) fertilizer in a pot experiment after 12 weeks (data of A.R. Garman).*

	Unfertilized	Fertilized
Upper Parliament Street	62.3	233.2
Garmoyle Road	102.1	303.6
Dansie Street	82.8	135.8
Park Street	92.2	196.3
Smithdown Road 1	96.0	167.5
Smithdown Road 2	102.6	283.0
Mean	89.7	219.9

established successfully on a wide range of sites by direct seeding in the wastes after surface cultivation and the application of fertilizer. Approximately 100 kg ha^{-1} of seed of a standard amenity grass mixture containing *Lolium perenne* L. and 500 kg ha^{-1} of 17:17:17 ($N:K_2O:P_2O_5$) complete fertilizer—equivalent to 85 kg N, 37 kg P, 70 kg K ha^{-1}—have been used (Bradshaw & Handley 1972).

However, although the grass has grown well for most of the first season and begun to form a closed sward, before closure is complete—about 75% cover determined by point quadrat—the rate of growth has decreased considerably in nearly all cases, and the grass has become yellowish green. This could be due to many causes but the symptoms suggest a nutrient deficiency. A series of aftercare experiments were, therefore, carried out on a number of sites in which N, P and K were applied in a factorial manner. These show conclusively that the cause of slow growth is nitrogen deficiency (Bloomfield *et al.* 1982) (Fig. 29.1).

We must, therefore, conclude that although other nutrient deficiencies can be overcome by the addition of fertilizer, the deficiency of nitrogen cannot. Although sufficient nitrogen is present at the outset, and is contributed from atmospheric sources to allow a scattered weed population to establish, there is obviously an insufficient store of nitrogen in the soil, even after the application of a further 85 kg ha^{-1}, to ensure an adequate supply of mineral nitrogen to a

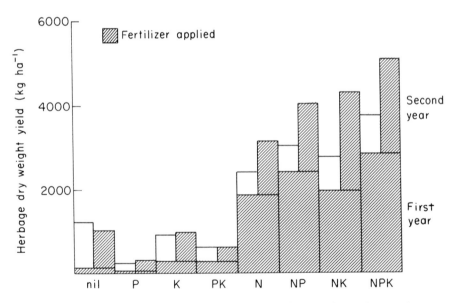

FIG. 29.1. The effect of addition of nitrogen, phosphorus and potassium on the growth of an established grass sward on an urban clearance site in Liverpool (50 kg N ha^{-1}, 22 P, 42 K applied each year in combinations shown) (Bloomfield *et al.* 1982).

continuous grass sward. This agrees with other work which shows that nitrogen is a crucial problem in the reclamation of derelict land (Handley *et al.* 1978).

Legume growth

It would, therefore, seem reasonable to incorporate legumes such as white clover (*Trifolium repens* L.) in the grass sward despite the fact that there is some antagonism to their inclusion in amenity grass seed mixtures. In fact *T.repens* is a common colonist of untreated clearance sites, forming slowly spreading patches. Analyses of the soils in clover and non-clover areas suggests the patches occur by chance rather than being due to any major environmental differences, although there is a slightly elevated level of extractable phosphorus. The importance of phosphorus alone in encouraging the growth of clover on these materials was indicated by an $N \times P \times K$ factorial experiment in which a mixture of *Lolium perenne* and *Trifolium repens* was sown on urban clearance land material: the addition of 18 kg P ha^{-1} increased the percentage of clover from approximately 5 to 45%.

As a vigorous component of the sward *T.repens* contributes directly to cover and sward density: its ability to spread laterally by stolons means that it rapidly colonizes bare patches, but its indirect contribution to the vigour of the grass component by its fixation of nitrogen is extremely important. This has been examined by a biological assay, using the growth of *Lolium perenne*, of soils taken immediately under, and adjacent to, individual 1–2-year-old patches of *Trifolium repens* occurring by natural colonization in an urban clearance area (Table 29.4). Soil analyses show that the levels of mineral nitrogen were $3 \times$, and of mineralizable nitrogen $2 \times$, in the clover patches compared with outside. In clover patches which have been established longer on material which has been fertilized, the increased levels of mineralizable nitrogen found under clover can be remarkable (Table 29.5), with corresponding substantial improvements of grass growth: the fall in mineralizable N in the oldest patches is due to the grass replacing the clover.

TABLE 29.4. *The growth (as dry wt kg ha^{-1}) of* Lolium perenne *on material taken from an urban clearance site under, and outside, patches of naturally occurring* Trifolium repens *(data of A.R. Garman).*

Patch	Under clover	Outside clover
1	1637	1280
2	1738	1077
3	1617	1034
4	2254	2148
5	1743	1209
6	1650	1733
Mean	1773	1414

TABLE 29.5. *The levels of mineralizable nitrogen in a reclaimed urban area (colliery spoil) under and outside naturally occurring patches of* Trifolium repens *of different ages (increase in mineral N* $\mu g\, g^{-1}$ *after incubation for 10 days at* $30°C$*) (data of K.C. Willson).*

| | Age of clover patch | | | |
	c. 2 yrs	c. 3 yrs	4–5 years	Mean
Outside clover	4.3	4.7	5.6	4.8
Under clover	85.4	141.5	23.4	83.5
Mean	44.9	73.1	14.5	

S.e. mean: ages 7.8; clover 9.3.

There is no doubt that legumes are an extremely important component of grass swards established on urban sites. Recent work has shown that even on poor derelict land materials, herbaceous legumes can accumulate more than 100 kg N ha^{-1} yr^{-1} (Dancer *et al.* 1977b). On urban amenity grassland sites the most suitable species is *T.repens* but it should be a dwarf cultivar such as Grasslands Huia or S184 and not a tall-growing cultivar. In rough grassland, other species are possible such as *T.pratense* L., *T.hybridum* L. and *Lotus corniculatus* L.

Tree growth

Trees and shrubs are an important component of urban reclamation schemes. Yet the performance of trees planted on urban sites has often been extremely disappointing. In a recent survey of newly planted trees in a variety of urban sites Capel (1980) showed that average survival after planting was approximately 60% and that average growth was only 50% of that shown by the best sites. Part of this can be attributed to vandalism, but it must be remembered that trees are as sensitive to lack of nutrients and water as other plants. Trees are often planted in poor soils but these are rarely as nitrogen deficient as derelict land materials. The effect of nutrient deficiency in urban sites can be shown by the growth of sycamore, *Acer pseudoplatanus* L. seedlings on urban materials: it is substantially improved by the addition of fertilizer (Fig. 29.2). Similar growth responses can be obtained when fertilizers are applied to standard trees, although these are slower to respond and effects may be masked if the planting pit has been back-filled with good soil. Fertilizer experiments on a variety of planted material have shown that growth can be improved by up to 100% by the addition of nitrogen fertilizer: the addition of other nutrients has little effect (Capel 1980) (Fig. 29.3). However, if there is grass or other vegetation around the base of the tree, the effect of the fertilizer may be nullified by increased competition for water from the increased growth of herbaceous vegetation. For this reason, underplanting trees in difficult sites with legumes has not always been successful (Bradshaw & Chadwick 1980).

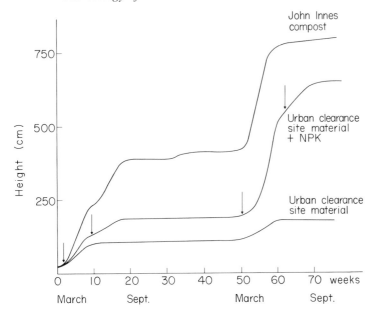

FIG. 29.2. The growth in height of seedlings of *Acer pseudoplatanus* on material from an urban clearance site with and without fertilizer, compared with growth on John Innes compost (in 125 mm pots; 100 kg N ha^{-1}, 22 P, 42 K applied as indicated by arrows).

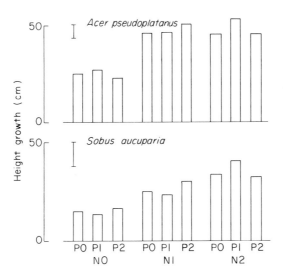

FIG. 29.3. The effect of addition of nitrogen and phosphorus on the growth in height over 3 years of two tree species recently established in urban clearance areas in Liverpool (N at rate of 0,200,400 kg ha^{-1} and P at 0,175,350 kg ha^{-1} applied each year to 1 m^2 around trees) (Capel 1980).

Soil and other amendments

Because of the apparently adverse nature of the soil in urban clearance areas many people responsible for derelict land reclamation are tempted to feel that a covering of topsoil or the use of some organic amendment is important despite the cost—the 1980 price of purchase and spread of 10 cm of topsoil in Britain is £2–3,000 ha^{-1}. Clearly there is some gain since stones and bricks become well covered. But the actual magnitude of the potential gain in plant growth is indicated in Fig. 29.4. The increase due to the use of topsoil is usually no more than that due to addition of fertilizer. It is interesting that there was no effect of peat, which suggests physical factors need not be important: however, peat might show some value under field conditions. Sewage sludge has clear benefits: this is likely to be due to its nutrient content. But sewage sludge could be difficult to apply in urban situations.

It is very important to realize that the topsoil which is supplied for reclamation purposes is often of dubious quality. A study of over 40 samples

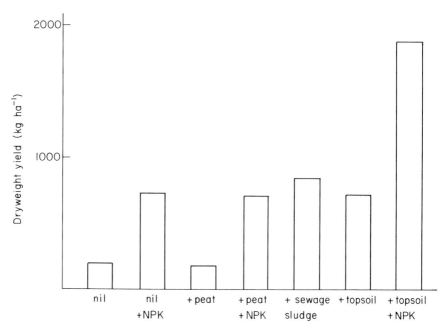

FIG. 29.4. The influence of various amendments on the accumulated growth of *Lolium perenne* and *Trifolium repens* on material taken from an urban clearance site (in 1,500-mm pots; 6 cm of amendment, mixed in except for topsoil; fertilizer 500 kg ha^{-1} 17:17:17 N:P_2O_5:K_2O; harvested after 10 and 18 weeks) (data of A.R. Garman).

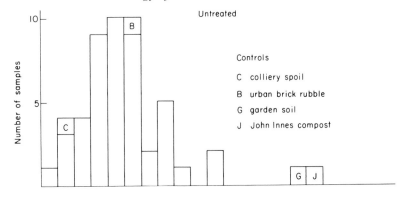

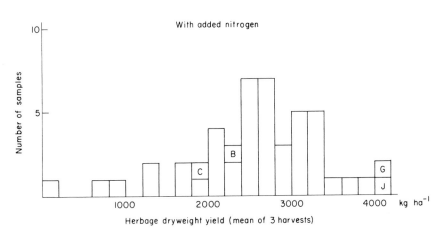

FIG. 29.5. The growth of *Lolium perenne* on 44 samples of topsoil supplied for reclamation purposes and on four control materials, with and without nitrogen (in 130-mm pots; mean of three harvests at 6, 12 and 35 weeks; 50 kg N ha^{-1} applied at 0, 6 and 12 weeks).

being used in urban reclamation shows that none were equal to a good garden soil and 50% were no better than brick rubble from an urban clearance site (Bloomfield *et al.* 1981) (Fig. 29.5).

CONCLUSIONS

From this set of simple experiments we are left with the strong impression that derelict sites in urban areas present far fewer problems for plant growth than we might have imagined. By appropriate cultivation, fertilization and use of legumes it appears that excellent swards can be established directly on the site materials. Topsoil is not necessary, and appears to have little value than as a physical cover.

This is borne out in practice: excellent swards have been produced on a large scale in different urban sites in Britain. Once the legume is properly established they require little or no maintenance, except an occasional application of a phosphorus fertilizer to maintain available phosphorus levels in the alkaline substrate and thereby ensure that the legumes persist. Areas to which topsoil has been added appear to perform no better, and often require heavy applications of a high N fertilizer unless a legume is present (Dutton & Bradshaw 1982).

The major advantage of a soil covering is that it covers stones, etc., and makes cultivation easier. However, cultivation is not difficult with a chain harrow, and there are now very effective stone-picking machines. The calcareous nature of the sites is extremely favourable to earthworms. Once they are established they can have a remarkable effect. Observations on a number of sites indicate that the surface-casting species bring up to the surface approximately 0.4 cm of fine material per year so that all stones soon become buried and a fine surface tilth is created.

For trees the problems are the same, but the techniques which must be used to overcome them must be different. Good soil surrounding the roots is essential to supply nutrients and to retain water, but annual applications of fertilizer help to achieve faster growth rates.

Urban derelict lands represent an interesting man-made habitat with very particular characteristics. Their intrinsic fertility except for nitrogen explains why natural plant colonization occurs readily and why legumes are common. It also explains why they are not difficult to reclaim once the problem of an adequate supply of nitrogen has been solved. Indeed, it is easier to establish vegetation on them than on most other derelict or degraded land. There is, therefore, no excuse for them remaining in a derelict state.

REFERENCES

Bloomfield H.E., Handley J.F. & Bradshaw A.D. (1982) Nutrient deficiencies and the aftercare of reclaimed derelict land. *Journal of Applied Ecology*, **19** (in press).

Bloomfield H.E., Handley J.F. & Bradshaw A.D. (1980b) Top soil quality. *Landscape Design*, **135**, 32–34.

Bradshaw A.D. & Chadwick M.J. (1980) *The Restoration of Land*. Blackwell Scientific Publications, Oxford.

Bradshaw A.D. & Handley J.F. (1972) Low cost grassing of sites awaiting redevelopment. *Landscape Design*, **99**, 17–19.

Capel, J.A. (1980) *The Establishment and Growth of Trees in Urban and Industrial Areas*. Ph.D. thesis, Univ. Liverpool.

Civic Trust (1977) *Urban Wasteland*. Civic Trust, London.

Dancer W.S., Handley J.F. & Bradshaw A.D. (1977a) Nitrogen accumulation in kaolin mining wastes in Cornwall. I. Natural Communities. *Plant and Soil*, **48**, 153–167.

Dancer W.S., Handley J.F. & Bradshaw A.D. (1977b) Nitrogen accumulation in kaolin mining wastes in Cornwall. II. Forage Legumes. *Plant and Soil*, **48**, 303–314.

Dutton R.A. & Bradshaw A.D. (1982) *Land Reclamation in Cities*. H.M.S.O., London.

Handley J.F., Dancer W.S., Sheldon J.C. & Bradshaw A.D. (1978) The nitrogen problem in derelict land reclamation with special reference to the British china clay industry. In *Environmental Management of Mineral Wastes* (Ed. by G.T. Goodman & M.J. Chadwick), pp. 215–236. Sijthoff & Nordhoff, Alphen aan den Rijn.

Roberts R.D., Marrs R.H., Skeffington R.A. & Bradshaw A.D. (1981) Ecosystem development on naturally colonised china clay wastes. I. Vegetation changes and accumulation of overall organic matter and nutrients. *Journal of Ecology*, **69**, 153–161.

30. RECULTIVATION: A PROBLEM OF STABILIZATION DURING ECOSYSTEM DEVELOPMENT

G. WEIDEMANN, H. KOEHLER AND TH. SCHRIEFER

Universität Bremen, FB3, Postfach 330440,
D-2800 Bremen, West Germany

SUMMARY

The reclamation of refuse tips and similar wasteland places is in practice too little guided by ecological knowledge, especially with regard to aspects of ecosystem function. This often results in damage to introduced plants during the early years due to the lack of an integrated successional development of all the components of the system to be established. An asynchrony exists between different systematic and ecological groups of organisms when colonizing formerly unoccupied sites. This asynchrony may be strengthened by site characteristics like exposure to climatic factors, soil compaction and reduced accessibility as well as by recultivation measures like the introduction of a sown or planted vegetation. It is proposed, therefore, that recultivation should be preceded by a period of undisturbed succession. This would allow for the slow colonization by, and succession of, those ecosystem components, which are responsible for nutrient recycling and rate regulation and thus for main conditions of ecosystem stability. Successional studies on a rubble and debris dump in Bremen are described. Two variants, treated as systems of their own, have been set up: one plot is left for undisturbed colonization (succession plot), while another has been sown with grass (recultivation plot).

INTRODUCTION

The reclamation of refuse tips is a public task appointed by law and supported by technical recommendations and great financial effort. Reclamation (or recultivation) aims at establishing a 'biologically healthy, fertile and permanently productive cultivated landscape' to be used for agriculture, forestry or recreation (Olschowy 1973, 1978). Recultivation means the establishment of a new ecosystem in a place where either the original ecosystem has been cleared away by human action as, for example, in opencast coal mining, quarries or gravel pits, or on newly deposited materials like spoil heaps and refuse tips. Recultivation measures on spoil heaps and refuse tips consist mainly of covering the pits with a 'soil' followed by sowing or planting. This practice is not guided by an ecosystem view of recultivation, and often results in the poor establishment of the introduced vegetation (see e.g. Kunick & Sukopp 1975; Neumann & van Ooyen 1979). This situation is usually repaired by new planting, but in our opinion this can be avoided if recultivation is preceded by a period of undisturbed succession, during which an ecosystem can be established.

THE ECOSYSTEM

An ecosystem can be defined as 'assemblages of organisms (i.e. biocenosis or community) and their associated environment (i.e. biotope or abiocene, Schwerdtfeger 1975) functioning collectively as a system to exchange material and energy' (Reichle 1975). According to Reichle, ecosystems are stable. Stability is used here for persistence (Orians 1975; Reichle, et al. 1975), and in this context refers to the functional properties of the ecosystem, that is to its ability to maintain its organization by energy and material transfers in spite of eventually changing the composition of its biological community.

Persistence of terrestrial ecosystems is, according to Reichle et al. (1975), based on four specific attributes. These are:

1. An energy base, composed of autotrophic green plants capable of fixing solar energy on which all ecosystem processes are dependent.
2. An energy and nutrient reservoir characterized by a large size and a slow response time consisting of soil and soil organic matter and, in the case of forests, of structural organic material.
3. Nutrient recycling as an ecosystem function, which provides that essential elements be retained within the ecosystem by bioretention.
4. Rate regulation, which controls the mineralization and thus mobilization of nutrients so that leaching is minimized.

Nutrient recycling and rate regulation are dependent on the existence of a complex interacting consumer and decomposer community (e.g. Crossley 1977; Kaczmarek 1971; McBrayer 1977; Weidemann 1978).

SUCCESSION

The above-mentioned attributes are the result of succession. The term succession mostly refers to directional changes in community composition (see e.g. Drury & Nisbet 1973; Miles 1979). But McNaughton and Wolf (1979) define succession more broadly as 'the directional change in community composition and associated biological and environmental properties of ecosystems'. Similarly, Connell and Slatyer (1977) describe facilitation as one type of mechanism of succession. Their model assumes that species of later successional stages can establish in unoccupied places only after these have been 'prepared' by pioneer species. The initial phases of succession on a refuse tip or on similar sites may be explained by this model, too. On the other hand there is evidence that in later stages of wasteland succession the tolerance and/or inhibition model of Connell and Slatyer apply (Gutte 1971). These models assume competition and the way of overcoming competition as the main mechanisms by which community composition changes.

RECULTIVATION

Only two of Reichle's (Reichle *et al.* 1975) pre-requisites of ecosystem persistence are satisfied by conventional recultivation measures: herbs, grasses, shrubs and trees form an energy base, and the cover; subsoil and rubble function as a nutrient reservoir and eventually as an energy reservoir if topsoil is included. But recycling and rate regulation, performed by a diverse biotic community are missing. It is assumed implicitly that the rest of the ecosystem will establish itself in due time in spite of the adverse conditions which are created by the site characteristics and by recultivation methods. These include the heap shape, which results in climatic and hydrological effects, and soil compaction which affects the moisture regime and the colonization. Later, methane production from anaerobic refuse may prevent the colonization of plants and animals and thus create gas deserts (Neumann 1976; Schriefer 1981). But this is a problem which can be solved, technologically, by gas drainage (Pierau 1975; Tabasaran 1976).

Modern municipal refuse tips are often heap shaped and raised to more than 50 m above the surroundings. This results in slopes with different microclimates and generally exposed conditions. Furthermore, groundwater contact is cut off, so that the water supply of the capping is totally dependent on precipitation. On the other hand the water balance of the cover is determined by soil type, soil density and by porosity. Sandy soils create dry conditions in combination with exposure to wind and sun. In the case of loamy soils, compaction by vehicles prevents rainwater infiltration, and surface run-off and evaporation are enhanced. Compaction of deeper layers may on the other hand result in waterlogging. Soil temperatures, too, may fluctuate widely until a closed vegetation cover has established. Consequently, damage to the vegetation of capped refuse tips from drought as well as from wetness have been reported (Kunick & Sukopp 1975; Neumann 1976).

The buildup of soil structure involves the formation of aggregates through the action of soil animals. By mixing of mineral particles with organic materials they produce soil crumbs which combine water-holding capacity with porosity. Under experimental conditions these soil formation processes may be finished within a few months (Kubiëna 1948), but on refuse tips this is not the case. Their development may be retarded even under undisturbed conditions, by the difficulties of organisms colonizing the site. But under undisturbed conditions all components of the ecosystem will develop in close dependency though at different rates. By recultivation, however, the development of the vegetation is accelerated and brought to a later state of succession. This results primarily in a strengthened asynchrony between vegetational and faunal development and secondarily in the instability of the whole system, since the regulating and controlling functions of the soil biota cannot be performed.

COLONIZATION OF RECLAMATION SITES BY ORGANISMS

There is some evidence from the literature and from our own work of the different rates of colonization by plants and animals on reclamation sites. Colonization of refuse tips and spoil heaps is initiated by annual plants. These are soon followed by a pioneer vegetation consisting of winter annuals and perennial herbs (Kreh 1935; Dunger 1968; Gutte 1971; Kunick & Sukopp 1975). Most of them have small mobile seeds with little or no dormancy, and are able to germinate under a wide range of temperatures (Bazzaz 1979) similar to those found on exposed tips. These pioneer phases show high species numbers presumably due to a lack of interspecific competition.

Among the herbivorous fauna of refuse tips, the Heteroptera have been studied (Soecknick 1980). He found that the spontaneous vegetation is almost immediately colonized by ecological and trophic generalists. Most species invade by flight from neighbouring ecosystems and species composition changes rapidly in parallel to vegetation succession.

Fast invasion and colonization of new sites and rapid change of species composition have also been reported for the epedaphic Collembola, which are easily transported by wind (Bode 1975; Dunger 1968, 1975; Hutson & Luff 1978; Hermosilla 1980). Among these are drought-resistant species with the short life-cycles typical of r-strategists (Hutson & Luff 1978). On the other hand, millipedes and woodlice, epedaphic macrohumiphages with high litter diminution capacity, invade slowly (Dunger 1968; Neumann 1971). Since they spread by walking, their colonization success is influenced not only by the trophic and microclimatic conditions of a site but also by its accessibility (Koscielny & Stach 1980). Pit heaps and refuse tips are often isolated islands within urban or industrial areas. Consequently, slow running and hygrophilic epigeic animals will have difficulties in reaching them.

Covering a tip with a fully developed soil from elsewhere brings a total spectrum of soil biota to the site. But this does not necessarily mean successful colonization. By turning over, transporting, compacting and exposing to extreme climatic conditions the soil fauna is heavily disturbed. Compaction has been shown to have a particularly adverse affect (Aritajat *et al.* 1977, Brockmann 1980). Nevertheless, some individuals belonging to many species will remain. In most cases, however, the capping of tips is not done with topsoil but with subsoil or with a material from deeper layers containing little or no biota. The methods of invasion include transport by wind as well as active invasion from the surroundings.

Passive transport by wind occurs in the aquatic soil microfauna which consists of Protozoa, nematodes, rotifers and tardigrades. Members of all of these groups, which belong to the initial colonizers in the xeroseries of soil development described by Kubiëna (1948), have been observed also at the zero-state of succession on our research site at Bremen. It has been stressed by Rusek (1978) that these animals are well adapted to the extreme fluctuations in temperature and moisture of newly exposed sites.

The members of the soil mesofauna presumably are carried to the site, but Acari establish more rapidly than Collembola (Hutson & Luff 1978). There is a distinct succession of ecologically different groups of Acari on reclamation sites beginning with the Acaridiae and the Tarsonemini, which are typical of poor soils with partially anaerobic conditions due to compaction (Hermosilla 1976). Oribatid mites, which depend to great extent on the availability of plant litter, are almost absent at the beginning of the colonization process (Dunger 1968; Hermosilla 1976; Hutson & Luff 1978).

The colonization success of the soil mesofauna (mainly Enchytraeids, Acari and Collembola) is dependent on the existence of sufficient pore space, since these animals are not able to produce soil pores by themselves. With either loamy or compacted soils, they need the channels produced by plant roots and hence the development of vegetation. At the zero-site on our tip at Bremen with a vegetation cover of less than 10% only 3,000–6,000 Enchytraeids m^{-2} have been counted (Weidemann, unpublished). In contrast on a 5-year-old plot with undisturbed successional vegetation about 29,000 individuals m^{-2} have been found (Brockmann 1980). Details for Acari are given by Brockmann and Koehler (pp. 336–337, this volume).

The only group of soil animals which is able to form new pore space is the earthworms (Lumbricidae). Their colonization success on tips covered with compacted soil is therefore of special interest, since by their activity pre-requisites for the successful colonization by soil mesofauna are provided. Earthworms may arrive on a tip passively with the covering material or with plant roots, or they may invade actively from the surroundings (Dunger 1967;

Schriefer 1979, 1981). The number of individuals introduced with cover material is of course dependent on its origin; material from deeper layers is virtually free of animals. But even if earthworms were contained in the cover material, they would mostly be killed by turbation and compaction. This danger is less acute when they are imported with the roots of trees and shrubs. Nevertheless, successful colonization is dependent on the ability of the animals to tolerate the different new environmental conditions. Schriefer (1979, 1981), however, demonstrated that colonization of pit covers may originate from planting. His findings suggest that the 'inoculation' of compacted tip covers with earthworms could be a method for improving soil conditions (see also Dunger 1969). Immigration from the surroundings and colonization of covered refuse tips or rubble heaps takes a number of years. Dunger (1968) reported an immigration speed of 10 m year^{-1} for *Allolobo-phora caliginosa* (Savigny) while Schriefer (1979) calculated a maximum speed of just 4 m year^{-1}. He found, exclusively, species with horizontal, near-surface burrows. As in the case of the macroarthropods of the soil surface, active immigration can only happen if there are no insurmountable areas between the new site and the earthworm-inhabited surroundings. Colonization success is dependent on the existence of appropriate abiotic, edaphic and food conditions. But since the development of vegetation cover is much quicker than immigration by earthworms, provided both processes are not hindered by gas deserts, these demands may be met within a few years. The question is, whether the development of vegetation, biomass as well as cover, is continuously possible on a particular site during that time without an effective soil fauna to decompose the litter of the pioneer vegetation and form an aerated soil structure.

The examples mentioned show clearly that different groups of organisms colonize a new site like a rubble heap or a refuse tip at quite different rates, and that these rates are further influenced by the mode of immigration of the organisms as well as by the accessibility and suitability of the site. On the other hand, the more or less isolated studies give little information on whether different rates of colonization by different functional groups of organisms influence the stability of the developing ecosystem. Hence it is necessary to study the succession of all relevant ecosystem components on newly covered heaps or refuse tips synchronously in order to find out which recultivation measures should be made use of, and when, so as to effectively shorten succession.

SUCCESSION APPROACH TO RECULTIVATION

The succession of different ecosystem components on disturbed and re-cultivated sites has, to our knowledge, never been studied in one place synchronously. The only comprehensive study including soil, vegetation, soil fauna and the activity of soil microflora has been carried out by Dunger (1968) on reclaimed dumps from opencast coal mining by comparing stands of different successional age in the same area. We have begun a detailed study at Bremen on a rubble and debris dump of 25 m in height, which is covered with a loamy sand and a sandy loam strongly compacted by vehicles. One plot has been left for undisturbed colonization (succession plot) while another has been sown with a mixture of different grass species after tilling (recultivation plot). Each variant is treated as a system of its own. The following state variables will be measured at appropriate time intervals for several years:

Soil

Particle size distribution; aggregate density and stability; porosity; moisture; temperature; acidity (pH); organic material content; C-, N-, P-, K-, $CaCo_3$-content.

Microclimate

Temperature above ground, within vegetation; relative humidity; evaporation.

Soil microflora

Soil respiration; biomass of bacteria, fungi, actinomycetes; enzyme activity (dehydrogenase, phosphatase); N-mineralization, binding, nitrification.

Vegetation

Species composition; coverage; net productivity.

Soil fauna

Species composition of main groups (enchytraeids, earthworms, Acari, Collembola, Isopods); species and functional diversity; biomass.

Furthermore, those climatic factors presumably most important for the developing ecosystem, namely temperature and precipitation, are being measured continuously.

CONCLUSION

The whole study aims at the parallel recording of the speed of succession of different ecosystem components (vegetation, soil microflora, soil epi- and endofauna as well as soil structure and hydrology), and at analysing how their assumed asynchrony will influence the development and stability of the whole system under changing environmental factors like precipitation and temperature. It is hoped that the results will give a deeper insight into the succession processes of ecosystems and, on the other hand, will provide an ecological basis for the recultivation of refuse tips and similar derelict land.

REFERENCES

Aritajat U., Madge D.S. & Gooderham P.T. (1977) The effects of compaction of agricultural soils on soil fauna. *Pedobiologa*, **17**, 262–282.

Bazzaz F.A. (1979) The physiological ecology of plant succession. *Annual review of ecology and systematics*, **10**, 351–371.

Bode E. (1975) Pedozoologische Sukzessionsuntersuchungen auf Rekultivierungsflächen des Braunkohlentagebaues. *Pedobiologia*, **15**, 284–289.

Brockmann W. (1980) Enchytraeiden (Oligochaeta) im Abdeckmaterial von Mülldeponien unter besonderer Berücksichtigung des Einflusses von Bodenverdichtungen. University of Bremen, FB 3, unpublished diploma thesis.

Connell J.H. & Slatyer R.O. (1977) Mechanisms of succession in natural communities and their role in community stability and organization. *The American Naturalist*, **111**, 1119–1144.

Crossley D.A. Jr. (1977) The roles of terrestrial saprophagous arthropods in forest soils: current status of concepts. In *The role of arthropods in forest ecosystems* (Ed. by W.J. Mattson) pp. 49–56. Springer, New York.

Drury W.H. & Nisbet I.C.T. (1973) Succession. *Journal of the Arnold Arboretum*, **54**, 331–368.

Dunger W. (1967) Die Entwicklung der Makro- und Megafauna in rekultivierten Haldenböden. In *Progress in Soil Biology* (Ed. by O. Graff & J.E. Satchell), pp. 340–352. Vieweg, Braunschweig, North-Holland Publishing Company, Amsterdam.

Dunger W. (1968) Die Entwicklung der Bodenfauna auf rekultivierten Kippen und Halden des Braunkohlentagebaues. *Abhandlungen und Berichte des Naturkundemuseums Görlitz*, **43**, 1–256.

Dunger W. (1969) Fragen der natürlichen und experimentellen Besiedlung kulturfeindlicher Böden durch Lumbriciden. *Pedobiologia*, **9**, 146–151.

Dunger W. (1975) On the delimination of soil microarthropod coenoses in time and space. In *Progress in Soil Zoology* (Ed. by J. Vanék), pp. 43–49. Junk, The Hague.

Gutte P. (1971) Die Wiederbegrünung städtischen Ödlandes dargestellt am Beispiel Leipzigs. *Hercynia N.F., Leipzig*, **8**, 58–81.

Hermosilla W. (1976) Beobachtungen an der Bodenfauna von rekultivierten Böden im Braunkohlentagebaugebiet der Ville. *Decheniana (Bonn)*, **129**, 73–75.

Hermosilla W. (1980) Die Mesofauna verschieden alter Rekultivierungsflächen im Braunkohlentagebaugebiet der Ville. *Decheniana (Bonn)*, **133**, 79–83.

Hutson B.R. & Luff M.L. (1978) Invertebrate colonization and succession on industrial reclamation sites. *The Scientific Proceedings of the Royal Dublin Society*, Series A, **6**, 165–174.

Kaczmarek W. (1971) Die Bedeutung der organischen Retention und der Bodenorganismen als Regulationsfaktoren im Stoffhaushalt der Landökosysteme. *Annales de Zoologie et Écologie Animale* Numéro hors-série, 473–480.

Koscielny L. & Stach M. (1980) Sukzession der Isopoda auf Mülldeponien. Universität Bremen, FB 3, Projekt Landschaftsökologie. Rekultivierung von Mülldeponien, unpublished report.

Kreh W. (1935) Pflanzensoziologische Untersuchungen auf Stuttgarter Auffüllplätzen. *Jahreshefte des Vereins für Vaterländische Naturkunde*, **9**, 59–120.

Kubiëna W.L. (1948) *Entwicklungslehre des Bodens.* Springer, Wien.

Kunick W. & Sukopp H. (1975) Vegetationsentwicklung auf Mülldeponien Berlins. *Berliner Naturschutzblätter*, **19**, 141–145.

McBrayer J.F. (1977) Contributions of cryptozoa to forest nutrient cycles. In *The role of arthropods in forest ecosystems* (Ed. by W.J. Mattson), pp. 70–77. Springer, New York, Heidelberg, Berlin.

McNaughton S.J. & Wolf L.L. (1979) *General ecology.* 2nd edn. Holt, Rinehard & Winston, New York.

Miles J. (1979) *Vegetation dynamics.* Chapman & Hall, London.

Neumann, U. (1971) Die Sukzession der Bodenfauna (Carabidae (Coleoptera), Diplopoda und Isopoda) in den forstlich rekultivierten Gebieten des Rheinischen Braunkohlenreviers, *Pedobiologia*, **11**, 193–226.

Neumann U. (1976) *Untersuchungen über die Begründung und Entwicklung von Vegetationsdecken auf Müllablagerungen.* TU Berlin, Institut für Landschaftsbau, Dissertation D 83.

Neumann U. & van Ooyen G. (1979) *Rekultivierung von Deponien und Müllkippen.* Beihefte zu Müll und Abfall, 16.

Olschowy G. (1973) Industrieanlagen. In *Landschaftspflege und Naturschutz in der Praxis* (Ed. by K. Buchwald & W. Engelhardt), pp. 276. BLV, München, Bern, Wien.

Olschowy G. (1978) 11.4.6 Bergbau und Landschaft. In *Natur- und Umweltschutz in der Bundesrepublik Deutschland* (Ed. by G. Olschowy), pp. 461–474. Parey, Hamburg, Berlin.

Orians G.H. (1975) Diversity, stability and maturity in natural ecosystems. In *Unifying concepts of ecology* (Ed. by W.H. van Dobben & R.H. Lowe-McConnell), pp. 139–150. Junk, The Hague.

Pierau H. (1975) Entgasung von Abfalldeponien—Schadgase verlieren ihre Gefährlichkeit. *Kommunalwirtschaft*, **4**, 1–8.

Reichle D.E. (1975) Advances in ecosystem analysis. *Bio-Science*, **25**, 257–264.

Reichle D.E., O.Neill R.V. & Harris W.F. (1975) Principles of energy and material exchange in ecosystems. In *Unifying concepts in ecology* (Ed. by W.H. van Dobben & R.H. Lowe-Connell), pp. 27–43. Junk, The Hague.

Rusek J. (1978) Pedozootische Sukzessionen während der Entwicklung von Ökosystemen. *Pedobiologia*, **18**, 426–433.

Schriefer T. (1979) *Lumbriciden auf Mülldeponien.* University of Bremen, FB 3, unpublished diploma thesis.

Schriefer T. (1981) Regenwürmer (Lumbricidae) auf unterschiedlich abgedeckten Mülldeponien. Bestandsaufnahme und Besiedlungsmechanismen. *Pedobiologia*, **21** (in press).

Schwerdtfeger F. (1975) *Ökologie der Tiere Bd. 3: Synökologie.* Parey, Hamburg & Berlin.

Soecknick R. (1980) *Heteroptera as colonizators of spontaneous vegetation on refuse tips.* University of Bremen, FB 3, doctoral thesis in preparation.

Tabasaran O. (1976) Überlegungen zum Problem Deponiegas. *Müll + Abfall*, **8**, 204–210.

Weidemann G. (1978) Über die Bedeutung von Insekten im Ökosystem Laubwald. *Mitteilungen der deutschen Gesellschaft für allgemeine und angewandte Entomologie*, **1**, 196–204.

31. THE TEACHING OF URBAN ECOLOGY
TO FUTURE TEACHERS

WALTER K. R. E. VAN WINGERDEN*

*Instituut voor Lerarenopleiding Vrije Leergangen Free University,
Postbox 90048, Amsterdam, The Netherlands*

SUMMARY

The programme of a course in urban ecology which is held yearly at a teacher training institute (Amsterdam) is presented and commented on. The course contains learning activities with respect to information on species and abiotic factors in built-up environments, and an exercise in the development of the teaching of ecology in the urban environment. The exercise consists of three phases: 1, an inventory of topics; 2, the elaboration of a topic into a pupil exercise; 3, the application and the improvement of the pupil exercise.

INTRODUCTION

Students at the so-called 'New Teacher Training Institutes' in the Netherlands are prepared to teach pupils, between the ages of 12 and 16, in two disciplines. Students in biology have a course on urban ecology at the beginning of their third year of study. Such a course is important to future teachers as in the Netherlands the greater part of the schools are situated in the built-up environment. Furthermore, most of the pupils live and play in urban areas (i.e. the environment best known to them).

The urban ecology course lasts 4 days during 2 consecutive weeks. When the students enter the course they have a basic knowledge of ecological processes in populations and ecosystems. Furthermore, they are able to recognize a considerable number of plant and bird species, and have some knowledge of soil- and water-inhabiting invertebrates.

The purpose of the course is to acquire knowledge and skills in order to be able to teach ecology in the built-up environment as well as to be able to recognize the typical ecological characteristics of the urban environment. The course consists of two parts:

1. Information on plants, animals and the abiotic factors in the urban environment, their inter-relationships, the ecosystems that they form and their significance to man.

* Current address: Research Institute for Nature management, Kemperbergerweg 67, 6816 RM Arnhem, The Netherlands.

2. An exercise in the development of the teaching of ecology in the urban environment.

The latter point will be dealt with first.

EXERCISE IN THE DEVELOPMENT OF THE TEACHING OF ECOLOGY IN THE URBAN ENVIRONMENT

The exercise consists of three subsequent phases.

Phase 1: the inventory of topics

We start with the presentation of an inventory scheme (Fig. 31.1, modified after Bleyerveld *et al.* (1977)), in which the different elements of the urban environment are indicated as well as the different levels at which these can be dealt with. Roughly three levels of elaboration can be distinguished:

1. Making observations, descriptions, inventories and classifications of dead and living things, in order to get information on the diversity of the urban environment.
2. The study of inter-relationships between species, as well as between species and abiotic factors and/or man.
3. A more comprehensive synthesis from which predictions of the effects of urban-planning on ecological systems can be made.

Subsequently, the students, in groups of two or three, survey a part of a district of Amsterdam in order to make an inventory of 10–15 topics appropriate for use in teaching (Table 31.1). The topics are expressed in the form of lesson themes. After they have finished the inventory the students indicate (by placing dots and lines in the inventory scheme (Fig. 31.1)) which elements from the urban environment and which level of elaboration their lesson themes concern. By doing this students become aware of the under- or over-representation of elements and/or levels of elaboration in their list of lesson themes. Subsequently, the students should ask themselves whether the district in question does not contain the under-represented elements or whether they have been overlooked. In the example (Table 31.1 and Fig. 31.1) a lesson theme on invertebrates is lacking. Furthermore, the category of the more comprehensive synthesis is under-represented. The themes concerning higher plants are over-represented, as is usually the case in our course.

Phase 2: the elaboration of a lesson theme into a pupil exercise

First, we present and discuss a number of boundary conditions and guidelines

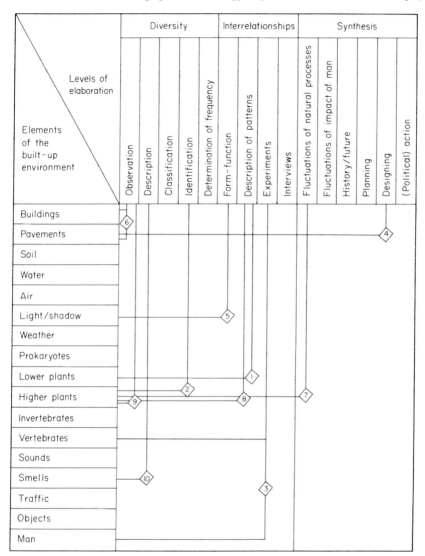

FIG. 31.1. An inventory scheme for lesson themes in urban ecology (modified, after Bleyerveld *et al.* (1977)). The figures refer to a corresponding list of 10 different themes (Table 31.1).

TABLE 31.1. *A list of lesson themes in urban ecology which is representative of the results of the student's inventory. The elements of the urban environment as well as the levels of elaboration are indicated in Figure 31.1.*

1. The determination of the distribution of lichens in a city district.
2. Recording of fern species along canals.
3. Observations on competition for pieces of bread, experimentally presented to birds; influence of the presence of man.
4. The construction of a new design for a street in which traffic is restricted to the one-way system, and room is reserved for plants and a playground.
5. The influence of the light/shadow period on the shape of weeds on brick pavements.
6. The measurement of surface temperatures in a city district.
7. The recording of the colonization by higher plants of a sand body prepared for building.
8. The drawing of a map of the distribution pattern of fruits from an isolated stand of elms in a city district.
9. Observations on the fate of leaves falling into the water of canals.
10. Registration of sounds and smells in a city park.

which fulfil the requirements of a good exercise. The boundary conditions are determined by the timetable and the facilities in our schools, as well as by the characteristics of the urban environment. Furthermore, the purpose of the exercise should be indicated. The text of the exercise should be clear at first glance with respect to location, route, methods and materials and the exercise ought to be capable of being finished within two lessons ($c.1\frac{1}{2}$ hours). The exercise should not expose the pupils to hazardous conditions, and should contain instructions on road safety. In addition, appropriate teaching methods for working out of doors should be discussed.

Subsequently, the students will extend the exercise. While doing this, they also add to their list of exercise themes, especially to those categories which are under-represented.

Phase 3: the application and the improvement of the pupil exercise

Two different ways are possible:

1. A group of pupils are put through the exercise.
2. A small group of fellow-students carry out the exercise, at the same time adding to the list of lesson themes, especially for the under-represented categories.

We prefer the first possibility but, for practical reasons, only have experience with the second. The fellow-students get about $1\frac{1}{2}$ hours to carry out the pupil exercise as well as to deliver critical comments which are added to the text of the exercise.

Afterwards, all students who were involved discuss the exercise together in order to improve it. Subsequently, the text of the exercise is prepared for insertion into the final report of the course, together with the list of lesson themes from the inventory. The students are able to use the final reports in the development of their future teaching.

INFORMATION ON PLANTS, ANIMALS AND ABIOTIC FACTORS OF URBAN ENVIRONMENTS

Theory

The following themes are dealt with:

1. Differences between towns and the country with respect to the level and fluctuations of abiotic factors (temperature, wind velocity, rain, humidity, etc.,) and their significance to the flora and fauna.
2. Ecological strategies of species living in urban environments.
3. The influence of spatial and temporal variation on the stability of urban ecosystems.
4. The significance of the flora and fauna to the human environment in cities.
5. Physical planning, taking into account the geological and ecological characteristics of the landscape.

We have used literature (e.g. Deelstra 1975) and lectures on those topics accompanied by questions which direct the students to further study.

Practical

During the last few years we have studied the vegetation of a fallow area on a sand body prepared for the construction of a road. From vegetation mapping along a height gradient, it appeared that at the lower end of the sand body the plants are relatively large and species diversity is low, whereas at the top, plants are relatively small and species diversity is considerably larger. Captures of soil-dwelling invertebrates are also made along the gradient.

After the fieldwork the application of these ecological data for the management of nature in cities is discussed, as well as teaching methods in fieldwork.

Furthermore, we pay attention to the non-indigeneous trees and shrubs as well to the cultivated varieties of native ones which in our country are frequently planted in the urban environment. The students construct a nature trail in a park and/or visit the municipal nursery garden. The nature trail and its use in teaching are discussed.

Finally, the students study a collection of plants from fallow areas and parks in order to learn to recognize the species. This is followed by a recognition test by means of which the students are able to ascertain whether they have studied the collected material sufficiently.

EVALUATION

The students are mostly satisfied with the programme and the teaching methods of the course, although they would prefer a longer period than the 4 scheduled days. Often they admit to becoming aware for the first time of the facilities that the urban environment has to offer for teaching. Many of them intend to tackle aspects of urban ecology in their future teaching. Most students are reluctant to give adequate comments or constructive criticism on the inventories and pupil exercises made by their fellow-students; this is a pity since it interferes with the improvement of their results.

ACKNOWLEDGEMENTS

The author wishes to thank Mr A. Andeweg, Mrs H.A. Achterstraat and Mrs D.M. van der Tol for contributing to the development of the Urban Ecology course and for commenting on the manuscript.

REFERENCES

Bleyerveld C.A., Both C. & Teernstra P.J. (final redaction by Payens J.P.D.W.) (1977) *Het gebruik van de schoolomgeving.* Publikatiefonds Bulletin voor Docenten in de Biologie, **12**, 1–212.
Deelstra Tj. (1975) De nederzetting, ecologisch bekeken. In *De Gouden Delta* (Ed. by H. Gysels), pp. 100–48. Centrum voor landbouwpublikaties en landbouwdocumentatie, Wageningen.

32. THE FIELD TEACHING OF ECOLOGY IN CENTRAL LONDON—THE WILLIAM CURTIS ECOLOGICAL PARK 1977–80

JEREMY COTTON

School of Biological Sciences, Thames Polytechnic, Wellington Street, London, SE18 6GF, UK

SUMMARY

The William Curtis Ecological Park in Central London was created in 1977 (the year of the Queen's Silver Jubilee) by voluntary effort. It is a pilot project for the study of urban ecology, and for the field teaching of ecology by inner urban schools and colleges at all levels. Some of the advantages and disadvantages of using inner urban sites for fieldwork, and the implications in terms of logistics and organization, are discussed on the basis of the first 3 years' work.

INTRODUCTION

The creation of the William Curtis Ecological Park may be regarded as an example of the de-urbanization of the former dock area of London in recent years. The London docks extended from London Bridge (at the City of London proper) eastwards for about 10 km. With the development of container transport the great majority of seaborne trade entering the Thames estuary passes through Tilbury, 30 km or more east of London Bridge. The old docks within 10 km of London have, therefore, declined during the last decade, and many sections are completely disused, with the buildings derelict or already demolished while awaiting redevelopment. The William Curtis Ecological Park occupies 0.85 ha (2 acres) of land on the south bank of the Thames between London Bridge and Tower Bridge (the most easterly of the bridges) immediately opposite the Tower of London. It is part of a larger area in which the warehouses were demolished and the foundations sealed in with rubble and ash to form a heavy goods vehicle park. A new set of proposals for redevelopment of the area are at present awaiting planning permission.

CREATION AND DEVELOPMENT OF THE ECOLOGICAL PARK

During 1977, the year of the Queen's Silver Jubilee, and as part of the London celebrations of that event, a programme was launched to find uses for some of the derelict and unused or under-used land in London. The Ecological Park was one of five projects launched under this scheme with a small amount of initial funding, most of the work being carried out by volunteers. Since then it has been managed by the Ecological Parks Trust who publish a report on the park every year (Ecological Parks Trust 1978, 1979, 1980) of which the first deals with the creation of the park in detail, and the later ones with subsequent management, ecological development and educational work.

In January 1977 the site was effectively *tabula rasa*—the basement of one of the former buildings had been opened up by archaeologists, but the remainder remained sealed; there were some dumps of rubble, rubbish and soil with colonizing weed species, and a line of shrubs (*Salix caprea* L., *Acer pseudoplatanus* L. and *Buddleia davidii* Franch.) along the fence south of the park. These, some small public open spaces nearby and the imported soil itself were the main sources of the organisms that recolonized the park. The layer of hardcore still underlies the whole park, impeding drainage but, more importantly, ensuring that any water-table is 'perched' and disappears in a normal summer.

In March 1977 the site of the Ecological Park was fenced and subsoil, mostly clay with little organic matter content from nearby building sites, was dumped and landscaped by contractors. From then on, all the work was carried out by voluntary labour, mostly the British Trust for Conservation Volunteers (Conservation Corps). The whole area of landscaped subsoil was cultivated and rubbish removed, it was sown with a seed mixture of *Festuca rubra* L. and *Agrostis stolonifera* L. and a wide range of tree species were planted. Throughout the whole period of the project no trees or other plants have been bought: all have been donated from a wide variety of sources. A hollow was dug for the pond and lined with a single sheet of PVC, protected above and below by matting and the combined lining covered with a layer of approximately 7.5 cm of fine sand as a rooting medium. The pond was then filled with water from a nearby tap, and planted with a range of aquatic and emergent plants. Some other terrestial plant species were also planted at various times during the 3 years, in addition to the natural colonization referred to above.

All this was done at high speed to ensure completion before the official opening ceremony, in connection with the Jubilee celebrations, on 17 May 1977. Management by the Ecological Parks Trust effectively began on 1 July 1977 with the appointment of the author as Warden Naturalist. A single warden was found to be inadequate under the local conditions, and the park is now managed by a minimum of two staff in winter and three in summer. The capital cost of creating the park, including fencing and the lining of the pond, was approximately £5,000; the erection of a teaching building and the cost of materials for construction of paths cost another £5,000 (approximately)—all at 1977 prices. Only the use of voluntary labour, and generous donations of trees, plant and other material enabled the park and installations to be completed within this small budget. Cost has so far prevented the installation of a permanent water supply, which is desirable but not essential.

The Ecological Parks Trust has kept a photographic record of the condition of the site before work started, and of the actual process of creation. An annual photographic record of the development of the vegetation was kept from September 1977 to September 1979. Scientific records have also been kept; some conclusions were published by Ecological Parks Trust (1980), but more detailed examination of the data is in progress.

One aim of the project was to attempt to re-create natural communities of plants and animals (which, on a small site, will be predominantly invertebrates). The pond has been the main success in these terms. All the plant species were introduced, but the majority have become established and spread; in some areas a natural zonation of the emergent vegetation has developed from a more random original planting. The pond was originally filled with water from the London mains supply, which is high in nutrients and in pH—in 1978 several measurements gave a pH of 10. The high nutrient levels resulted in excessive growth of filamentous algae (mostly *Cladophora* spp. Kütz) until 1979, when the replacement of the mains water supply with rainwater from nearby roofs reduced both nutrient levels and pH (measurements between 6.5 and 8.5 in March 1980). This, combined with an increasing population of snails (mostly *Limnaea stagnalis* L.) and some management, almost eliminated the algae and allowed the floating and submerged aquatics to replace them.

Some non-flying invertebrate pond animals were introduced; others apparently colonized from the Thames (see Ecological Parks Trust 1979). Colonization by flying invertebrates has been so rapid that no deliberate introductions were attempted. A number of small water bodies have been found near the park, which are likely to have acted as the sources of this colonization and account for its speed. Such small informal water bodies appear to be commoner in Central London than would be expected without a detailed survey. The Odonata provide an example of the rate of colonization. None bred in the pond in 1977; *Ishnura elegans* van der Linden and *Sympetrum striolatum* Charpentier laid eggs in 1978; both these species hatched from the pond in 1979 and both species, plus *Aeshna grandis* L. and *A.juncea* L. laid eggs that summer. Other species have been recorded, but have not yet bred. More details of these and other groups are given in the reports (Ecological Parks Trust 1978, 1979, 1980). This ecosystem has at least been able to support a range of vertebrates: a large population of Nine-spined sticklebacks (*Pungitius pungitius* (L.)), and breeding populations of Common Frog (*Rana temporaria* L.) and Common Toad (*Bufo bufo* (L.))—all introduced—while Mallard (*Anas platyrhynchos* L.) nested in the park and brought ducklings to the pond (once, probably, in 1978; twice in 1979; and twice in 1980) and Moorhen (*Gallinula chloropus* L.) nested successfully in the reed vegetation of the pond in 1980. The park still only contains small shrubs and most birds that nest successfully do so on the ground or in neighbouring buildings; Blackbirds (*Turdus merula* L.) nested in a building in 1979 and on the ground in the park in 1980, which might be regarded as an example of new behaviour developing under urban conditions.

By contrast with the pond, the development of terrestial communities has been slow. The physical structure of the clay subsoil used was already poor, because of the lack of organic matter content; it was then compacted by the heavy machinery used by the contractors, and by trampling by visitors and vandals. Nutrient levels were not measured, but can be assumed to be low: no fertilizer was added. During 1977 the growth of the grass species sown was poor and communities of the Class Chenopodietea Br.-Bl. 1951, identifiable to associations described in Westhoff and den Held (1969), were allowed to develop. This began to loosen the soil and some organic matter, if only faeces of Collembola, accumulated. By 1979 grass growth was good and organic matter accumulated rapidly. In 1980 it was possible to take a first cut of hay. The importance of nitrogen was illustrated by the rapid growth of a wide range of leguminous species in the absence of marked competition from non-nitrogen-fixing species.

One feature of Central London is the urban microclimate. This is reflected both in the similarity of the plant associations to those described from the Netherlands, and in the number of plant species established in London which are not native to the British Isles. Many of these are native to Southern and Central Europe, and more often to South-East than to South-West Europe. I am hoping to analyse this in more detail elsewhere. This microclimate, combined with the perched water-table already referred to, results in drier soil conditions during the summer than are usually found in Britain. As a result Alfalfa (*Medicago sativa* L.) has proved a more suitable legume on this site than *Trifolium repens* L. (the species used in Liverpool). The latter has usually been checked, and has died of drought on a number of occasions during dry spells in summer.

EDUCATIONAL USE

Background

The possible use of inner urban sites for fieldwork depends on the nature of the demand, the potential of the sites concerned and the existence and potential of alternative facilities—in other words, on the market, the product and the competition. Table 32.1 shows the structure of education in England and

TABLE 32.1. *Examination courses, school structure and age ranges—England and Wales. (Nomenclature for Inner London Education Authority area.)*

Age range	Description of schools		Examinations	No. of subjects taken
6–7	Primary	Infants	—	—
7–11		Juniors	—	—
11–14	Secondary	Middle school	—	—
14–16			CSE, GCE 'O' Level	5–8
16–18		Sixth form	GCE 'A' Level	2–3
16+	Further education		'O' Level, 'A' Level, etc.	
18+	Tertiary or higher education		Courses above 'A' Level	

Wales (there is a completely independent system in Scotland) using the nomenclature of the Inner London Education Authority (details of organization vary between local authorities). GCE 'A' Level, the sixth-form course (designed for university entrance) is highly specialized, each pupil only studying two or three subjects. The number of pupils in any one school studying a field subject such as biology is usually, therefore, small. Even when students studying in further-education colleges are added, the total market for fieldwork at 'A' Level remains very small, while the higher education market is even smaller.

Actual use of the William Curtis Ecological Park

The majority of schools within a convenient distance use the park for some 'A' Level work, but mostly for initial training in field techniques in preparation for their main field courses at residential field centres outside London. The park has also been used for higher education project work. The main potential use, however, is by primary and secondary schools for the 8–11 and 11–16-year-old age groups. A few infant classes (6–7 years old) have visited the park but the attention time of children at this age is too short for much structured learning to be possible.

Most use of the Ecological Park in 1978 and 1979 was at primary level. Schools within a convenient distance made repeated visits, whereas those from further away usually made only one visit a year, often combined with a visit to some other site (e.g. the Historic Ships Collection at St Katherine's Dock). Some of the schools who derived most benefit from use of the park then attempted to create their own ecological parks or nature study areas on or near the school site. It seems probable that at primary level such school-linked areas, which can be visited at short notice and without preliminary organization, will be of more value than specialized centres.

During 1980 some primary school use continued, but secondary use increased, especially at middle school level (11–13). Specialization begins at 13 or 14, so that at this lower level all pupils in the school are still studying together and can be introduced to field studies. This preliminary experience at the Ecological Park indicates that field studies at this level can be extended beyond the simple materials already in use, and that fieldwork for the 14–16 age group can usefully be organized for the different academic streams. Virtually no actual fieldwork was attempted with 14–16 year olds as the teachers themselves wanted to build up more experience and confidence before attempting fieldwork at more than an elementary level. This lack of confidence among teachers is dealt with by Booth (1979) and Sinker (1979). It is more acute among teachers in inner-urban schools, both because these have less opportunity for fieldwork, and because existing textbooks and courses at universities and colleges of education apply to non-urban ecosystems. At such schools pupils in the 11–16 age group may do no fieldwork, while at 'A' level the teaching of ecology may be left completely to field centre staff, so that it becomes completely separated from the remainder of the course, as well as being the pupils' first experience of field techniques.

Potential use of urban sites

The main advantage to schools of sites with specialist staff such as the William Curtis Ecological Park or the Epping Forest Conservation Centre (Moxey 1979) is that teachers are able to develop their own experience and confidence under guidance. Such sites can only be used on a regular basis within the school timetable by schools within easy reach—in the case of the William Curtis Ecological Park, a maximum of 15 minutes' travelling time allowed an hour of teaching in a standard 'double period' of 1 hour 25 minutes. This allows use of the park without re-arranging the timetable or involving other members of school staff in 'covering'. It is, therefore, possible for any and every class in the school to include field studies in the timetable, making repeated visits for a particular project or making visits at all seasons of the year.

Schools further from a specialist centre can organize fieldwork at sites nearer the school on a similar regular basis provided the necessary textbooks and information on urban ecology are available, and provided the staff have developed the necessary experience and confidence. Such sites would be needed in large numbers, and so would not normally have specialist staff, or more than the minimum of security and management. This would prevent inclusion of vulnerable habitats such as ponds. Such sites are also likely to be small and with a limited flora, fauna (mainly invertebrates) and limited populations of any species, compared with the number of pupils involved.

The use of such sites is, therefore, likely to emphasize the use of small-scale simple systems, such as the plant–insect relationships covered by recent papers (Fry & Wratten 1979; Edwards & Wratten 1980). It may also lead to teaching methods designed to give the maximum educational value with the minimum disturbance or destruction of habitats and populations. At the William Curtis Ecological Park such methods were developed for use in the pond, eliminating the use of nets: demand was greater for pondwork than for any other form of study (Ecological Parks Trust 1980; Cotton 1979). These proved to be more successful in educational terms than using nets, as well as in terms of conservation of habitat and material.

REFERENCES

Booth P.R. (1979) The Teaching of Ecology in Schools. *Journal of Biological Education*, **13**, 261–265.

Cotton J. (1979) Field teaching in inner cities: The William Curtis Ecological Park. *Journal of Biological Education*, **13**, 251–255.

Ecological Parks Trust (1978) *The William Curtis Ecological Park, First Report 1977–78.*

Ecological Parks Trust (1979) *The William Curtis Ecological Park, Second Report 1978–79.*

Ecological Parks Trust (1980) *The William Curtis Ecological Park, Third Report 1979–80.*

Edwards P.J. & Wratten S.D. (1980) *Ecology of Insect–Plant Interactions.* (Studies in Biology No. 121) Edward Arnold, London.

Fry G.L.A. & Wratten S.D. (1979) Insect–plant relationships in ecological teaching. *Journal of Biological Education*, **13**, 267–274.

Moxey P.A. (1979) Working towards an ecological awareness. *Journal of Biological Education*, **13**, 256–260.

Sinker C.A. (1979) Sites for ecological work (Appendix to P.R. Booth (1979) above). *Journal of Biological Education*, **13**, 265–266.

Westhoff V. & den Held A.J. (1969) *Plantengemeenschappen in Nederland.* W.J. Thieme, Zutphen.

The reports of the William Curtis Ecological Park are available from The Ecological Parks Trust, c/o The Linnean Society, Burlington House, Piccadilly, London W1V oLQ.

IV

ABSTRACTS OF POSTER PAPERS

Water regime and metabolism of several roadside tree species as influenced by the use of de-icing salt in winter

A. SPIRIG AND M. ZOLG   *Institut für Ökologie, Technische Universität Berlin, Rothenburgstrasse 12, D-1000 Berlin 41.*

The effects of de-icing salt on the water regime and the chemical composition of leaves of several roadside tree species (*Aesculus hippocastanum* L., *Quercus robur* L., *Tilia × euchlora* C. Koch, *Platanus acerifolia* (Aiton) Willd.) were investigated throughout two vegetation periods (1975–76). Salt-treated sites were on the dividing strip of a road. The soil types of the salt-treated and control sites were comparable.

Aesculus hippocastanum and *Tilia × euchlora* showed a marked increase in sodium and chloride, *Platanus acerifolia* a slight increase in chloride only. *Quercus robur* showed no difference to the values measured for the controls.

Species with high chloride contents had high contents of potassium, nitrate and soluble organic nitrogen compounds; carbohydrates, especially sucrose and starch, were reduced (Zolg 1979). The magnitude of the effects seemed to depend on the salt sensitivity of the respective species and the degree of injury.

All trees were subject to a certain degree of water stress in summer (Spirig 1980). However, the differences in water potential and water saturation deficit between the salt-stressed and the unstressed sites were not significant. Species with high chloride uptake showed a marked decrease in transpiration rate. These results suggest only a limited change in the overall water balance of the salt-stressed trees compared with the controls.

Two conclusions can be drawn: 1, the hypothesis of a salt-induced 'physiological dryness' has to be abandoned; and 2, the changes in chemical composition of the leaves induced by salt damage (premature browning and abscision of leaves) cannot be explained as an indication of early senescence, but as a sign of a pathological process.

REFERENCES

Spirig A. (1980) *Zum Wasserhaushalt verschiedener Strassenbaumarten unter dem Einfluss der winterlichen Streusalzanwendung.* Diss. Eidgen. Techn. Hochsch. Zurich.
Zolg M. (1979) *Ökologisch-chemische Untersuchung der Auswirkung der Streusalzanwendung auf einige Blattinhaltsstoffe verschiedener Strassenbaumarten.* Diss. Techn. Univ. Berlin.

Effect of the interaction between road salt and road dust upon water relations of young trees

W. FLÜCKIGER, S. BRAUN AND H. FLÜCKIGER-KELLER   *Botanical Institute, Schönbeinstrasse 6, 4056 Basel, Switzerland.*

In field and laboratory experiments the water relations of clones of young trees grown in pots were studied in relation to the impact of road salt and dust on leaf surfaces. At the control site the salted plants showed a significantly increased stomatal diffusive resistance during hot summer days and an increased water potential compared to unsalted plants. A similar result was observed in laboratory experiments. However, the salt effect on water relations was conspicuously reduced when plants were exposed along a motorway. Scanning electron micrographs (Flückiger *et al.* 1977) and laboratory experiments (Flückiger *et al.* 1978, 1979) revealed that road dust and exhaust gases inhibit stomatal closure. Plants along the motorway and leaves dusted artificially with exhaust dust showed a generally significant decrease in stomatal diffusive resistance and a reduced water potential during hot summer days. Exhaust gases from a combustion engine significantly reduced the stomatal diffusive resistance even at a dilution of $1:200$. Experiments with leaflets of salt-treated ash trees (*Fraxinus excelsior* L.) showed that dusted leaflets had 35% more salt per unit dry weight after 3 weeks of dust application. These plants showed much earlier leaf necrosis than those which were not dusted. Similarly, dusted leaflets on the same leaf showed an earlier necrosis than undusted leaflets. It is thought that road dust and exhaust gases may increase the salt damage to plants by affecting the water relations.

REFERENCES

Flückiger W., Flückiger-Keller H., Oertli J.J. & Guggenheim R. (1977) Verschmutzung von Blatt- und Nadeloberflächen im Nahbereich einer Autobahn und deren Einfluss auf den stomatären Diffusionswiderstand. *European Journal of Forest Pathology*, 7, 358–364.

Flückiger W., Flückiger-Keller H. & Oertli J.J. (1978) Inhibition of the regulatory ability of stomata caused by exhaust gases. *Experientia*, 34, 1274.

Flückiger W., Oertli J.J. & Flückiger H. (1979) Relationship between stomatal diffusive resistance and various applied particle sizes on leaf surfaces. *Zeitschrift für Pflanzenphysiologie*, 91, 173–175.

Planning motorway planting in relation to de-icing salt

J. R. THOMPSON AND A. J. RUTTER   *Imperial College at Silwood Park, Sunninghill, Ascot, U.K.*

Many European motorways are planted with trees and shrubs, and these have both landscape and wildlife conservation value. Their frequently unsatisfactory performance is often attributed to the widespread and sometimes heavy use of de-icing salt, mostly NaCl. Four aspects of this problem have been considered:

1. Salt application rates on motorways. During the winters 1967/68 to 1979/80 and depending on their severity, mean application rates ranged from 3.65 to 12.59 t per lane km. Within a given winter, amounts in the northeast were occasionally over 10 times greater than those in the south.

2. The fate of applied salt. There were large and rapid fluctuations in the sodium and chloride concentrations of the soil surface layers depending on the amount of salt applied and the rainfall. Surface values were higher in the spring and lower in autumn than those in deeper layers. Concentrations were highest in the central reservations, but on verges, samples taken 2 m from the hard shoulder never exceeded about 500 μg g^{-1} Na.

3. Development of a mathematical model. Verified by sampling, this model predicts the sodium and chloride concentrations in soil from amounts of salt applied and net rainfall. By combining maps of salt application rates and winter rainfall, zones of increasing salt hazard (1–4) were identified:

Zone 1: areas close to London, Bristol and the Lancashire coastal plain.

Zone 2: all low land lying approximately south of the Humber in the east and of Carlisle in the west.

Zone 3: isolated areas of high ground in the south and east; most of the West Pennines and the East Midlands north of Northampton.

Zone 4: North-east England including the Eastern Pennines to just north of Leeds.

4. Experiments on container-grown shrubs. Salt was applied either to the roots or shoots at realistic concentrations and the effects measured. For planting on central reservations, the following species can be recommended from the viewpoint of resistence to salt:

Species	Recommended for Zone			
	1	2	3	4
Hippophae rhamnoides L.	●	●	●	●
Salix atrocinerea Brot.	●	●	●	●
Thelycrania sanguinea L.	●	●	●	●
Rosa rubiginosa L.	●	●	●	
Viburnum opulus L.	●	●	●	
V.lantana L.	●	●		
Acer campestre L.	●	●		
Prunus spinosa L.	●	●		
Salix viminalis L.	●	●		
S.caprea L.	●			
Crataegus monogyna Jacq.	●			

Anthropogenic influences on the oribatid mite population (Acari: Oribatei) of a roadside

CHRISTA HARTNIGK-KÜMMEL *Im Grund 3, D-7507 Pfinztal (Wö), West Germany.*

To investigate whether the physical and chemical changes in the soil caused by road building and traffic effects exert an influence on the soil arthropod fauna, monthly samples from November 1974 until October 1975 were taken from a depth of 0–6 cm at three sampling plots: 1, beside a busy street; 2, at a distance of 50 m in a forest; and 3, beside a paved woodland lane.

From a total of 75,513 soil arthropods extracted, 90.1% were mites, 8.5% collembola and 1.4% other arthropods; the mites were dominated by oribatids (72.5%). The latter were determined to species level and their population structure was compared.

The abundance of oribatids (as well as of other mites, collembola and other arthropods) is highest in plot A (25,932 individuals), lowest in plot C (7,472 individuals); plot B has 15,894 oribatids. Depth distribution is also different: in general there is a higher percentage of arthropods at a depth of 3–6 cm in A than B and C; in the case of oribatids more than 36% occur at a depth of 3–6 cm in A and C against only 21.5% in B. Species number is slightly higher in B (31) than in A (30), whereas C has the lowest number (27). Plot B is more diversified (0.77) than A (0.67) and C (0.56) as determined by Shannon-Wiener's calculation with $\log_{10}$. Species similarity between A and B is as high as between A and C, but less between B and C; dominancy and constancy similarity is highest between A and B, less between B and C, and least between A and C.

Compared with the forest plot, both roadside plots are changed in qualitative and quantitative respects. Under favourable circumstances the road-induced changes lead to a higher productivity (plot A) but, under unfavourable conditions they result in a depletion in quality and quantity (plot C).

The influence of emissions from a magnesium factory on ruderal communities

T. KRIPPELOVÁ   *Experimental Biology and Ecology Station, Sienkiewiczova 1, 88534 Bratislava, Czechoslovakia.*

Since 1961 the effects of pollution from a magnesium factory on the vegetation of Košice have been studied. Košice is the second largest industrial centre in Slovakia, and the city is expanding rapidly. The growth of the city has caused many environmental problems, but a major one is the pollution from a magnesium factory which was built in 1957. This factory is situated in the northern part of the city, and the prevailing northerly winds carry the pollutants across the urban area.

Particulates accumulate on the soil surface, forming a crust in some places with a high magnesium content (65–80% MgO), and there are marked changes in the biological, chemical and physical properties of the soils. Surface soil pH may be as high as 9.5 and the impermeable crust prevents seed germination. Magnesium displaces other cations from the soil exchange sites and thus causes mineral deficiencies. Polluted soil can only be reclaimed with great difficulty.

The influence of the emissions on the vegetation is clearly demonstrated in the ruderal communities of the alliance Polygonion avicularis. Characteristic species of these communities (e.g. *Lolium perenne* L., *Polygonum aviculare* L. and *Poa annua* L.) decline and are replaced by halophytic species (e.g. *Puccinellia distans* L. and *Chenopodium glaucum* L.). *Puccinellia distans* has been increasingly abundant in Košice since 1957, and by 1966 the ruderal vegetation had been so altered in some areas that a new association, the Puccinellio–Chenopodietum glauci (Krippelová 1971), was described. By 1976 its locations in the city were considerably increased, and at present (1980) there is a zone running north–south through the city in which the locations of the association have merged to form a broad belt. The emissions have thus caused a marked and rapid change in the ruderal communities. In the most polluted sites the vegetation is very sparse and only *P.distans* and *Agropyron repens* (L.) Beauv persist.

Bioindication by transplantation?

WOLFGANG PUNZ *Institut für Pflanzenphysiologie der Universität Wien, A-1010 Wien, Austria.*

In transplant experiments, lichens from unpolluted areas are transferred to polluted sites and after a certain exposure-time, several morphological/physiological changes are observed which may be used for bioindicative purposes. But there are always several factors interacting to produce these effects. These factors include altered microclimates, different pollutants acting at various concentrations (and often interacting with each other), and seasonal differences in the sensitivity of lichens to pollutants (see e.g. Punz 1979a, b). The change in the morphological and physiological characteristics of lichens observed ('Schadbild') must, therefore, be considered as a function of several factors, and it is difficult to estimate which factor is responsible. It is better to restrict such studies to sites where differences in microclimate can be minimized and where large differences in the concentration of one pollutant is the most likely cause of the response. Considerable experimental work is required to assess the accuracy of bioindicator methods in more complex situations.

REFERENCES

Punz W. (1979a) Der Einfluss isolierter und kombinierter Schadstoffe auf die Flechtenphotosynthese. *Photosynthetica*, **13**, 428–433.
Punz W. (1979b) The effect of single and combined pollutants on lichen water content. *Biologia plantarum*, **21**, 472–474.

Productivity and indicator value of *Melilotus* during succession on refuse tips as related to ecosystem development on raw soils

J. MÜLLER *Universität Bremen, FB3 Postfach 330 440 D-2800 Bremen 33, West Germany.*

The development of vegetation on a 5–8-year-old refuse tip is characterized by a stage dominated by *Melilotus officinalis* (L.) Pall. and *M.alba* Medic. (Melilotetum albiofficinalis after Kienast 1977), following a short-lived grassland community (see Weidemann *et al.*, pp. 305–313, this volume). Heights of up to 1.50 m have been recorded for the two *Melilotus* species in the literature. However, the investigated community shows maxima of up to 2.70 m. Consequently, the biomass is very high with an average of 2.5–3.5 kg dry wt m^{-2} (max. 5.5 kg dry wt m^{-2}) depending on the site. The adjacent *Tussilago farfara* communities have a lower biomass (0.8–1.0 kg dry wt m^{-2}—see Hahn *et al.* 1979). In these neutral to basic soils (pH 7) the growth and infection of *Rhizobium meliloti* is favoured. This results in good nitrogen fixation. The high biomass correlates with a high nitrogen supply, and also high rates of nitrogen mineralization. The latter allow the immigration of species with a higher nitrogen requirement than the *Melilotus* species. However, the clumped occurrence of the nitrophilous *Urtica dioica* within the *Melilotus* community cannot be related to significantly higher nitrogen concentrations in the soil but to localized areas of high phosphorus availability.

The *Melilotus* species are important, deep-rooting pioneer plants which may be useful in the reclamation of other sites.

REFERENCES

Hahn W., Wolf W. & Schmidt W. (1979) Untersuchungen zum Stickstoff-Umsatz von *Tussilago farfara*- und *Agropyron repens*-Bestäden. *Verhandlungen der Gesellschaft für Ökologie*, 7, 369–380.
Kienast D. (1977) Die Ruderalvegetation der Stadt Kassel. *Mitteilungen der floristisch-soziologischen Arbeitsgemeinschaft*, N.F. 19/20, 83–101.

Colonization of secondary raw soils on refuse tips by soil mesofauna

W. BROCKMANN AND H. KOEHLER *Universität Bremen, FB3, NW2, Achterstrasse, D-2800 Bremen 33, West Germany.*

The influence of the organic content of the soil on the process of colonization by Acari and Collembola was investigated in the soil covering a refuse tip. The soil of a number of quadrats was prepared by mixing untreated litter from a grassland with abundant Acari and Collembola into the top 5 cm. Other quadrats received sterile litter or were just mixed to a depth of 5 cm (controls).

The development of the Acari and Collembola communities was maximal on the fresh litter plot and minimal on the control after 8 weeks (May–June 1980). Colonization from outside occurred through phoresy and wind on all sites, and also in the untreated litter site through survivors imported in the litter (Hutson & Luff 1978). Rabbit droppings were found on the two litter sites only, where they probably favour the overall development of the soil fauna.

A comparison between two differently treated refuse tip plots (one with a natural succession and the other sown to grass and grazed by cattle) indicates the negative effects of cattle trampling on the soil and enchytraeid fauna. The trampling ($> 5\,\mathrm{kg\,cm^{-2}}$) causes a reduction of the pore volume (macro-pores, $> 50\,\mu$) (Slager 1964). In the upper soil layer (0–5 cm) the macro-pores were reduced by about 30%, followed by an 85% decrease of enchytraeid abundance.

REFERENCES

Hutson B.R. & Luff M.L. (1978) Invertebrate colonization and succession on industrial reclamation sites. *Scientific Proceedings of the Royal Dublin Society*, **6**, 165–174.
Slager S. (1964) A study of the distribution of biopores in some sandy soils in the Netherlands. In *Soil micromorphology* (Ed. by A. Jongerius), pp. 421–427. Elsevier, Amsterdam.

The exploration of thermal conditions in urban areas by methods of vegetation science

KARL-JOSEF DURWEN, ROSEMARIE DURWEN, KARL-FRIEDRICH SCHREIBER AND RÜDIGER WITTIG *Institut für Geographie der Universität, D-4400 Münster, and Botanisches Institut der Universität, D-4000 Düsseldorf, West Germany.*

The climate of cities differs from their environs, for example in higher mean annual and daily temperatures, fewer frosty days and a reduction in the daily amplitude of temperature (see e.g. Kratzer 1956). In addition to these general climate distinctions, differences within the city like heat-islands or ventilation-paths are relevant to town-planning. To obtain reliable results over a wide area by measurements from stationary or mobile recording apparatus (e.g. Eriksen 1964) requires considerable resources. Thermal pictures taken by aeroplanes (e.g. Gossmann 1977) are not only very expensive but are moreover difficult to interpret as they only show surface temperatures at an instant in time. However, plants can reflect different environmental conditions by their distribution or state of development, and may thus be employed as inexpensive bioindicators if they are sufficiently widely distributed.

In the city of Münster three different methods were applied and compared:

1. The 'relative thermal division' based on phenological observations, especially of blossom development (e.g. Ellenberg 1954; Schreiber 1977);

2. The calculation of the indicator-values for the 'temperature figure' according to Ellenberg (1974) from floral lists of spontaneous vegetation spread all over the urban area;
3. A gridded map showing the spread of thermophilous plants.

A seven-point scale was devised for 'relative thermal division' and this was used to map the urban areas (Durwen 1978). The spectra of indicator-values showed the difference between the city and its environs with higher values for built-up areas, and a delimitation between the relative thermal grades 5 and 6 is evident.

The frequency of thermophilous species, for example *Hordeum murinum*, showed a strict correlation with the limit 5–6 and a less significant one for the transition from grade 6 to 7.

As the blossom development obviously reacts favourably to local modifications of thermal radiation and irradiation caused by buildings, the phenological method (method 1) is well suited to monitor the thermal division of cities. On the other hand, methods based on the distribution of thermophilous species (methods 2 and 3) reveal the climatic conditions in general specified at the beginning.

REFERENCES

Durwen R. (1978) Kartierung der relativen Wärmeverhältnisse Münsters mittels phänologischer Spektren. Diplom-Arbeit, Münster, pp. 88, 2 maps.
Ellenberg H. (1954) Naturgemässe Anbauplanung, Melioration und Landespflege. *Landwirt-schaftliche Pflanzensoziologie*, 3, 1–109.
Ellenberg H. (1974) Zeigerwerte der Gefässpflanzen Mitteleuropas. *Scripta Geobotanica*, 9, pp. 97.
Eriksen W. (1964) Beiträge zum Stadtklima von Kiel. *Schriften des Geographischen Instituts der Universität Kiel*, 22, pp. 192.
Gossmann H. (1977) Radiometrische Oberflächenmessung und Thermalbild als Hilfsmittel der Umweltforschung. *Geographische Rundschau*, 3, 101–112.
Kratzer, A. (1956) Das Stadtklima. *Die Wissenschaft*, 90, pp. 141.
Schreiber K.-F. (1977) Wärmegliederung der Schweiz 1:200,000 mit Erläuterungen. *Grundlagen für die Raumplanung*, Bern.

The management of a semi-natural suburban garden for wildlife

H. GYSELS *Onderzoekscentrum voor landschapsecologie en milieuplanning, Rijksuniversiteit Gent, B-9000 Gent, Belgium.*

For 12 years part of a plot in a new garden (7 km south of Ghent, Belgium), originally an old meadow, was subjected to mowing twice a year (a continuation of the old management practice). No fertilizers were added and the mown grasses were removed in order to impoverish the soil generally. To increase its species diversity, a number of wild flowers and young trees were sown or planted. Some low-lying land was partially filled in with two different types of soil. A common lawn seed mixture was sown on these soils, which germinated together with pioneer-weed species.

In the lowest part of the garden, formed by the remainder of a ditch, bordered by bushes and young trees (*Alnus glutinosa* Gaertn., *Prunus spinosa* L., *Populus alba* L. and *P.canadensis* Moench, *Salix aurita* L. and *S.babylonica* L.), marsh and wet meadow plants are doing well, for example *Osmunda regalis* L., *Iris pseudacorus* L., *Lotus uliginosus* Schkuhr., *Cardamine pratensis* L., *Lythrum salicaria* L., *Symphytum officinale* L. and *Cirsium palustre* Scop., besides *Juncus effusus* L., *Carex acutiformis* Ehrh. and *Glyceria fluitans* R.Br.

On higher sandy areas, dry meadow plants *Chrysanthemum leucanthemum* L., *Ranunculus acris* L. and *Trifolium pratense* L. grow in competition with a vegetation more characteristic of the wayside, for example *Achillea millefolium* L., *Centaurea jacea* L. and *Medicago lupulina* L. The grasses *Lolium perenne* L., *Cynosurus cristatus* L., *Anthoxanthum odoratum* L. and *Alopecurus pratensis* L. are common. In more shaded situations *Ornithogalum umbellatum* L., *Heracleum sphondylium* L. and *Melandrium rubrum* Fr. add to the diversity, and after 12 years the first orchid (*Epipactis helleborine* Crantz) has appeared spontaneously.

Where the soil is composed of a mixture of sands, clay, ashes and small stones, a ruderal vegetation has developed (*Malva sylvestris* L., *Potentilla reptans* L., *Verbascum thapsus* L., *Veronica chamaedrys* L., *Glechoma hederacea* L., *Artemisia vulgaris* L. and *Tanacetum vulgare* L.).

Animal visitors include *Talpa europaea* L., *Microtus agrestis* (L.) and *Erinaceus europaea* L.; *Rana temporaria* L. lives and hibernates in the ditch. *Saperda carcharias* (L.), a wood-eating beetle, attacks the popular stems and *Dendrocopus major* (L.) comes to pick up its larvae. Among 51 visiting bird species, some of which nest (eg. *Parus major* L. and *Turdus viscivorus* L.), *Hippolais icterina* (Vieill.) and *Jynx torquilla* are the most unexpected.

The natural development of the garden shows how small rural sites can be preserved and managed under the changing circumstances caused by suburban expansion.

Zoological studies connected with a proposed housing estate in Białołęka Dworska, Warsaw

ALINA BREJNIAK AND MACIEJ LUNIAK *Institute of Zoology, Warsaw, Poland.*

This housing estate is intended as an experimental site concerned with environmental management on behalf of the housing industry in Poland. The estate is planned for 25,000 inhabitants and will cover an area of 2 km^2 in the suburbs of Warsaw. This area and the adjacent forest are included in the project. A group of scientists representing various fields participates in the work. Zoological studies carried out in 1976–79, before the onset of the building programme, yielded a picture of the fauna which will be a basis for future comparisons. Data have been collected on 1,915 invertebrate species (255,000 specimens) and 81 vertebrate species. A prognosis for the fauna changes has been prepared for differing variants of the design. Recommendations have been made for providing desirable conditions for animal communities.

Proposals for implementation include: 1, a continuous network of green areas ('ecological corridors') and their connection with the adjacent forest; 2, the reduction of garden maintenance; 3, the restoration of the former stream; 4, the creation of ponds, breeding sites and refuges for animals; 5, the construction of two passages under the main street to enable animal migration; and 6, the introduction of certain animal species.

Throughout the construction of the estate (1981–84) and for a long time afterwards, changes in the fauna will be observed and a management programme will be implemented. Efforts will be made to increase environmental awareness of the inhabitants and to engage them in nature protection.

Railway vegetation in Britain

CAROLINE SARGENT AND J. O. MOUNTFORD   *Institute of Terrestrial Ecology, Monks Wood Experimental Station, Abbots Ripton, Cambs., U.K.*

The conservation value of the estimated 80,000 ha of railway verge in Britain is being investigated under contract to the Nature Conservancy Council. The land has limited public access and provides a continuous network supporting a disturbed and complex vegetation system which may be peculiar to the railway. Increasing adjacent land pressures and changes in vegetation management practices have made a thorough description and quantification desirable.

The division of British Rail into five administrative regions has provided a basis for the distribution of sampling effort: Eastern, London Midland and Scottish Regions were each the subject of a single field season (respectively 1977, 1979, 1980), whilst Southern and Western Regions were combined and surveyed during 1978.

A classification of the verges, dependent on mapped geographical attributes, was made. This produced 25 track classes, which are distinguished by climate, geology, topography and railway usage, and which are variously distributed throughout the five regions (Sargent & Mountford 1980). Random vegetational sampling has been proportionately distributed within the track classes with the intention of improving the precision of sampling estimates.

Southern and Western Region vegetation data have been ordinated (Reciprocal Averaging; Hill 1973) and classified (Indicator Species Analysis; Hill *et al.* 1975) and 14 working vegetation types recognized. Essentially, the sorting techniques have differentiated between semi-natural and more disturbed (Grime 1979) vegetation forms. Thus, for example, 'hay meadows' and chalk grasslands are distinguished from those with many ruderals or much invasive bramble.

The better railway grasslands tend to occur on cuttings, which are more regularly and systematically cleared than other railway formations, whilst embankments frequently support scrub, with woodland developing on lower slopes when sufficient land is available.

The railway influence—chemical spraying, ballast tipping, dumping of nitrogenous and oily wastes, *ad hoc* scrub removal and burning—produces certain vegetation types which occur consistently throughout Southern and Western Regions (and probably much of the British Rail network) and which do not correlate with local environmental conditions. When track (geographic) and vegetation classifications are compared, a pattern does not emerge unless more disturbed vegetation forms are excluded.

However, vegetation types developing in response to these influences are particularly, and possibly uniquely, characteristic of the railway, and include many of the more interesting and unusual railway plants (Sargent & Mountford 1979)

REFERENCES

Grime J.P. (1979) *Plant strategies and vegetation processes.* John Wiley & Sons, Chichester, New York, Brisbane, Toronto.
Hill M.O. (1973) Reciprocal averaging: an eigenvector method of ordination. *Journal of Ecology*, 61, 237–249.
Hill M.O., Bunce R.G.H. & Shaw M.W. (1975) Indicator species analysis, a divisive polythetic method of classification, and its application to a survey of native pinewoods in Scotland. *Journal of Ecology*, 63, 597–613.
Sargent C. & Mountford J.O. (1979) Third interim report to the Nature Conservancy Council on the biological survey of British Rail property. (NCC/NERC Contract No. F3/03/80:ITE Project No. 466). Unpublished.
Sargent C. & Mountford J.O. (1980) Fourth interim report to the Nature Conservancy Council on the biological survey of British Rail property. (NCC/NERC Contract No. F3/03/80:ITE Project No. 466). Unpublished.

Environmental study of Kenitra (Morocco)

SERGE KEMPENEERS *Centre d' Étude de l'Environnement Urbain Université Libre de Bruxelles, Belgium.*

The environmental study for the development plans of Kenitra (Morocco) includes a biological evaluation, a landscape evaluation and a bioclimatological study in order to define constraints and planning potentialities.

Buildings and green areas were mapped (200 km²). Data (temperature, humidity, wind speed and direction) were collected along a traverse at predetermined sampling points.

The biological evaluation was principally from a study of the vegetation. A scale of five values was used. The highest values were attributed to the mattoral of *Juniperus phoenicea* Pall. Fl. Ross, dune vegetation, Mamora forest, and the marsh of the Fouarat valley. The high littoral dunes reduce the oceanic influence. This is especially perceptible when east winds blow through the Rharb plain. A slight heat island was also observed ($dT_{u-r \ max} = 3°C$).

A rapid landscape evaluation was made using the quality of view and the topography of the landscape. Maps of biological quality and landscape quality (constraints maps) were drawn and the potentialities for each zone were indicated. A functional approach to the city shows possible acute waste and pollution problems in the future. Proposals for the best use of the individual zones were made.

Two avian raptor populations in urban forests of Berlin: *Milvus migrans* and *Falco subbuteo* (Aves:Falconiformes)

DIETRICH FIUCZYNSKI   *Klingsorstrasse. 27, D-1000 Berlin 41.*

Voous (1977) proposed 'to ban or rigorously restrict or regulate the admittance of human recreation' in some areas near urban centres after comparing numbers of birds of prey in the 'Reichswald'. The Dutch part of the 'Reichswald' has intensive holiday and week-end recreation and has low raptor populations, while the German part, with markedly less human influence, has high bird numbers.

In contrast to these observations, Black Kite *Milvus migrans* Boddaert and European Hobby *Falco subbuteo* L. populations in forests in the Berlin city neighbourhood are not affected by human recreational activities in and around the woods and on lakes and rivers. However, in Berlin Scots Pine forests (151 km²) both species have decreased—from 18–21 pairs of Black Kites (1959–61) to 3 pairs (1979), and from 26–31 pairs of Hobby Falcons (1959–61) to 18 pairs (1979)—but a density of 12 Hobby pairs per 100 km² forest (1979) is still among the highest recorded for Germany. This decrease is not apparently due to pollution as biocide load in both species is small (DDE 1.5–9.5 μg g⁻¹, PCB 1.0–21.9 μg g⁻¹ wet weight in Hobby's eggs; mercury ranges from 0.3 to 11.2 μg g⁻¹ in feathers of Kite adults and juveniles) (Fiuczynski & Nethersole-Thompson 1980; Fiuczynski, in press). Food resources (fish in the river for the Kite, small birds in the city for the Falcon) are plentiful. Human disturbance is unimportant in spite of the intensive use of the forests for recreation and tourism. Similar observations north of Berlin in the Oranienburg-Bernau region show population changes on a larger scale and over a wider area.

REFERENCES

Fiuczynski D. Berliner Milan-Chronik (*Milvus migrans* und *M. milvus*). *Beitr. Vogelkd., Jena,* **27** (in press).
Fiuczynski D. & Nethersole-Thompson D. (**1980**) Hobby studies in England and Germany. *British Birds* **73**, 275–295.
Voous K.H. (**1977**) Three lines of thought for consideration and eventual action. In: *World Conference of Birds of Prey, Vienna 1975* (Ed. by R.D. Chancellor), pp. 343–347. Basingstoke, Hampshire.

Succession of bird communities in an urban recreational area in Holland

G. Th. de Roos   *Agricultural University, Department of Nature Conservation, Dorpsstraat 198, 8899 AP Vlieland, The Netherlands.*

Soon after the creation of a recreation project on a bog area (370 ha, including 37 ha of water and reedlands) within the capital of Leeuwarden, investigations concerning the succession of breeding bird communities were undertaken.

Before the creation of the project, only marsh- and water-bird communities with species such as *Anas querquedula* L., *Podiceps cristatus* L., *Acrocephalus scirpaceus* Hermann and *Emberiza schoeniclus* L. were present. After afforestation with deciduous trees, species such as *Acrocephalus palustris* Bechstein (10 pairs/10 ha), *Sylvia communis* Latham (7/10 ha) and *S.borin* Boddaert (16.5/10 ha) increased enormously. (Highest numbers appear in brackets.) Similar changes for *Locustella maevia* Boddaert (5/10 ha) and *Acrocephalus scirpaceus* (4 pairs/km reed-edge) were also observed. With the development of the woodland canopy, the original marsh-herb layer disappeared and a typical deciduous woodland bird community with species such as *Troglodytes troglodytes* L. (4/10 ha), *Turdus merula* L. (4/10 ha), *Phylloscopus trochilus* L. (30.5/10 ha), *P.collybita* Vieillot (2/10 ha), *Columba palumbus* L. (7/10 ha), *Streptopelia turtur* L. (2/10 ha) appeared. The density of the original species decreased; examples for the status of the two species in 1980 are: *Acrocephalus palustris* (2/10 ha) and *Sylvia communis* (1.5/10 ha). The recreation pattern is also a determining factor (De Roos & Schaafsma 1980).

REFERENCE

Roos G. Th. de & Schaafsma W. (1980) Is recreation affecting the number of bird's nests? *Statistica Neerlandica,* **34** (in press).

Aerial dispersal of spiders in a city

G. VISSE & W. K. R. E. VAN WINGERDEN *Instituut voor Lerarenopleiding V.L.-V.U., sectie Biologie, Postbox 90048, 1006 BA Amsterdam, The Netherlands.*

Aerially dispersing spiders were captured on a roof (height, 10 m) in the Hague during a 3-month period (29.8.79–29.11.79). The captures were made with the help of an iron wire (2 × 11 m in a cross-position) covered with glue. Altogether 314 spiders were caught of which 83.9% belong to the family Linyphiidae, and 67.1% to the genus *Erigone* V. Andouin 1826. The following species of the latter genus were present: *E.atra* (Blackwall) (26 ♀, 45 ♂), *E.dentipalpis* (Wider) (30 ♀, 16 ♂), *E.vagans* Andouin (1 ♀) and *E.arctica* (White) (1 ♂).

The numbers of adults of *E.atra* and *E.dentipalpis* are most probably high enough to found new populations, even if the females are not fertilized before dispersing (in breeding experiments 10 dispersing females did not produce viable eggs). Even the numbers of subadults are high enough to establish new populations.

Therefore, these species are expected to be among the first (re)colonizers of urban habitats; their chance of founding new populations is favoured by the availability of their habitats (grassland, annual plants, detritus).

The Orthoptera of the city of Giessen (Hesse, FRG)

SIGFRID INGRISCH *Institut für Zoologie, RWTH Aachen, Kopernikusstrasse, 5100 Aachen, West Germany.*

The presence of insects in urban areas depends on the geographical position of the city, and on the demands of the species. Due to the mild climate, the Orthopteran fauna of Giessen is relatively rich. Thirty-two species of the insect orders Orthoptera (Saltatoria) (24 species), Dermaptera (4 species) and Blattoptera (4 species) are present in Giessen. These are 46% of the species living in Hesse (cf. Ingrisch 1979).

One cricket (*Acheta domesticus* L.) and two cockroaches (*Blatta orientalis* L. and *Blattella germanica* L.) live as synanthrops in houses. One earwig (*Labia minor* L.) is confined to farms of the suburbs. The remaining 28 species normally occur in more or less natural habitats of the outskirts. Nine orthopterans and 2 dermapterans can also be found in gardens and on waste grounds in the suburbs. Their presence is due to small relict habitats which are little influenced by human activity.

Apart from synanthropous species the occurrence of orthopterous insects in the centre of the city is limited to small plots of green. Only *Forficula auricularia* L. may invade houses. It is striking that three tettigoniids but only one acridid are present in the centre of Giessen. This is due to the fact that these bush-crickets spend at least part of their life-cycles on trees and are less influenced by human activities than grasshoppers. *Meconema thalassinum* (De Geer) and *Leptophyes punctatissima* (Bosc) deposit their eggs on the bark of trees. They are, therefore, able to reproduce in the city, while *Tettigonia viridissima* L., a ground-laying species, invades each year from the outskirts to the centre. The cutting of grass in parks prevents the presence of grasshoppers, and the only site for *Chorthippus parallelus* (Zetterstedt) is in grassy areas beside a watercourse.

The comparison of the Orthoptera of Giessen with that of other cities of Central Europe (e.g. Weidner 1939, Knoerzer 1942, Röber 1951, Kühnelt 1955) shows that similar faunas occur in the city centres, while in the outskirts the species composition depends more on the geographical position of the city.

REFERENCES

Ingrisch S. (1979) Die Orthopteren, Dermapteren und Blattopteren (Insecta: Orthoptera, Dermaptera, Blattoptera) von Hessen. *Fundortkataster der Bundesrepublik Deutschland* (Ed. by P. Müller) Teil 13; 99 pp., Saarbrücken & Heidelberg.

Knoerzer A. (1942) Grundlagen zur Erforschung der Orthopteren und Dermapteren Südost-bayerns. *Mitteilungen der Münchner Entomologischen Gesellschaft*, **32**, 626–648.

Kühnelt W. (1955) Gesichtspunkte zur Beurteilung der Grossstadtfauna (mit besonderer Berücksichtigung der Wiener Verhältnisse). *Österreichische Zoologische Zeitschrift*, **6**, 30–54.

Röber H. (1951) Die Dermapteren und Orthopteren Westfalens in ökologischer Betrachtung. *Abhandlungen des Landesmuseums für Naturkunde in Münster/Westfalen*, **14**, 3–60.

Weidner H. (1939) Die Grossstadt als Lebensraum der Insekten, ihre Biotope und ihre Besiedlung. *Verhandlungen des VII. Internationalen Kongresses für Entomologie 1938*, **2**, 1347–1361.

The influence of waste water and thermal pollution on the benthos of an urban canal

C. FRANK AND T. KOEHN *Fachbereich Biologie, Freie Universität Berlin, FB 23, WE 5, Haderslebener Strasse 9, 1000 Berlin 41.*

The Teltow-Canal in West Berlin is polluted by industrial effluents, cooling-water discharges and polytrophic effluents from sewage treatment plants and irrigated sewage fields (mean input in the summer of 1975: 6.42 tons day^{-1} nitrogen, 4.18 tons day^{-1} orthophosphate; the mean flow being 9.24 m^3 s^{-1}, Kloos (1978)).

The macrobenthos of the canal was investigated between November 1978 and February 1980. Water temperatures were between 2.6 and 27.2°C, the maximum increase was 5.5°C caused by the power plant Steglitz and 12.9°C caused by the plant Lichterfelde.

Warm water and the oxygen enrichment by the plants accelerate self-purification. The oxygen content above the sediment was between 1.38 mg l^{-1} and 9.56 mg l^{-1}, and saturation between 16.6 and 116.0%. Tubificids showed a maximum of approximately 270,000 ind. m^{-2}. Dominant species were: *Limnodrilus hoffmeisteri* Claparede, *Limnodrilus claparedeanus* Ratzel and *Tubifex tubifex* Müller.

Chironomid larvae are abundant only in muddy sediments, the maximum was 44,100 ind. m^{-2}. Upstream from the power plant Lichterfelde, *Chironomus riparius* Meigen dominates with at least 99.5% of all chironomids.

Downstream, species diversity increases and *Chironomus plumosus* Linné, *Cryptochironomus defectus* Kieffer and *Procladius* sp. replace *Chironomus riparius*.

The chironomid larvae show deformations of the mentum (gaps and overlapping teeth) (Koehn & Frank 1980). The percentage of deformed larvae ranged from 7.7 to 39.3% (*C.riparius*) and from 5.9 to 40.3% (*C.plumosus*).

Significant differences in the rates of deformation at different stations could not be verified. Larvae with and without deformed mentum were reared in the laboratory and showed after one generation only between 0 and 2% deformation.

Warwick (1980) found a percentage of 0.09% deformed larvae in sediments from approximately A.D. 1087 and 238 B.C. in comparison to 1.99% in 1972.

Hamilton and Saether (1971) and Hare and Carter (1976) ruled out domestic and agricultural sewage as inducin agents for the deformations. The contamination of the sediment and the water by industrial pollutants, such as heavy metals, phenolics and oil, are most probably the cause of the deformations.

REFERENCES

Hamilton A.L. & Saether O.A. (1971) The occurrence of characteristic deformities in the chironomid larvae of several Canadian lakes. *Canadian Entomologist*, **103**, 363–368.

Hare L. & Carter J.C.H. (1976) The distribution of Chironomus (s.s.)? cucini (salinarius group) larvae (Diptera, Chironomidae) in Parry Sound, Georgian Bay with particular reference to structural deformities. *Canadian Journal of Zoology*, **54**, 2129–2134.

Kloos R. (1978) Die Berliner Gewässer: Wassermenge, Wassergüte. *Besondere Mitteilungen zum Gewässerkundlichen Jahrsbericht des Landes Berlin.*

Koehn T. & Frank C. (1980) *Effect of thermal pollution on the chironomid fauna in an urban channel.* Chironomidae (Ed. by D.A. Murray), pp. 187–194. Pergamon Press, Oxford.

Warwick W.F. (1980) *Pasqua Lake, Southeastern Saskatchewan: a preliminary assessment of trophic status and contamination based on the Chironomidae (Diptera).* Chironomidae (Ed. by D.A. Murray), pp. 255–267. Pergamon Press, Oxford.

V

INDEXES

AUTHOR INDEX

Figures in italic refer to pages where full references appear

SUBJECT INDEX